NEVER
TO BE TAKEN
ALIVE

NEVER
TO BE TAKEN
ALIVE

A Biography of

General Gordon

Roy MacGregor-Hastie

St. Martin's Press
New York

This book is dedicated to The Right Honourable Mrs. Margaret Thatcher, FRS, MP, Prime Minister, who would not have been too late.

NEVER TO BE TAKEN ALIVE. Copyright © 1985 by Roy MacGregor-Hastie. All rights reserved. Printed in the United States of America. No part of this book may be used or reproduced in any manner whatsoever without written permission except in the case of brief quotations embodied in critical articles or reviews. For information, address St. Martin's Press, 175 Fifth Avenue, New York, N.Y. 10010.

Library of Congress Cataloging in Publication Data
MacGregor-Hastie, Roy.
    Never to be taken alive.

    1. Gordon, Charles George, 1833-1885.   2. Generals—
Great Britain—Biography.   3. Great Britain.   Army—
Biography.   4. Colonial administrators—Sudan—Biography.
5. Sudan—History—1862-1899.   I. Title.
DA68.32.G6M33   1986   941.081′092′4 [B]   85-25163
ISBN 0-312-56478-3

First published in Great Britain by Sidgwick & Jackson Limited.
First U.S. Edition
10 9 8 7 6 5 4 3 2 1

Contents

List of Plates and Maps

All maps drawn by Neil Hyslop

Gordon at eleven (*Courtesy of M.A. Larkin, Secretary of the Gordon Action Group, Gravesend*)

Fullands School, Taunton (*Somerset Archaeological & Natural History Society*)

The ruins of Sebastopol, 1855 (*Victoria and Albert Museum*)

Gordon's map of Sebastopol (*Public Record Office, Crown Copyright MR 189 (28, 30) ex WO 78/1026*)

Caricature of Mis(s) Management (*British Museum*)

Gordon at thirty-two (*Royal Engineers Museum, Chatham*)

Romolo Gessi, 1856 (*Biblioteca Classense, Ravenna*)

Gordon in oriental dress (*Royal Engineers Museum, Chatham*)

Map of Shanghai (*Public Record Office, Crown Copyright, MR 866 ex WO 78/987A*)

Pages from Gordon's essay on the Garden of Eden (*Courtesy of the Headmaster, The Gordon Boys' School, West End, Woking, Surrey*)

Gordon in 1880 (*National Portrait Gallery*)

Romolo Gessi in 1877 (*Biblioteca Classense, Ravenna*)

Map of Gordon's journey in Ethiopia (*Public Record Office, Crown Copyright, FO 925/26*)

The Mahdi (*Mansell Collection*)

Punch Cartoon, 'Too Late' (*Mansell Collection*)

Gordon's statue in Khartoum (*Radio Times Hulton Picture Library*)

Gordon's statue in London (*Department of the Environment, Crown Copyright*)

Acknowledgements

Many people have been very helpful and deserve my thanks. In particular I am indebted to: the Library of the Royal Military Academy, Sandhurst, and especially the Deputy Librarian, Mr M.G.H. Wright; Miss G.L. Beech of the Map Department, Public Record Office, Kew; Mr Colin Crook, Group Librarian at Gravesend, and his staff; Mr S.D. Thomson, City Archivist, Southampton; Ms Elizabeth Roads at the Court of the Lord Lyon, Edinburgh; Mr Edward Firth, BA, DLC, Headmaster, the Gordon Boys' School, Woking; Mr Leo Fuchter, Assistant Curator of the Royal Engineers' Museum, Chatham; Councillor John Lovell, Mayor of Gravesham; Councillor Dorothy Brown, Mayor of Southampton; Dr Dante Bolognesi of the Biblioteca Classense, Ravenna; Dr Annamaria Paissan Schlechter, Director of the Biblioteca Comunale, Trento; Dr Baldi and all the staff of the Rovereto Civic Library; Mrs Christine Kelly, Archivist of the Royal Geographical Society, London; Mr David Bromwich, MA, ALA, Local History Librarian at Taunton; Mr Tony Richardson of the Library and Records Department at the Foreign Office; Mr Victor Smith of the Kent Defence Research Group; Fr Giovanni Peruzzi, OFM, in Khartoum; Dr Wan Fei-jan, former President of the People's Court, Peking; M.A. Larkin; Ms Megan Tafner; and innumerable friends at the American University, Cairo.

Foreword

Of all the men whom Queen Victoria hated – and she was a good and frequent hater – none aroused her wrath as easily and as often as William Ewart Gladstone. He was not respectful, even to the memory of Prince Albert, 'the best of men'. Some, indeed, said he was not even respectable. He was unkind to Benjamin Disraeli when he was alive and unmoved by 'Dear Dizzy's' death. He was ironic about her title, Empress of India. Worst of all – worse even than the fact that he kept on becoming her Prime Minister – was his 'betrayal' of Charles George Gordon, one of her heroes. As the Queen-Empress wrote to General Gordon's favourite sister, Augusta, in 1885:

> How shall I write to you, or how shall I attempt to express *what I feel*? To *think* of your dear, noble heroic Brother, who served his Country and his Queen so truly, so heroically, with a self-sacrifice so edifying to the World, not having been rescued. That the promises of support were not fulfilled – which I so frequently and constantly expressed on those who asked him to go – is to me *grief inexpressible*! indeed, it has made me ill.

The death of Gordon, Governor-General of the Sudan, at the head of the staircase to his apartments in his palace in Khartoum, inspired many a late Victorian poet and artist and the modern feature film *Khartoum*. In all probability he did not die there, but that is part of the mystery. Where is his body? His head was last seen stuck on a spear in the camp of his conqueror, the Mahdi of the Sudan. And, a hundred years later, what has happened to all the schools, boys' clubs, stained glass windows and other memorials which bore his name so proudly after his martyrdom? Much remains a mystery, and he was more than just an eminent Victorian.

This soldier who 'served his Country and his Queen so truly' was

viii

not, in fact, on active service in the British Army. He was in the employ of a foreign power, as he had been for most of the illustrious part of his life. He was a senior civil servant of the Khedive of Egypt, as he had been on and off for more than a decade. He held the rank of field-marshal in the Turkish Army, and the equivalent rank of Ti Tu in the army of Imperial China. He had ʋeen offered the highest civil or military rank in the service of the King of the Belgians but he was only a retired major-general and colonel of Engineers at home, a rank lower than that attained by his late father after a lifetime of pedestrian service in the Royal Artillery. He had been a member of the French Legion of Honour for nearly thirty years, held the highest decorations in the Imperial Chinese State and Army, the Turkish Empire and Egyptian State, but the British Army never awarded him more than a few wretched campaign medals and clasps in life and nothing posthumously. His brother, a superior military storekeeper, ranked above him in the Order of the Bath.

This great soldier, one of the best to graduate from the Royal Military Academy, Woolwich, had his appointment to the Royal Engineers held back because the authorities mistrusted him. This suspicion persisted even after a long and brilliant career, at the end of which he had been a general officer in four armies. He would have been the ideal man to modernize an army which still clung to the memory of Wellington and Waterloo, but he was sent anywhere and everywhere his ideas could not upset the status quo at the War Office.

Again, Queen Victoria often referred to him as an exemplary Christian and an example he certainly was to many. But he was not a Broad Church Anglican. He was a Christian fundamentalist who fought and crushed an indigenous Christian fundamentalist uprising in Imperial China, though he was humane enough to understand the causes of the uprising and beg for mercy for its leaders. Having refused the Mahdi's offer of mercy, he died at the hands of this Islamic fundamentalist who ante-dated the Ayatollah Khomeini by a century. But to which Christian denomination did Gordon belong at his death? Nobody knows. Some members of his Scottish family, the Gordons of Park, went over to Protestantism with the advent of the Hanoverians, but his best friend was a Catholic and he may well have been on his way to mass at the Austrian church in Khartoum when he was hacked to death by the Mahdi's warriors. When a memorial service was held in Khartoum, thirteen years after his death, the service was conducted by Catholic, Anglican, Presbyterian and Methodist chaplains in concert, just to make sure that the right words were said over the unquiet spirit.

And this best friend – was he a fine upstanding British bulldog, faithful at his master's heels? No, for a quarter of a century Gordon chose to share moments of farce, tragedy, heroism and disaster with an Italian adventurer, sometime interpreter in the Crimea, sometime Garibaldino, sometime general in the Sudan, explorer of Lake Albert, who turned cannibal on his stranded barge in Equatoria. British biographers have tended to ignore Romolo Gessi. He was, after all, a foreigner, an Italian, not always scrupulously honest and certainly not well connected; and, to be fair, it is only recently that the city of Ravenna has put together a bibliography of writings by and about this Italian Geographical Society Medallist who was one of the city's most famous sons.

Gordon himself was a Fellow of the Royal Geographical Society in London for eight years and an Honorary Corresponding Fellow until his death. He was, however, an unusual member. He resigned on one occasion because the RGS wanted to lionize him and get him to give illustrated lectures. They missed an important point: not only did he not like being lionized, he did not see the world as being illustrated. In his schooldays and at the Royal Military Academy, Woolwich, he showed a talent for drawing, but in black and white. That is how he saw the world – as a place to be mapped, not one to be painted. He was one of the most widely travelled men of his times, but he paints no word pictures of glamorous places. 'To write of the varied scenery one has passed through', he wrote in 1867, '. . . is unprofitable.' Viewers of any of the innumerable television programmes or films of recent years, about or set in China, the Balkans, Turkey, Egypt and South Africa, will have seen these places on screen in colour. Gordon saw them all in reality, but in black and white, more often than not in terms of human geography, of people who were right or wrong, which for him was black or white. He was not a man for delicate shading, as geographer or Christian. He seldom condemned anybody – though Gessi was more often black than white – but he made it clear that he knew which sort of colour was before him. He made only one tourist trip during his stay in China – a brief excursion to the Great Wall. In Asia Minor he was interested in the site of the grounding of Noah's Ark, and not in the view from Mount Ararat. In Cairo and Constantinople he complained of the people and did not notice the minarets. His life story was not a travelogue.

For Gordon, money was black and he tried to keep his distance from it, though he was offered a great deal from time to time. He was always upset when accused of enriching himself as a soldier of fortune. Yet he was indirectly the victim of British, Austro-Hungarian, French and Italian intrigues over the control of the Suez Canal, as much as he was directly the victim of the Mahdi. As a very young man he met Luigi Negrelli, the Italian engineer whose idea the Suez Canal was, and De Lesseps who built it and is said to have offered Gordon and Gessi jobs. Gordon's arch-enemy in Cairo was the British banker, Baring, who advanced himself to the peerage as a diplomat. And the extent of Gordon's military success in China and its importance can only be gauged against the background of political and commercial intrigue by the European Powers and the United States of America, at a time when American Methodist missionaries and opium traders of every nationality lived cheek by jowl in Shanghai, the city Gordon saved from the Taiping rebels, the subjects of the Heavenly Kingdom of Great Peace.

'A gallant Englishman for whom we must all pray', was how one clergyman described Gordon during the last days at Khartoum. Of course, he was not English and the story of his Banffshire family is as murky as any to be met with on the dark pathways of Scottish Highland history, on which even Scottish historians have been known to lose themselves. Gordon's ancestors deserted the Highlands a century before he was born, but as a child he was horrified by accounts of the Clearances, and he was drawn to the Scottish and Irish rural poor until the end of his days. In 1880 he was still trying to find ways of keeping the Irish on the land, but nobody heeded his proposals. His great-grandfather deserted not only the Catholic Church but also the Stewarts, and committed himself to the Hanoverian cause, becoming a close friend of 'Butcher' Cumberland, George II's son who defeated the Jacobites so savagely at Culloden. The shadows of this decision were still long in Charles's childhood. With his piercing blue eyes and wavy, reddish hair, he resembled portraits of the Gordon Marquis of Huntly, who supported Charles I against the Covenanters and for his pains was executed in Edinburgh.

As Queen Victoria turned the pages of Gordon's own Bible, given to her by his sister, she chose to ignore most of this. The War Office and Foreign Office would have liked to ignore him in death as they had often done in life, but for a decade after his martyrdom, for which they were responsible, the criticism continued. From time to time nowadays a book inspired by one or other of these august institutions appears, putting the official point of view, but the effort is rather half-hearted. Perhaps they hope that in death, as in life, he will eventually go away. It has been suggested that this is the reason why Gordon's statue in London has been moved from its place of honour in Trafalgar Square to where it now stands, rather dejectedly, on Victoria Embankment. Senior civil servants do not have to pass it now on their way from the clubs in St James's and Pall Mall to Whitehall and Downing Street. It is a pity. The world is in need of new heroes, and Charles George Gordon had the stuff in him to make several.

ONE

A Gordon for Me

A Gordon for me, a Gordon for me,
If y're nae a Gordon, y're nae guid tae me;
The Black Watch are bra', the Seaforth and a',
But a Bonny Wee Gordon's the pride of them a'.

Popular song

Charles George Gordon was born in London on 28 January 1833 at
No. 1 Kempt Terrace, Woolwich Common. His father, Major
Henry William Gordon, was off duty that rainy afternoon, and
waited downstairs until he was summoned to see the newborn baby.
He recalled afterwards that the child did not bawl, but fixed him
with bright eyes which had an almost adult expression. After the
ritual noises of approbation Major Gordon went out to give the
news to his brother officers and make arrangements for the
baptism, something his wife liked done as soon as possible.

Elizabeth Gordon, the daughter of Samuel Enderby of Croom's
Hill, Blackheath, did not suffer during the pregnancy or birth. She
had been producing children for fifteen years, from Henry William
in 1818 to Charles in 1833, and her final tally was to be five sons
and six daughters. She seems, unusually for the times, to have
reared them all to healthy adulthood. For an army officer's wife,
who did not always go with him on foreign postings, it was a
comfort to have a lot of children around, and her elder daughters
were almost companions.

Life together at Woolwich was very pleasant. Elizabeth preferred
it to their first home in Brompton Lines (now Brompton Barracks)
at Chatham. Woolwich, with its great Arsenal, *was* the Royal
Artillery, and her husband's career as a gunner was helped by being

1

at the centre of things. The youngest son of his own family, Henry William Gordon had always been intended for the Army and after the early death of his promising elder brother seems to have been deliberately groomed for the military distinction for which his brother had already shown potential. After school in Exeter, he went up to the Royal Military Academy, Woolwich, on 10 March 1801 and was commissioned ensign in the Royal Artillery on 17 August 1803 at the age of seventeen. Notwithstanding his youth, he was rapidly advanced to lieutenant and plunged into the thick of the second phase of the war against Napoleon. In 1805 he served in the expedition to Naples and took part in the occupation of Sicily. A year later he was appointed Adjutant of his regiment and fought very bravely at the Battle of Maida and the attack on the Rock of Scylla, for which he was awarded a medal and clasp. On 3 August 1810, barely seven years after being commissioned, he was 2nd Captain and Adjutant. After Waterloo, he found he had acquired a reputation as a good administrator, and for much of his life he shuttled between Chatham, Woolwich and garrisons abroad, refurbishing and rebuilding barracks and batteries.

At the time of Charles George's birth Henry William had been a major for three years and had already been told that a lieutenant-colonelcy would be his in a few years' time. He and his wife had an adequate income, rounded out by her father, who was a great favourite with the children. Elizabeth would always get up at dawn with her husband, and after breakfast see him off to his duties. She would spend the morning managing her large household and then have lunch with the children. On most days her husband would be home at two o'clock in the afternoon, and at teatime the family and servants (and any gunners she could catch) would be assembled. Then Elizabeth would read aloud for a couple of hours from the Bible or from her large collection of religious tracts. Her sister-in-law, Henrietta Augusta, had married the Rev. William Gwynne, an Evangelical, and their joint activity – she lived only a mile away – seems to have been intense. Henrietta Augusta, William and Elizabeth believed that the Bible was essential reading for everybody, was literally true, and, failing approved works, was sufficient in itself for the education of a godly, upright and worthy person. Elizabeth's mother had put her on this straight and narrow path, during the long absences abroad of her father; he was a prosperous merchant, with warehouses in Glasgow, Liverpool and Bristol, and personally controlled his trade with the West Indies and the United States of America.

After these devotions, the children would be sent away as the adults got ready for dinner. The Gordons seem to have been well liked, in spite of the fact that they were very devout and seldom entertained. A contemporary description of Henry William is very flattering:

> He was a man of much individuality. He was a good and complete soldier with a cultivated knowledge of his profession. He will be long remembered by those who served under him for his firm yet genial character, and his very striking figure. He was of a peculiar type . . . [with] his lively and expressive face, great round head – bald from early manhood, and surrounded by short, curly hair, black in his best days – his robust playfulness of manner, and the twinkle of fun in his clear blue eyes. In his company it was not possible to be dull; he had a look which diffused cheerfulness and an inexhaustible fund of humour. On occasions he could be stern, for the essence of his character was a decision which turned to severity when others deviated from their duty, or did it amiss.

This Victorian paterfamilias, successful and respected, rigid yet playful, with his devout, prolific wife, surrounded by merry children, seems to be the archetypal pillar of English society in his day. Yet along the corridors of the house in Woolwich, in all their houses at home and abroad, stalked the ghosts of the Covenanters and the '45. For all his Englishness, Henry William (named after George II's grandson, the Duke of Gloucester) was part of the history of the decline and fall of Stewart Scotland, as his own father (godson of 'Butcher' Cumberland) had never ceased to remind him.

When Protestantism came to Scotland, it had an appeal at first only in the Lowlands, to the lawyers, the merchants and the small farmers. Above the Highland Line it made converts only among the Campbells, and this was good enough reason for nearly everybody else to reject it; since the reign of James IV (1488–1513) the Campbells had acted as royal policemen in the Highlands, enriching themselves at the expense of the MacGregors, MacDonalds and Murrays, who were regularly punished for crimes which did not exist. By the middle of the sixteenth century the Gordons were the only clan strong enough to act as a counterweight to the Campbells; their chief threw in his lot with Mary Queen of Scots, and rode into Edinburgh with her in 1566 to ensure her safekeeping at the time of the birth of her heir, who was to become James VI of Scotland and I of England. James VI raised the Gordon chief to the marquisate of Huntly at the end of the century, to keep a balance of dignity between the Catholic Huntly and the Protestant Campbell, Earl of Argyll.

James went to London in 1603, to inherit the Kingdom of England and Wales, leaving Scotland in the middle of an uneasy peace. When his son, Charles I, found himself in difficulties with his Parliament at Westminster, his Scottish subjects at first remained neutral in the debate on the Royal Prerogatives. However, when Charles tried to introduce a new book of service into the Established Church and have it read, too, in Scotland, there were riots in Edinburgh – at St Giles church 'Dost thou say mass in my lug?' and 'Belly God' were shouted at the Bishop. What is sometimes called the Presbyterian Revolution began on that day, Sunday 23 July 1637. A 'National Covenant for Religeon [sic] According to the Word of God' was signed in 1638 and people were forced to subscribe to it all over the Lowlands; an act of open rebellion against the King and his Episcopalian policies, it was followed by two so-called Bishops' Wars. The then Marquis of Huntly came out for King Charles and again under Montrose in the Civil War; he lost his head at the Mercat (Market) Cross in Edinburgh, saying: 'My only regret in dying is that I have not been the first to suffer for a cause which makes death so sweet to me.' When some Covenanting ministers tried to make him change his religion, he dismissed them contemptuously with the words that as he had 'never been accustomed in life to give ear to false prophets, so now [he did] not wish to be troubled by them at [his] death'. Gordon of Invermarkie, Gordon of Newton Gordon and Gordon of Harthill also died at the Cross; Huntly's son, Lord Gordon, had fallen dragging a Covenanting general from his saddle in battle.

At King Charles II's Restoration in 1666 the Gordons had the satisfaction of seeing Argyll and several other Campbells beheaded, but during the next few years of relative peace and prosperity the lines of religious loyalty of all the clans became blurred. The majority remained Catholic and Royalist; some became Episcopalian and Royalist; a few became Presbyterian and anti-Stewart; some kept their religious views to themselves and fought in foreign armies, Catholic and Protestant – it was the beginning of the long era of the Scottish soldier of fortune.

After 1689, and the deposition of the Catholic James VII of Scotland and II of England, most of the Gordons made their peace with William of Orange, who raised several regiments in the Highlands. These regiments were much admired by writers of the day. The diarist John Evelyn wrote that he had observed 'some regiments of Highland dragoons . . . on their march through England. They were of large stature, well proportioned and disciplined. One of them, having reproached a Dutchman for cowardice . . . was attacked by two Dutchmen, when with his sword he struck the head off one and cleft the skull of the other to the skin.'

On the death of Queen Anne, however, the old questions of loyalty to the House of Stewart, and that of religious denomination, came to the fore again. The throne of the United Kingdom was offered to the Elector of Hanover, though without enthusiasm; had the Old Pretender renounced his Catholicism in 1714, the Stewarts would have been restored in his person. There was a sharp division of loyalties along religious lines, among the Gordons as among the members of the other clans. Gordons were out in the 1715 Rebellion on both sides, more for James than for George. When Charles Edward Stewart made a last attempt to restore his family to the throne in 1745–6 most of the Gordons came out for him – Lord Louis Gordon, Gordon of Killihuntly, Gordon of Cobardie, Gordon of Abachie, Gordon of Glenbucket and Sir William Gordon of Park, the majority of whom died in exile after the defeat of the Young Pretender. However, at the Battle of Prestonpans, which Charles Edward Stewart won in 1745, Sir William Gordon of Park's cousin was an officer in the 47th Foot (Colonel Lascelles) on the Hanoverian side and was captured on the field. This cousin, David Gordon, is often referred to as 'the first known ancestor of "Chinese Gordon" ', and though the family history, *The House of Gordon*, states that 'his origin has baffled every inquiry', the fact that he had 'turned' – become Protestant – may explain why not too many inquiries have been made, since David's father was almost certainly out in the '15 for James.

The 'turning' of a member of such a prominent Gordon family made a deep impression. Nearly all those who did not go into exile 'turned', so a few years later MacDonnell of Glengarry could write to the Young Pretender's brother, Henry Stewart, Cardinal York, asking for a fragment of the True Cross: 'Our name is the only Catholic one now in Scotland, since the family of Gordon changed.'

David Gordon, born 1712, an ensign and Assistant Adjutant of the 47th in 1741, and lieutenant and Adjutant when he was captured, was an important convert to the Hanoverian cause. He was rescued after Prestonpans by the Angus Militia, having resisted pressure by his cousin Sir William to 'turn again and fight with the sons of [your] forefathers'. He was welcomed back by the Duke of Cumberland himself, with whom he seems to have enjoyed a close friendship; 'Butcher' Cumberland, after all, had been godfather to David's son, born in 1739. David Gordon was, of course, a useful propagandist. He spoke bluntly of his conversion and new loyalties. He reasoned that as the only career open to the Gordons was that of soldiering, which they did well, and as the Stewart cause was lost, he would do well to make shift to throw in his lot 100 per cent with the Hanoverians; symbolically, his son was named William Augustus after the 'Butcher' himself.

Promoted captain, David Gordon was well enough thought of to be a principal witness at the 'Board of General Officers Appointed to examine into the conduct of Sir John Cope, Colonel Peregrine Lascelles and Brigadier General Thomas Fowke, from the time of the breaking out of the Rebellion in 1745 till the action of Prestonpans'. It stuck in the throat of the Duke of Cumberland that there could have been such a Jacobite victory, in the words of Sir William Butler,

> of two and a half thousand ill-disciplined Highlanders who utterly routed and destroyed in five minutes fighting a force of old and seasoned regular troops, fresh from the Flemish wars, capturing guns, camp and baggage, killing or taking prisoners more than two thousand infantry, and doing it all so instantaneously that the second line of clansmen, placed only fifty paces in rear of the first, and following that first line in its charge as fast as Highland legs could run, never got blow of scythe or sword at the English enemy, and had to content themselves with prisoners and plunder.

The Duke hoped that the Board would find out who had failed in his duty. According to Sir William Butler, Captain Gordon gave evidence that 'about daybreak on September 21st he received orders from Major Severn to make the line of foot stand to their arms, which the whole of them accordingly did. Lt-Colonel Whitford's narrative was read and the witnesses said that as far as it came to their knowledge the narrative was true, and believed the other part of it to be true having nothing to say on contradiction to it.' After the defeat of Charles Edward Stewart at Culloden, David Gordon hoped to be rapidly advanced in the service. Unfortunately for him, the fact that he had been taken prisoner at Prestonpans and given evidence at a Board which condemned some of his senior officers, not to speak of a certain jealousy on the part of those who thought he had already been too rapidly advanced by the Duke of Cumberland, stopped his career where it was. He was posted first to Ireland, on garrison duties, then to Nova Scotia, where he died in 1752 as a result of an accident outside Halifax. The Duke did not neglect his widow, Sarah, who was given a pension of £26 a year, on which she lived modestly until her death; she is buried in Marylebone churchyard.

Young William Augustus had followed his father into the Hanoverian service, and was made an ensign in the 40th Foot at the age of sixteen. He was promoted lieutenant in 1756, and fought against the French in Minorca during the Seven Years' War, later serving with distinction in Canada, at the siege of Louisburg, 'in that part of the army commanded by General Wolfe, and in the battle and siege of Quebec [1759] in the Corps distinguished by the name of Louisburg Grenadiers, and later at Montreal and at the conquest of Martinique and Havana [1762] where he acted as Assistant Quarter Master General'.

Unfortunately for William Augustus, his godfather died in 1765 and thus he lost his protector. Had the Duke of Cumberland lived to become king or regent – there was a party which preferred him to his nephew, who was crowned George III in 1760, and his other nephews were minors – things might have been different. As it was, after the Seven Years' War William Augustus was retired as a captain on half pay. This was a double irritant. His cousin, the young Sir William of Park, was already a colonel in Lord Ogilvie's Irish Regiment in the French service (what use had it been for his father to sell sword and soul to the Protestant Hanoverians?), and he was frustrated by inaction and lack of money at a time when he had fallen in love with the sister of the Rev. Slaughter Clarke, Rector of Hexham in Northumberland and wanted to marry her. He petitioned William Pitt the Elder on 26 August 1766:

Pardon a soldier of Fortune presuming to take this liberty on a business which he would have ventured doing personally, did his income of £40 per annum permit his being in London and at the same time keep up the character due the cloth he has had the honour of wearing almost from infancy; he has already rather broke in upon it by eight months' application to get in again to the service . . . failing which he attempted that of Portugal, and lastly the East India Company; but in vain, tho' he can safely say that he had the countenance of all those officers under whose command he served in America. . . . I may truly say the inactive life I at present lead is irksome to me, indeed to anyone who has been ever used to employment, and not only renders me unhappy, but greatly breaks my health. Therefore, my Lord, I hope you will take my particular hard case into your well known consideration.

His letter achieved its desired effect and he was back on active service in the 11th Foot the following year. His faith in the

Hanoverians returned, and on marrying Anna Maria Clarke he saw to it that his children all bore the names of George III's brothers and sisters: his three sons were christened Augustus Henry, Henry William and William Augustus, and his four daughters Augusta Maria, Anna Maria, Henrietta Augusta and Charlotte Matilda. However if he hoped this would be a talisman he was doomed to disappointment – Charles George Gordon's uncles and aunts were for him a model of frugality. It cannot have been easy to keep a large family on a captain's pay, even though his wife's father, a London merchant, made them an allowance, and things became even more difficult when William Augustus senior was retired again in 1776. Anne Maria, however, was both a religious and an enterprising woman. After failing to get a post for her husband at his old school in Great Windmill Street, London, she managed to get him appointed to manage several schools in Yorkshire and Lincolnshire. His duties seem to have been light – he was a sort of itinerant bursar, but he was pleased to have both some formal employment and time on his hands; his wife filled the latter with readings from various religious tracts published by her brother.

The Rev. Slaughter Clarke was a well-known Evangelical preacher who frequently left Hexham for the south-west, where he had many admirers. He now advised his brother-in-law to go there too because his prospects would be better, and in 1786 William Augustus and his family moved to Devon. They settled in Exeter and for the next ten years seem to have been poor but happy. In 1796, however, this happiness and unity were destroyed by tragedy. On 25 February his wife died, and shortly afterwards his favourite son, another William Augustus, was killed when he was thrown by his horse at the Cape of Good Hope where he was stationed. Only nineteen, he was already a captain in the 95th Foot. He died, Butler writes, 'universally lamented by his regiment; he was a very promising young man and in consequence caused a feeling of regret in all who knew him that such early worth should have been so prematurely ended'.

This double bereavement left William Augustus senior uncertain about what direction his life should take, and he applied for various posts as younger officers left home for service against Napoleon. He tried for the job of Barrack Master in Exeter and for a commission in the Devonshire Militia. He was given the latter, but only as a lieutenant, though 'it was to be regretted that he had not made an earlier application when a captain's commission would have been allotted to him'. He died in 1809 and was buried at his wife's side in St Thomas's churchyard, Exeter. His only consolation during these

HANOVER

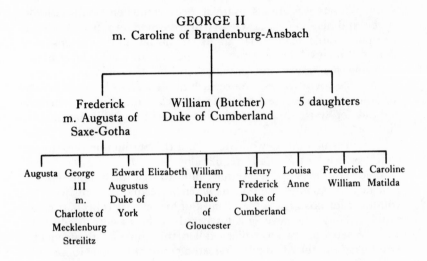

GEORGE II
m. Caroline of Brandenburg-Ansbach

Frederick
m. Augusta of
Saxe-Gotha

William (Butcher)
Duke of Cumberland

5 daughters

Augusta

George
III
m.
Charlotte of
Mecklenburg
Streilitz

Edward
Augustus
Duke of
York

Elizabeth

William
Henry
Duke
of
Gloucester

Henry
Frederick
Duke of
Cumberland

Louisa
Anne

Frederick
William

Caroline
Matilda

GORDON

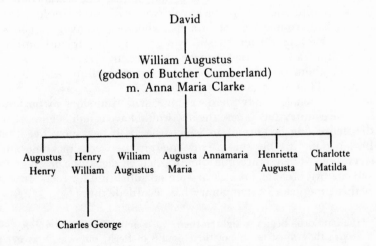

David

William Augustus
(godson of Butcher Cumberland)
m. Anna Maria Clarke

Augustus
Henry

Henry
William

William
Augustus

Augusta
Maria

Annamaria

Henrietta
Augusta

Charlotte
Matilda

Charles George

last years was the glowing opinions he heard expressed of his son
Henry William.

Henry William was always aware of the wretched end to his father's
career, and his son Charles George heard echoes of it from him and
his innumerable 'Hanoverian' aunts. It was one of the reasons why
Henry William had become a gunner, a specialist, instead of
following his father and grandfather into the infantry. It was
responsible for a fear of failure in himself and in his own which
made him such a severe if loving father; when the children behaved
and did not 'waste time in play', his eyes would twinkle, but if they
did not . . . Charles George soon got a clear idea of right and
wrong, in which the Law of Moses and the Sermon on the Mount
were fused with the family regulations.

Major Gordon's ambition urged him to 'seek the bubble reputation in the cannon's mouth', or when no cannons were firing to
volunteer for postings to places most of his brother officers tried to
avoid – though he never got further than the Eastern Mediterranean. When Charles was still a toddler, the whole family moved to
Dublin, where the rifled muzzle-loading guns at Pigeon House Fort
in the Bay had to be relined. The child, who sometimes claimed
total recall, said later that he did not remember much about the
place but liked the people; however, his brother Henry said that the
'baby' did not like life at the Fort very much and was always
frightened by the daily shoot and parade noises. The servants made
a fuss of him, in spite of their cold war with Mrs Gordon. She
always had trouble with the maids, who were Roman Catholics,
because they would not sit still while she read to them from her
Protestant tracts and tried to make them see the error of their ways,
offering them the straight and narrow path and an escape from
Popery. They were not converted.

For the whole family there were frequent excursions by boat, or
into the countryside. There the boy would have caught a glimpse of
the depressing conditions in which the Irish peasantry lived, as
Butler puts it, 'on the narrow margin between rackrent and
starvation'. The picturesque whitewashed cottages, the green grass
and the brightly coloured carts were no substitute for food. It was
at this time, as a contemporary has recorded, that

> the landlords began to tighten their grasp upon the soil. *Coûte que
> coûte*, they must have, not their pound of flesh, but what was in
> reality the price of flesh and blood of the entire family; for already

the highest authority in the land had declared that the process of eviction was tantamount to a sentence of death. Then began the old scene: the "driver", the server, the bailiff, the policeman were abroad, and behind them in gloomy procession came the antithesis of justice – resistance. Against the driver appeared the blackened face, against the server rose the "moonlighter", the notice to quit was followed by the threatening letter.

From time to time there were riots, carriage burnings and angry processions, often led by priests. Charles George saw the troops stood to and sent to disperse the ...ob. The sight impressed itself on the infant mind and in later life The Irish Question was one he always followed closely – so closely, in fact, that forty years afterwards he made his own detailed proposals for answering it. His parents were uncertain in their attitude to the riots. They were in sympathy with the poor and out of sympathy with unscrupulous landlords, but Elizabeth was fiercely anti-Catholic and the Irish peasants were 'Papists'. Again her husband was part of the establishment in Ireland, and the establishment was being attacked; his duty was clear – to help stop anti-government violence and enforce the law, however unjust.

When he was promoted lieutenant-colonel in 1837, and posted to Leith Fort near Edinburgh, Henry William Gordon came face to face with a similar tragedy in his country of origin. What became known as the Highland Clearances had begun in 1814, Bliadhna an Losgaidh or the Year of the Burning. A Gordon by descent, the Marchioness of Stafford – Countess of Sutherland in the Scottish peerage – had begun it to 'improve' her dowry, the vast spaces of the Highlands which already brought her £15,000 a year. It meant getting the clansmen off the land and replacing them with sheep; fishing would be developed also as a cash crop and the displaced crofters would, in theory, become fishermen. Even seen from England, where she lived, with her husband, an art collector, the idea was at best Utopian. Resistance to the clearances was met with force, and the Staffords' principal factor, James Loch, earned an unenviable reputation for severity. The clansmen and their women and children were driven from their homes, which were burnt so that they could never return. Bands of women who resisted were clubbed by the sheriff's officers, and troops were brought in to deal with the worst pockets of resistance.

Some attempts were made to resettle the clansmen in Australia and New Zealand, and the Earl of Selkirk even founded a colony on the Red River prairie in Canada, but the suffering was widespread

11

and intense as the dispossessing went on into the fourth decade of the nineteenth century. There is some irony and satisfaction, perhaps, in recalling that the clansmen who were driven out of their homes by sheep later themselves raised such vast numbers of sheep in Australasia that they ruined the Scottish industry that they had been displaced in order to create.

There was also a religious dimension to the Clearances. Stafford was English and a Protestant, and Loch took care to drive off Catholics first. In reprisal, the Catholic MacDonnell of Glengarry drove off his Protestant tenants. The Kirk was very embarrassed by the whole affair. Why had ministers not protested? The answer was very simple: their livings were in the gift of the absentee landlords. The embarrassment of the Kirk eventually led to a schism and the setting up of the Free Church of Scotland, free from all patronage and appointments not approved by the congregation of parishioners.

The Gordons were in Leith while the discussion which led to the schism was going on, and like everybody else heard lurid tales of the Clearances. The family was in sympathy both with the plight of the dispossessed in the Highlands, and with the reform of the Kirk. The democratization of the latter, as had happened with the Methodists, would make it easier for ordinary members of the congregation to ensure that no 'false doctrines' were smuggled in at the door of the sacristy. Charles listened to these thoughts voiced at the daily Bible reading and commentary. He used to say that he had had a bellyfull of injustice by the time he was eight years old.

Having repaired the guns at Leith Fort, Lieutenant-Colonel Gordon was offered what the family thought was a romantic posting, in contrast to the grimness of Dublin and Leith with their social problems. He accepted a short stay on that unlikely-sounding outpost of Empire, the island of Corfu, where there were batteries to be resited. The younger children, who were to accompany their parents, were very excited by the prospect and by the sea voyage, though Charles was seasick all the way. They found the island warm and welcoming, and quite different from anything they had ever seen or heard. Charles was astonished to find that not only did the islanders speak Greek, but his mother spoke some words of the language, too, though he never knew how she came by this accomplishment. With his brother Enderby he explored the narrow streets of Corfu town, which had just over fifty thousand inhabitants at the time. The Gordons lived in a whitewashed house above the port, to which an English tutor came every day to give lessons to the two boys and three sisters. In the afternoon there was plenty of time to explore the island with a battery sergeant-major who had been there since 1827, when the British had snatched it from the Turks – who had moved in after Napoleon's brief occupation – and used it as a garrison to ensure the survival of Greek independence. They saw the ruins of a civilization which had flourished there since the island was known as Corcira, and Enderby, who was an amateur historian, explained the surviving artifacts of Venetian rule, which had lasted from 1386 to 1799.

Charles enjoyed it all. He was said to be very impressionable and a little guileless at that age, and often reckless – 'he used to fling himself into deep water,' wrote Butler, 'although quite unable to swim', and wait patiently until rescued. There was no respite, even on Corfu, from the daily Bible readings and discussions, from which he acquired a vast treasury of biblical lore; the only difference was that they took place later in the day, and in the light which came through the oddly shaped windows of the former Venetian merchants' apartments. Charles said in later life that he was astonished to learn that not every family spent at least twenty hours a week with the Old and New Testaments.

At the age of nine the boy was slight, wiry, normally mischievous (he enjoyed taking mice with him into other people's houses) and self-sufficient. He had had half a dozen homes in his short life, so his self-sufficiency was not surprising; he later credited the constant movement with his parents from posting to posting with his 'lack of preference for any race', laudable but surprising in one who was to become the hero of the British jingoist. But however formative these wanderings were his parents thought it was high time he went to school in England. Augusta, three years his senior, had already become the close friend and confidante of her brother that she was to remain throughout his life. She wept, but to no avail. He would have to go to a good school, so that he could be got ready to follow his father into the Army. The problem was, which school should he be sent to?

As Lytton Strachey wrote in *Eminent Victorians*, in the essay on Dr Arnold, Headmaster of Rugby, who had died in 1842:

The public schools of those days were still virgin forests, untouched by the hand of reform. Keate was still reigning at Eton; and we possess in the records of his pupils, a picture of the public-school education of the early nineteenth century, in its most characteristic state. It was a system of anarchy tempered by despotism. Hundreds of boys, herded together in miscellaneous boarding-houses, or in that grim 'Long Chamber' at whose name in after years aged statesmen and warriors would turn pale, lived, badgered and overawed by the furious incursions of an irascible little old man carrying a bundle of birch-twigs, a life in which licensed barbarism was mingled with daily and hourly study of the niceties of Ovidian verse. It was a life of freedom and terror, of prosody and rebellion, of interminable floggings and appalling practical jokes. Keate ruled, unaided – for the under-masters were few and of no account – by sheer force of character. But there were times when even that indomitable will was overwhelmed by the flood of lawlessness. Every Sunday afternoon he attempted to read sermons to the whole school assembled; and every Sunday afternoon the whole school assembled shouted him down. The scenes in Chapel were far from edifying: while some antique Fellow doddered in the pulpit, rats would be let loose to scurry among the legs of the exploding boys. But next morning the hand of discipline would reassert itself; and the savage ritual of the whipping-block would remind a batch of whimpering children that, though sins against man and God might be forgiven them, a false quantity would only be expiated in tears and blood.

This was not the sort of school which commended itself to the Gordons. They did not object to a certain amount of flogging – William flogged his sons regularly when they transgressed. They did not object to the Latin, though this was not necessary in an army class. What they wanted was a good Evangelical atmosphere, ideally in the West Country, with some Army connection, and modernity without frivolity.

Their choice fell on Fullands School at Taunton. Aunt Henrietta Augusta took an interest in mental health and knew a Dr Edwin Fox, a pioneer in the establishment of private asylums. Fullands had been a private asylum for some years – it was a large house, a mile and a half outside the town of Taunton, just far enough for any strange noises to pass unheard. Dr Fox had now been offered even more convenient premises in Brislington, and therefore sold Fullands to a Mr George Rogers. Mr Rogers was on the lookout for pupils at the same time that the Gordons were on the lookout for a school, and Henrietta Augusta acted as intermediary. She recommended Mr Rogers for his academic achievements and his piety, though he seems to have had no university degree and was not in Orders. Rogers was assisted by his son, Herbert, who also had the curacy of St Mary's, Taunton.

Charles George Gordon did not enjoy his four years at Fullands. Charles Dickens had reached a zenith of popularity with the publication of *Pickwick Papers*, *Nicholas Nickleby* and *Oliver*

Twist. Then, in 1841, there had appeared *Barnaby Rudge*, subtitled, *A tale of the Riots of 'Eighty, led by Lord George Gordon.* Young Gordon was to be teased later at Woolwich about the high treason of his distant relative, but at Fullands, perhaps because the publication of Dickens's novel was so recent, the young Mr Rogers went out of his way to hint that if Charles George did not behave he would end up at the bar of the Court of King's Bench or even worse. A certain amount of literary insensitivity does not surprise at a military academy; but in a recently founded school, anxious to make a name for itself in an era of reform, it was a little odd. The boy was put off Dickens for life.

If he hated Rogers and Dickens, Charles George Gordon hated sport even more, and of all sports cricket was the most. In this he was as unfortunate as in the chronology of Dickens's works. As the author of *Somerset and Dorset Notes and Queries* wrote:

> Mr E. Western – one of the masters – familiarly and affectionately known as "Teddy" – acted as secretary of the club and kept wicket for the school eleven, and on some other occasions. For it was by no means only school matches that were played on the Fullands ground; and if for no other reason, Fullands School deserves to be remembered as undoubtedly the "cunabulum" of Somerset cricket. Here during the season the whole of the ground was kept carefully mown, and tended throughout the year, at a time when most other clubs were content to mow a square patch in the middle of a field. It was here that almost all the earlier (so-called) "County" matches were played, when Somerset was struggling to emerge from the position of a second class to that of a first class cricketing county.

Quite a lot of the boys' time was taken up removing leaves from the cricket field, and harsh punishments were meted out to those who dared to sit on it or play lesser games near the pitch area. However, as Charles George later recalled, it was possible to pretend to be tending the sacred grass and idle away an early summer afternoon with impunity.

Every Sunday, Gordon once said, bitterly, 'Rogers shows off his lunatics, hoping to find more parents mad enough to send their children to his asylum.' *Somerset and Dorset Notes and Queries* puts it rather more kindly:

> Fullands was then in the parish of Wilton, but it was a long way round to Wilton Church, and on Sundays the boys of the school were taken instead to St Mary's, Taunton, which was much nearer [and the young Rogers was curate]. They were marched into the

15

town in column of fours, and made an imposing spectacle en route, which perhaps also served in a measure as a useful advertisement. On these occasions, they wore "mortar board" caps, of university pattern, with tassels of orange and black. These were the school colours, and appeared again in the striped jerseys used for football, and the "blazers" worn on the cricket field.

This regular long march, three miles there and back, took place in fair weather and foul and only very seldom was it said to be 'too inclement' – or, as the boys put it, 'they were afraid the chains would rust and break'.

One of the Rev. Herbert Rogers's activities did impress Gordon, and was, perhaps, responsible for a later interest of his own. For some reason there were many orphans in and around Taunton, and young Rogers founded a home for them, St Saviour's, at the corner of Park Street. Boys at the upper end of Fullands were encouraged to go and take part in 'improving' services at the home. Charles George Gordon, who had grown up with lengthy passages from the Bible ringing in his ears, was a sensitive reader in spite of his slight lisp, and often intoned parables which the Rev. Herbert would expound on evangelically. The orphans were also allowed to watch cricket matches, which impressed the Fullanders, and their food was said to be better than that served at the school.

It was some lay helper at St Saviour's who discovered that the boy had a talent for drawing, not a subject to which much attention was paid by day. It was a strangely expressed talent. He did not want to draw or paint the old houses or the rolling hills of Somerset. What interested him was the making of street maps, with great attention to accuracy and detail.

There were occasional excursions to Exeter, to the tombs of his uncle and grandparents at St Thomas's, and this meant good teas with aunts and older cousins. With all these activities and the exciting uncertainty of never knowing in advance where he would be spending his holidays, four years passed, if not pleasurably, at least quite quickly. He counted the days until he would follow his father to the 'Shop', the Royal Military Academy, Woolwich, and set himself to earn those good reports which would make his admission there automatic, and as early as possible. The age on joining at Woolwich ranged in those days from fourteen years to fifteen years and nine months. Charles George was fourteen and a half when he was 'appointed', so he succeeded in his task. As he said goodbye to his friends at Fullands, he told them: 'I will never come this way again.' And he never did.

TWO

Coddling Young Soldiers

'This Gentleman Cadet will never make an officer.'
Eardley-Wilmot, Captain of the Cadet Company,
RMA Woolwich, 1850.

The Duke of Wellington is supposed to have said that his victory at Waterloo was 'the nearest run thing you ever saw in your life', and this is the opinion of most military historians. It was not just a question of the late arrival of the Prussian Blücher, though this was not just better late than never but decisive. It was rather a question of indifferent leadership by monarch and ministers, a deeply rooted conviction that to be a good officer it was enough to be a gentleman, and the lack of any systematic training for officers or men.

George III did not feel that a sovereign's place was on the battlefield, nor was it a place for his heir. Three of Prince George's brothers were lieutenant-generals, and the Duke of York a field-marshal, but 'Prinny' was only a colonel of Dragoons (he had his own decorative regiment). When he asked his father 'to be allowed to shed the last drop of my blood in support of your Majesty's person, crown and dignity', he was told not to be ridiculous; the 10th (Prince Regent's Own) had to fight without him. By the date of Waterloo, George III had become a blind, bent old man, wandering about Windsor and the old Palace of Whitehall in a violet dressing-gown with the Order of the Garter pinned to it; ironically, at Whitehall he occupied the rooms used by Charles I on his way to execution. The Duke of York was still in disgrace over the sale by his mistress, Anne Clarke, of commissions and promotions. Six years were to pass before a member of the royal family bothered to visit the battlefield; the then George IV, with Wellington as his guide, wandered about in the rain, missing the warmth and comfort of Dessin's Hotel in Calais where he had left a pretty French-woman.

It was as well that the British Army had no major war to fight between 1815 and 1854. The professional soldiers who came home victorious from Waterloo kept a tight hold of the Army and its administration and looked askance at any proposed change, not to speak of reform. It was only in 1850 that the old Duke of Wellington felt that maybe a younger man should succeed him as Commander-in-Chief. Lord Hardinge held the post till 1856 when the job went to George, Duke of Cambridge, a cousin of Queen Victoria and a dolt. Britain took part in the Crimean War with a military organization which was largely non-existent. The Commander-in-Chief was quite independent of the government as such, though he relied on it to procure funds for the Army in Parliament. Infantry and cavalry regiments were expected to be largely self-supporting. Colonels, and the ladies who had the ears of colonels, designed uniforms which looked pretty on parade; the Light Cavalry was always the most spectacular with its Roman and Etruscan, hotel pageboy and fur teacosy headgear, lances and pennants, swords and standards, sabres, ribbons and frogging. Commissions and promotions were sold openly to rich aristocrats and the money was used to buy equipment for the enlisted men; officers were expected to kit themselves out, and have an allowance large enough to live in style. There was no real training programme approved at the centre. Drill and flogging were supposed to create discipline, and it was only in 1845 that flogging was limited to 100 strokes (a soldier died after 150 lashes and there was a public outcry). It was not until 1870 that the purchase of commissions was abolished, and flogging went on until 1881.

Then there were the part-time soldiers, raised by local squires and burgesses. In addition to decorative duties, hunting and beating for shoots, they were called out – especially in the industrial North and Midlands – to put down rioting workers; they were seen as a sort of private police force at the disposition of local magistrates. In theory, the yeomanry and militia formed a reserve on which the professionals could call in time of war, but it was not until 1851 that the need for a nationally organized militia or territorial army was recognized; opposition to it brought down Lord John Russell's government.

There were no mercenaries or soldiers of fortune in the British

Army, which made it almost unique. When Henry William Gordon was commissioned 2nd lieutenant in the Royal Artillery on 17 August 1803 he was soon to find himself in action against Scottish troops in Napoleon's armies, and there were many Scottish officers on the other side in the service of the Tsar. Swiss, Italian and assorted German officers and rankers fought everywhere, and there were Irish regiments in Spain. It was probably the Hanoverian fear of the Stewarts for so many years which led to the homogenization of nationality in the British Army – in Hanover, where there were no such threats to the throne, mercenaries were used.

Of course, there were bright spots on the escutcheon. Henry William Gordon appears on 10 March 1801 on the Muster Rolls of the Royal Military Academy, Woolwich and spent just over two years in this establishment. Some effort had been made since 1764 to train at least those officers who would 'supervise the engines of war', the Royal Artillery and Royal Engineers in particular. Neither the RA nor the RE was held in very high esteem by the 'proper soldiers' of the infantry and the cavalry; gunners and sappers were supposed to remove obstacles in the path of heroes, build roads and bridges, make maps, fortify, and blow up the enemy's fortifications. 'Proper soldiers', on horseback or on foot, would wait, arguing about who should be Right of the Line (which made for some untidy engagements), then charge when the way was clear and they could get on with the real business of war. It was the Peninsular campaign which made those who wanted to see that gunners and sappers were 'proper soldiers', too. However, for young men with a practical bent who came from families which could not afford to buy them commissions, the Royal Military Academy was as good as a gateway to glory as any other, and there was so great a demand for graduates until about 1811 that the internal equilibrium of the establishment was upset.

After the Napoleonic Wars there was a pause, as wounds healed and Europe digested the implications of the Congress of Vienna. There was some suspicion of those who wanted to increase the amount of education offered at the Academy. Some people were afraid that the gentlemen cadets would become spindly bookworms. The number of classes was reduced in 1823 and gymnastics made compulsory the following year for all senior classmen.

By the end of 1826 the Lieutenant-Governor could report that a new seriousness of attitude was developing in the cadets, but he became over-ambitious. In 1829 compulsory study for an hour each evening, in the cadets' rooms, was introduced, and the orderly officer was required to check on those suspected of idleness; to

19

reassure those who had been frightened by this intellectual trend, riding was made compulsory for the practical class in the following year. The Office of Ordnance (War Office) urged the Lieutenant-Governor 'to seek at all times a balance between the exercise of the mind and that of the body'. The aged Archbishop of Canterbury tried several times to enforce religious observances, but many of the cadets came from Nonconformist families and this was a failure; no Roman Catholics were openly admitted to the Academy.

In 1832 an attempt was made to divide the gentlemen cadets into groups according to ability, abolishing the divisions into Lower Barracks and Upper Barracks, or academies within the Academy, but merit was not yet thought worthy of such recognition. More specialization, however, was thought necessary. In 1832 those cadets who had already been nominated to the Royal Engineers were sent for six months to RE Chatham to take a course in surveying. They formed a tight-knit community in their quarters at 14 House, Brompton Barracks, with their own mess and study room. Their parents had to pay fees to the RE Agent, but the cadets, received 4s a day, partly as a reward and partly to compensate for extra expenses; no fees were paid to the Academy during this period. This 'work experience' lasted for three years, until in 1835 it was felt that their absence weakened the Academy *esprit*. During this experiment, prizes – three for each Academy – were presented to students in the junior entries, and prizewinners wore a strip of gold lace on their collars; there was some argument about whether or not this would lead to what Kipling later called a 'middle class lust for mere marks'.

In 1836 German was introduced to the curriculum. For a time it was more popular than French, which was still thought to be faintly unpatriotic and the language of 'the enemy'. A sudden surge of interest in and affection for the monarchy followed the accession of Queen Victoria in 1837. Lord Melbourne, the Prime Minister, made it known that the young sovereign was accomplished: 'She speaks German well, and writes it; understands Italian, speaks French fluently, and writes it with great elegance.' Victoria herself commented that 'Reading History is one of my greatest delights' – in a couple of months she disposed of Sully's *Memoirs*, Clarendon's *History of the Rebellion* and Russell's *Modern Europe*. For a while it became fashionably necessary for young men and women to seem to be virtuous and studious. French came back into favour.

In 1840 another attempt to foster more intellectual pursuits at RMA was made when in February the Lieutenant-Governor passed on to the gentlemen cadets at Woolwich a new order:

The Master-General has approved of a new distribution of the cadets for the purpose of carrying on the studies. The division into Academies is to cease, and the cadets are to be formed into classes as follows, viz: five classes of mathematics, four classes in fortification, and four classes formed for the study of languages, history and geography; surveying will be taught, as heretofore, to a class formed from the others. The present arrangements are not to be considered as permanent, but will be liable to such changes as may appear necessary in the general working of the plan. Thus the system of individual instruction and division of the cadets into Academies for study, with advancement from Academy to Academy, chiefly according to mathematical talent, provided a certain number of plates in fortification were drawn, which has been followed for very many years, is changed to class instruction; that is, each branch of study is to be carried on independently of every other; and the cadets divided into classes according to their efficient advancement in each study, each class being divided into sections according to progress, each section to be called up once in each attendance, so that each cadet will be regularly carried through every branch of study, and be advanced from class to class without reference to advancement in any other; none to be considered eligible for final examinations in the theoretical course till he has reached the 1st class of mathematics and of fortification, and be either in the 1st class of French, or qualified to be so; and in order to obtain a commission he must also receive certificates of diligence and fair progress in other branches of study.

The strict enforcement of the regulation that 'should any cadet fail to qualify himself in the theoretical course within four years, his name will be submitted to the Master-General for removal from the Institution' certainly raised standards and thinned out the ranks. Another regulation made it compulsory for all cadets to be examined at the end of their first year, so that those who were 'not likely to qualify for commissions in the time allowed' could be asked to leave.

These rigorous new rules created a demand for a sort of military preparatory school, so that when the boys arrived at RMA Woolwich they would have some idea of what was expected of them. The Board of Ordnance itself opened the first school, at Carshalton House, near Croydon; there were 100 boys, with a headmaster and two assistant masters to teach them. To get into the school it was necessary to have the placet of the Master-General, and there were soon accusations of favouritism, if not bribery and corruption, because after going through Carshalton House entry to RMA was assured.

Charles George Gordon might well have gone to Carshalton House had it opened sooner; in fact it took its first entry in 1847, and on 8 July he was appointed to RMA, joining it on 15 September, forty-four years after his father had left. His father, in fact, had grave doubts about whether the boy would survive; he once said that 'while he is at the Academy, I feel like I am sitting on a powder keg'. He showed some academic weaknesses, but – worse – signs of stubbornness and contempt for authority. However, like most of the boys at Woolwich he was the son of an army officer, a colonel marked down for advancement to general officer, and his brothers had passed through the Academy with some distinction and had gone on to become professional soldiers. Young Henry, in particular, had made his mark in the practical class of his day, and had won a number of prizes and merit badges.

Their younger brother arrived just in time to experience two revisions of the regulations and the curriculum. Starting with his intake, cadets in the practical class would be divided into two streams – the lower one would be known as the competitive class and because, by definition, less able, would do no riding. The other change was a new standard timetable for both the practical and the theoretical classes, which would make it much more difficult for junior instructors to change the timetable to suit their own social engagements, or even their preference for this subject over that. The Lieutenant-Governor would still be able to make changes as he thought fit and to extend the time a cadet spent at the Academy, according to opportunities for promotion in the Army outside, the performance of cadets in the examinations, and what would later come to be called 'character assessment'.

In effect, the Academy was now divided into one practical and four theoretical classes. As far as the theoretical classes were concerned, a cadet had to keep pace with his contemporaries in every subject. Those who were good in mathematics, but not so good in fortification or French, could not be in the top class for one and the bottom class for the others. The allowance for individual abilities was made by sectioning each class according to talent displayed. This, again, made for homogeneity in teaching and pace of progress.

Young Gordon did not find the academic work difficult and soon showed his natural talent for drawing as well as for getting good marks for fortification and French. As a 'snooker' or first-year, freshman, cadet he was, however, on the receiving end of a certain amount of bullying. The death of Dr Arnold, Headmaster of Rugby, in 1842, and the subsequent near deification of the man and universal emulation of his methods, had convinced all educators, including the teachers of civilian subjects at Woolwich, that there was only one way to keep discipline in any sort of educational establishment. Arnold had taught, and demonstrated, that by setting older boys to discipline younger boys the teaching staff could be withdrawn from the battlefield of the classroom to purely academic duties, and only the headmaster needed to intervene, occasionally, to back up his sixth-form prefects or praepostors and, even more occasionally, flog boys who had been flogged by older boys without any improvement in their conduct. The 'set an older thief to catch a young thief' theory had something to commend it but it was open to abuse. In its RMA Woolwich variant, it was always open to abuse. The 'sixth-form prefect' in this case was a second-or third-year cadet, given the internal rank of corporal; those promoted to this rank were given special shoulder straps known as 'swabs', which they wore at all times.

Charlie Gordon, as he was called by one and all by the end of his first year, objected to what he called the abuse of privilege by some of the corporals. He resented the sneering remarks made by those set to supervise prep. in class study rooms, and he resented the enforcement of all petty restrictions. The food at RMA Woolwich left much to be desired, and what was on offer was served very slowly. Boys in the first terms only had an hour for what was called dinner, and this often turned out to be just long enough to down the pudding and get to study or class rooms. This was irritating because most of the cadets either had extra food in their trunks, with which they supplemented what was served, or used their pocket money to buy cakes and pies at a sort of tuck shop kept by former NCOs and their wives. Cadets who were last out of the mess had no chance at all of getting at their trunks or to the counter in the tuck shop, and so faced relative starvation until the late supper served to the theoretical class. Inevitably, as soon as the last plate in the mess had been polished clean and the Cadet Captain had given the cadets permission to leave, there was a rush for the door during which some of them were crushed or had their uniforms torn. On one occasion the officer on duty told a corporal to stand at the head of the stairs leading out of the mess and make sure the cadets walked in a slow and dignified manner to their next appointments. As his brother relates:

> This was too much for Charlie Gordon, who, putting down his head, butted with it, and catching the Corporal in the pit of the stomach, not only sent him down the stairs, but through the glass

door beyond. The Corporal jumped up, and Charlie Gordon was placed in confinement and nearly dismissed. He was, however, allowed to remain though deprived of all his honours, and the captain of the cadet company [Eardley-Wilmot] predicted that he would never make an officer.

After the butting incident he became the target for all sorts of verbal disparagement and physical abuse. When he was heard to say of the Lieutenant-Governor, who had lost a leg at Waterloo: 'Never employ anyone minus a limb to be in authority over boys – they are apt to be irritable and unjust', he was accused of what would now be called 'subversive' ideas and attitudes. The revolutions of 1848 in Europe provoked a reaction among the establishment everywhere, and nowhere was it more violent than in the British Army. The Lieutenant-Governor addressed the gentlemen cadets on the need to root out any tendency to think that the young knew better than the old, the humble better than the noble. Sometimes men's motives might seem to be estimable, but who knew where rebellion might lead? Think of Cromwell, a soldier like them, creator of the New Model Army.

Unfortunately for Charles George Gordon, the Queen had discovered Scotland. Prince Albert and the children wore the tartan. The Queen learned to dance the strathspey and her husband even struggled with Gaelic for a year. All 'Scottish' boys were pleased by this, but young Gordon had been taught to be faintly ashamed of his Highland connection and very sensitive about his name. Again, the riots of the Protestant Association came up in conversation, and he was asked if he were a relative of the Lord George Gordon who had led them. This time it was worse than at school. He was reminded that the King, George III, had had to put himself at the head of his Guards and restore order after the mob had attacked the military in Fleet Street, while the Law Lords vacillated and magistrates locked themselves in their counting houses. The Lieutenant-Governor hoped there was no trace of this sort of excess in the character of any of the gentlemen cadets.

Again, discussing the French Revolution of 1830, Dr Arnold was quoted:

> An officer observed a boy (of twelve) insulting the soldiers, and though the action against the rioters was then raging, merely struck him with the flat of his sword, as the fit chastisement for boyish impertinence. But the boy had been taught to consider his person sacred, and that a blow was a deadly insult; he therefore followed the

officer, and, having watched his opportunity, took deliberate aim at him with a pistol and murdered him.

The corporals interpreted this homily in their own way. When Charlie Gordon was released from confinement they flogged him unmercifully on every occasion, believing that they had a *nihil obstat* from the authorities. After all, a boy who could butt a corporal through a glass door could do worse. 'Where is the wisdom of encouraging a fantastic sense of the degradation of personal correction? What can be more false, or more averse to the simplicity, sobriety and humbleness of mind which are the best ornaments of youth and offer the best promise of a noble manhood?'

Young Gordon's reaction to the bullying was to draw in his head and reinforce the shell about him, which was thought very odd and frightening. Bland Strange (later Major-General RA) records that 'One of Gordon's peculiarities was that he would at times, without apparent reason, withdraw himself from his friends, not speaking for days.' It was an effective form of self-defence. He was slight in build, though wiry, and could not offer much in the way of physical resistance. He would stand fast and fix his persecutors with his hard blue eyes until they stopped beating him and went away, discomfited.

It was during this period that Gordon began his lifelong correspondence with his elder sister Augusta. The Penny Post was still something of a novelty, though Rowland Hill had introduced it in 1839; there was no collection box at the Academy and Charlie had to go into Woolwich to buy his stamps and send his letters – this was regarded with some suspicion by the authorities, who opened several of his letters. The letters from Augusta were full of speculation about the nature of Heaven, Hell and even Purgatory. His sister seems to have been interested in religion almost to the exclusion of everything else, though perhaps this is not surprising. Young ladies could not make careers for themselves, except as wives and mothers, but they were encouraged to profit by their education, which may have had a bias towards literature and the arts, including the domestic arts, but was in many ways better than that given to boys of the middle and upper classes. Many of them were voracious readers, and not just of 'romances'. Augusta may have acquired a greater than usual interest in religious works, but the whole of the nineteenth century was so much awash with this sort of writing that it would have been astonishing had she not followed her mother in her choice of reading. Augusta was especially keen on books of sermons and commentaries – especially Scott's *Commentaries* – which came out in instalments; she would read them and send them on to her brother with her own commentaries on the *Commentaries*. She also read the newspapers and had her own opinions on events in the everyday world.

At this stage in his life Charlie was neither devout nor observant. There was a chapel at RMA and cadets were encouraged to attend an early form of ecumenical service, but many of them went home for the weekend. Charlie preferred to spend Sunday walking the streets, sometimes listening to an open-air preacher, but as often as not showing a pagan delight in the passing show or lunching at some small restaurant with one of his friends, as a change from the food in the mess. He would write to Augusta on Sunday evenings, sometimes teasing her about her beliefs, sometimes asking for her assessment of his own heroes, among whom was Garibaldi.

As he grew older, he often cast himself in the role of a brigand or romantic rebel. He enjoyed stirring up trouble, especially during the interminable parades, and would always get himself shuffled into the rear rank where he would be invisible to the sergeants taking the drill or the officers taking the parade. Charlie had his nicknames for them all and salacious stories of what they did off duty. He disliked the doctor and his mode of speech, perhaps because he had a slight lisp like Charlie's own. In any event, their voices were very similar, which made mimicry easy. Bland Strange reports that

> on one occasion an order was read out that, on the recommendation of the doctor, Gentlemen Cadets were forbidden to bathe later than the month of October.
> ' "Damned nonthence, coddling young soldiers!" lisped Gordon. "Let us bathe all winter, and prove that it's wholesome and the doctor's a fool".
> 'The front rank grinned and got an extra drill for unsteadiness. Gordon stepped to the front, took the blame upon himself and also got a drill for his pains. Next morning after 'oxters' [as the defaulters drill was called], they doubled over to the cadets' pond and bathed, continuing to do so all winter, though they had sometimes to break the ice.

Because their names came in sequence on the Muster Roll, Charlie often found himself in the company of Adam Lindsay Gordon, who was later to become famous as an Australian stock-rider and versifier – a sort of Antipodean Kipling. Bland Strange says: 'He was the exact opposite of Charles Gordon – a dreamy lad, with a far-off look in his eyes, indicative perhaps of the touching and semi-philosophical ballads, so dear to every Australian heart (redolent as they are of fatalism and wattleblossoms) though scarcely indicative of the man who beat "The Favourite" [a well-known Australian poem].' Adam Lindsay often teased his namesake for bearing the same Christian names as George Gordon, Lord Byron, and creating the fiction that he was some sort of relative; this was sure to 'draw' Charlie, who had been brought up to believe that Byron and Shelley were unmentionable subjects – though in later years Byron was promoted to join Garibaldi as a liberator of oppressed peoples.

Once he was a senior cadet, Charles George became a severe disciplinarian and 'eccentric in his mode of punishment as in all else'. The joking in the ranks ceased, and he looked forward to receiving his commission in 1851. There were some doubts about whether or not he would pass out high enough on the list to get 'sappers' – to be appointed to the Royal Engineers. He was a very poor mathematician, and though the Master-General had tried to lessen the emphasis on this subject, old teaching and examining habits died hard. In 1850 he had won a medal for French (medals were introduced in 1849 for those who had most distinguished themselves in mathematics, fortification, geography, history, French and German), and as he had to wear this on his uniform in the practical class it helped to compensate for weakness elsewhere. He was also very hard-working and good at surveying and fortification, which told in his favour. However, he was not to be commissioned with his intake. During the year 1850–1, the Board of Ordnance held one of its periodical inquiries into the bullying at the Academy. Several of the younger boys had gone home with visible injuries, one with a broken arm and nearly all with bruises. All armies attract sadists, but this was a more serious case than had been reported, for a long time. Questions were even asked in the House of Commons by MPs who had campaigned against the brutality at Keate's Eton.

The Commission of Inquiry took evidence from all the younger boys and tried to get them to name the aggressors; this was not easy because the 'sneaky snookers' would certainly be beaten for it when the members of the Commission went away. But one boy, with a badly bruised back, accused Charlie Gordon of having hit him several times with the back of a clothesbrush, and this accusation was followed by others. Relieved to have at least one culprit named, the Commission of Inquiry recommended that Gordon be dismissed, but the Lieutenant-Governor thought this unfair, as the other 'bullies' had not been identified, and proposed that dismissal be commuted to backterming – retarding the culprit's commission for six months, subject to good behaviour. When the Lieutenant-Governor told Charlie Gordon of his decision, he is supposed to have torn off his corporal's shoulder straps and thrown them on the floor, saying: 'If I am not fit to become an officer this term, I am not fit to wear these.' For this outburst he got nine extra drills.

But there was nothing to be done. He had passed through four classes in mathematics, fortification and French and completed his theoreticals (without public examination, notes the Register) on 18 June 1851. His practical examination was delayed until 22 June 1852, and he had obviously caught up in any weak subject because he was promoted Royal Engineers on the following day. He went home on leave and was made much of by Augusta and his other sisters and brothers.

There is a note of mystery about this last year at Woolwich. The backterming is well known, and recorded in F.G. Guggisberg's *The Shop*, a history of the Royal Military Academy, Woolwich, but there are no records at all for 1850–1 in the Woolwich Letter Books or elsewhere. It is difficult to refute the accusation that when Charles George Gordon had become a hero somebody made off with the pages covering the crucial period. Perhaps some mistaken person thought that Gordon's Academy career needed a little help for historians, or maybe even the Academy tried to hide – not for the first or last time – evidence of ineptitude. Whatever the truth of the matter, and of the justice of the accusations made against Gordon, he certainly never forgave the British Army establishment and spent most of his active service with foreign armies or political administrations, usually as a result of solicitation on his behalf or by Gordon himself.

After a long leave at home he was posted to Chatham. Like most subalterns, he was given an assortment of uninteresting tasks, including repairs to the fabric and plumbing of RE establishments. One of these was Carshalton House, the RA and RE prep. school at Croydon. Captain Peter MacLean, RA, who had served with Charlie's father, was Headmaster, and though he had put the boys in uniform and given the school a decidedly military flavour he was genuinely interested in his pupils. For 2nd Lieutenant Gordon this was a novelty and diluted some of his rancour. What was particularly interesting was not just that the boys were treated as human beings, but that MacLean believed it possible to take in a number of boys from other than the military upper middle classes; this was something really revolutionary in the middle of the nineteenth century and Gordon was impressed by the 'eagerness of the poor boys'. One day at Croydon, Gordon met Henry (later Cardinal) Manning, not long received into the Catholic Church and busy conducting a sort of census of Old Catholics and Oxford Movement converts. Manning, too, was interested in boys who could be schooled and improved. Protestant opinion in England and Scotland had been outraged in 1850 when the Pope had decided that the Roman Catholic population had grown to such an extent that it was now worthwhile organizing the two kingdoms into diocese, and in 1852 there was still an odour of anti-Popery by the sites of potential bonfires, but Gordon found Manning 'a pleasant fellow, really determined to raise the sights of the poor from Hell to Heaven'. Augusta, who was as snobbish as she was devout, was scandalized by the ideas of both MacLean and Manning.

When he was not repairing the roof at Carshalton House, Gordon was round and about the Medway towns, rebuilding barracks. It was in the long intervals between urgent tasks that he stimulated his early interest in surveying and mapmaking. Though he was often not actually asked to make these maps, the work itself and the necessity it implied for fatigue, mud and outside living gave him the excuse to avoid the social life of the garrison. He was not yet a good catch for garrison mothers – the ideal stage in the career of a prospective bridegroom was at promotion to captaincy – but there were balls and receptions which he could not otherwise have avoided.

Like any other sister, Augusta was rather worried about these early clues to the lifelong bachelordom of her favourite brother. She had grown up as the grisly progeny of George III shuddered and pirouetted to the grave, the worst of all advertisements for holy matrimony, but now they had all gone except the widowed Duchess of Gloucester. The young Queen Victoria had been married to her Albert for more than a decade, and the Great Exhibition of 1851 had enthroned him in the popular mind; the new Prime Minister, the Earl of Aberdeen, had said that the royal union was one any Scots girl would envy. Public morality had become stricter, with the rise of the middle classes, and marriage as such had become romantic and desirable. Augusta had several candidates for her brother's affections. She had laid her own plans, with her father's approval, for Charlie's introduction into female society and his horror of 'parties and fuss' did not make things any easier. But he was young, and at least nobody could say that he lived the life of a young libertine. In her letters she urged him to try to meet Christian families – she knew that Kent was stoutly Protestant – and to avoid, in particular, the young naval officers in the area who had '*such a bad reputation*'.

Augusta's warnings were unnecessary, just as her advice was ignored. Her brother met nobody socially. He would have liked to 'do some good works' but was almost painfully shy, and did not know how to approach those who were involved in such 'good works' locally. He cloaked his shyness with a brusqueness which was often misinterpreted, and seems to have been very lonely at the depot, given to long walks and nature study. His commanding officer found his conduct irreproachable and could not understand the implications of his behaviour at Woolwich, assuming, as he re-read the confidential reports, that the young man had fallen foul of somebody with more malice than judgement. If he had anything to complain about, it was that Gordon made him feel slightly uncomfortable, not good enough to be his formal superior.

After a year and a half, as Gordon was to come up for his lieutenancy, it was felt that he should be moved. There was no motivation for the posting to Pembrokeshire, except perhaps that it was far away and, for somebody not apparently subject to temptation, a place notoriously barren of the temptations of the flesh would be as much a home as any.

British military thinking has always been based on the principle that it is not only desirable but essential to bolt the stable door after the horse has fled. The naval and military stations in Devon and Cornwall had been built after the fright of the Spanish Armada in 1588, to the neglect of the Thames estuary, up which the Dutch had sailed, victorious, a hundred years later. Then work started on naval and military stations on the Thames estuary, which was why Napoleon, another century later, decided that the Welsh coast and the Bristol Channel would make a good invasion site. Fifty years after the Napoleonic threat of invasion had gone, Bristol and the south-west of Wales were being fortified.

The Royal Engineers depot was at Pembroke Dock, which might be described as the Cleddau estuary advanced redoubt for the defence of Pembroke. Pembroke had been important in Norman times and boasted one of the largest castles in Britain, fallen into ruin since the Civil War, though the seven bastion towers and 75-foot keep were still visible and recommended as an object for study by young sappers. Nothing of exceptional political or military importance had happened since 1457, when Henry VII had been born there, but then a few half-drowned Frenchmen and obdurate Jacobites had landed farther up the estuary half a century before, taking advantage of Britain's preoccupation with Napoleon, so the Board of Ordnance under Wellington thought it well worth refortifying the Dock.

From a military point of view, Gordon soon realized that what he was doing was a waste of time, but he liked the countryside and met a Captain Drew of the 11th, with whom he explored it. Drew, an amateur archaeologist, was writing a paper on the Druids, who had dragged huge dolerite stones round St Brides Bay to Milford Haven to be floated down the Avon on their way to Stonehenge. He and Gordon cast about St Davids looking for prehistoric relics, but Drew passed on much more than an interest in archaeology; he was a fundamentalist Christian, with his Evangelical roots in the Old Testament which he read aloud to Gordon as they picnicked together on the headlands. Drew was horrified to learn that his young friend seldom went to church, just as his young friend was startled to learn that Drew went to whichever church took his fancy, had a good preacher and an apparently devout congregation. Whatever new version of Christianity Drew preached, it was certainly attractive. Not only did Charlie Gordon take his first Communion that Easter, 1854, but he took to reading and prayer of a sort which had been Augusta's regular diet for years, such as Arnold's *Passages in a Wandering Life*, and *The Remains of the Reverend R. McCheyne*. He wrote to his sister:

> No novels or worldly books come up to the *Commentaries* of Scott. . . . I remember well when you used to get them in numbers, and I used to laugh at them; but, thank God, it is different with me now. I feel much happier and more contented than I used to do. I did not like Pembroke, but now I would not wish for any prettier place. I have got a horse and gig, and Drew and myself drive all about the country. I hope my dear father and mother think of eternal things. . . . Dearest Augusta, pray for me I beg you.

Gordon's joy at the performance of his first Easter devotions must have been somewhat clouded by the fact that on 28 February Great Britain and France had declared war on Tsarist Russia. The Ottoman Turkish Empire had been slowly disintegrating since the middle of the eighteenth century. Napoleon's Middle Eastern campaigns had encouraged rebellious subjects in their dreams of independence, and after the war some of these dreams had come true. Egypt under Mehemet Ali had won so many concessions of autonomy from the Sublime Porte in Constantinople that the country was now only a nominal vassal state. The Greeks had won their independence in 1827, and the Romanians were not far away from uniting the provinces of Moldavia and Wallachia.

It was Tsar Nicholas I who now tried to give the disintegrating edifice another shove. Russia had been disappointed in 1813 when the Turks had defeated the Serbs under Kara George, who believed, as Russia did, that a union of all the Slav peoples was desirable. Pan-Slavism in a crude form was unthinkable anyway, because so many Slavs lived under Austro-Hungarian rule. However, there was the Orthodox Church to protect, and though the Patriarch of the Russian Provinces was not the Ecumenical Patriarch or 'Pope', Russia felt a special duty to protect the faithful in all the provinces. Indeed, there was a duty to protect the faithful wherever they were, including the Holy Land, by caring for the Holy Places. As one writer (Kelen) has said, Tsar Nicholas 'whipped up an argument between Greek Orthodox and Roman Catholic priests into the Crimean War'. He was punished for it because 'having done so, he insisted on reviewing his troops while suffering from a high fever; thus he died of mindless heroism'.

Mindless and heroic or not, the governments of Britain and France felt that the only way to curb Nicholas's ambitions and pretensions was to go to war. This decision was discussed in every military household. According to Charles George's father, Britain ought to have arranged an invitation by Greece to 'liberate' the whole of the Balkans, guaranteeing the independence of all the states there. Turkey would not have objected very vigorously and the wind would have been taken out of the Tsar's sails. However Palmerston had taken a stronger line, and the Tsar was to be fought on the Crimean peninsula. Maybe, later, there would be a march on Moscow from the south; France was certainly keen to avenge Napoleon's defeat there in 1812.

Drew, whose instructions to get ready to leave for active service arrived almost immediately, thought there would be one decisive battle in the Crimea, then an occupation of the Balkans. That was why, he said, British and French bases were being set up at Varna and Constanţa on the Black Sea coast. Young Gordon, who was only twenty-one and neither good at history nor strong on politics, had no strong feelings about the war, merely one of disappointment that he would be deprived of the company of Drew, and the professional soldier's instinctive desire to get on to a battlefield as quickly as possible because that is where the glory and promotion are found – for the survivors.

Augusta, notwithstanding the fact that she had grown up in barracks and was surrounded by soldiers in her family, was not very keen to see young Charlie leave for the front. The more she read in the papers of the mess and muddle there, the less attractive the prospect became, and letters from her other brothers, already in the Crimea, worried her. Apparently the issue of winter boots in September 1854 turned out to be a masterpiece of mismanagement. Many sizes of boots had come only for left feet, and one lot had soles made of waxed paper instead of leather. Henry Gordon wrote that a large consignment of flannel shirts and drawers in boys' sizes had reached Varna, together with a crate of nutmeg graters, tents made for Sir John Moore at Corunna and a box of maps of the Crimea dated 1796. There would be worse to come.

But there was no stopping Charlie when Drew had gone, and he began to bombard friends at the Board of Ordnance with requests for a posting to the Crimea. With the help of a family friend, Sir John Burgoyne, he was attached to a Royal Engineer unit that specialized in mapping minefields. He celebrated Christmas with his family early, and on New Year's Day 1855 arrived at Balaclava, where the Allied fleets were moored.

THREE

The Crimea and After

'I see that Dr Hall [Principal Medical Officer for the Army] is now KCB. I can only suppose this to mean Knight of the Crimean Burial Grounds.'
Florence Nightingale to Sidney Herbert,
Minister for War

Lieutenant Gordon arrived in the Crimea with all the feelings of hope and excitement proper to a young soldier a month away from his twenty-second birthday. He had even enjoyed the journey from England, perhaps because he had been able to do part of it overland. 'I am extremely lucky in going by Marseilles,' he wrote on 12 December, 'as I am such a bad sailor.' His superiors, and Sidney Herbert, the Minister for War, had decided that wooden huts should be built for the troops, though the winter was far advanced and the Battles of Alma, Inkerman and Balaclava had already been fought by troops billeted in tents. Government contractors, anxious to line their own pockets, had managed to persuade Mr Herbert that there were no forests east of Ramsgate, so Gordon had been put to loading expensive oak planks on to colliers at Portsmouth; as Sir William Butler notes: 'The huts reached their destinations after the army they were to shelter was in its grave.' Gordon had then been sent across the Channel, then by rail to Lyons, steamer to Valence and rail again to Marseilles, because the British government was anxious to show the French government that it took seriously all its offers of co-operation. He wrote to his mother on the way that he was 'very tired, but I have seen along the way the pretty towns and villages, vineyards and rivers, with glimpses of snowy mountains beyond'. He left Marseilles the following Monday for Constantinople, spent Christmas Day on board, and duly arrived at Balaclava.

Balaclava on New Year's Day was not the most attractive place in Europe. He wrote to his mother on 5 January 1855:

> We have only put up two huts as yet but hope to do better soon. Lieutenant Daunt, Ninth Regiment, and another officer of some Sixtieth Regiment, were frozen to death . . . and two officers of the Ninety-third Regiment were smothered by charcoal. The streets of Balaklava are a sight, with swell English cavalry and horse artillery carrying rations, and officers in every conceivable costume foraging for eatables.

Another amazed spectator – though not in the Crimea itself – had been Miss Florence Nightingale, who had arrived on 4 November 1854 with her thirty-eight nurses to take up her appointment as Lady Superintendent in charge of nursing at the main hospital at Scutari-Constantinople. Lytton Strachey sums it up very well:

> What had occurred was, in brief, the complete breakdown of our medical arrangements at the seat of war. The origins of this awful failure were complex and manifold; they stretched back through long years of peace and carelessness in England; they could be traced through endless ramifications of administrative incapacity – from the inherent faults of confused systems to the petty bungling of minor officials, from the inevitable ignorance of Cabinet Ministers to the fatal exactitudes of narrow routine. In the inquiries which followed it was clearly shown that the evil was in reality that worst of all evils – one which has been caused by nothing in particular and for which no-one in particular is to blame.

Miss Nightingale was quicker to place the blame: 'I have been well acquainted with the dwellings of the worst parts of most of the great cities of Europe, but I have never been in any atmosphere which I could compare with that of the Barrack Hospital at night.' She went on to describe the senility of many of the army doctors; the idiocy of the supply officers who could not unpack without a Board, which entailed assembling a number of officials to observe the proceedings; and the unreal world inhabited by Lord Stratford de Redcliffe, British Ambassador in Constantinople, who wanted to devote the proceeds of *The Times* relief fund to building a Protestant church at Pera.

Lieutenant Gordon was a very junior officer, had no friends at court and could only get on with the job in hand. This job was the siege of Sebastopol. On 15 January he wrote home to say that he had had his first good look at the place: 'I do not think I ever saw a prettier city. It looks quite open and a Russian steamer was cruising about inside the harbour. Two of their steamers came out the other day and bombarded the French lines for two hours, but our vessels were unable to move out to attack them, as steam was not up. For the future it will always be up.'

Nobody seemed to know quite what to do to reduce the city. French and British engineers were put to mining and countermining along a front of 8 miles, everywhere in fact except along the strategically important south side of the harbour. Morale seemed to be low. On 14 February, after he had noted that 'young grass and crocuses are appearing', he wrote:

The night of February, 14th I was on duty in the trenches . . . I got, after some trouble, eight men with picks and shovels, and asked the captain of the advanced trench, Captain —— of the Fourth, to give me five double sentries to throw out in advance. It was the first time he had been on duty there; and, as for myself, I never had, although I kept that to myself. I led forward the sentries, going at the head of the party, and found the sentries of the advance had not held the caves, which they ought to have done after dark, so there was just a chance of the Russians being in them. I went on, however, and though I did not like it, explored the caves almost alone. We then left two sentries on the hill above the caves, and went back to get round and put two sentries below the caves. However, just as soon as we showed ourselves outside the caves and below them, bang! bang! went two rifles, the bullets hitting the ground close to us. . . . It was not a Russian attack, but the two sentries whom I had placed above the caves had fired at us, lost their caps, and bolted. . . . The Russians had, on the report of our shots, sent us a shower of bullets.

More farce was to come.

I met Colonel —— of the First Royals. I warned him if he went out, he would be sure to be hit by his own sentries or the Russians. He would go, however, and a moment afterwards was hit in the breast, the ball going through his coats, slightly grazing his ribs, and passing out again without hurting him.

Seeing the south side of the city and harbour neglected by the miners and counterminers, the Russians used the unusually mild February to throw up batteries of guns 600 yards in front of their existing earthworks; then they hurriedly fortified the intervening area. There was no British or French reaction, so in March they threw up another set of batteries 300 yards further on. This time the British noticed and Gordon wrote: 'This looks serious', but a cold snap had frozen his ink and 'getting a dip breaks the nib of my pen'. He was relieved when the weather broke finally at the end of March and he could go to visit his brothers:

26th March, 1855. Rode to Balaklava. Saw Henry and Enderby. Very hot. Races going on. Evening on duty in the trenches. Went down to advance to see work for the night. Captn Hill, 89th, left me to post his sentries. Fired on by R[ussia]n picket, struck and left by men. Went out for him after, but found only his coat. Constant alarms. Fired on working party from Redan [a Russian fortification] and shot from Creek.

It was decided to make the main assault on Sebastopol on 17 June. At three o'clock in the morning a great barrage of guns and mortars began (Gordon was on duty half an hour before, and in the trenches for seventeen hours), and went on all day. This was supposed to demoralize the Russians, and when their guns stopped firing early in the afternoon, it was assumed that the barrage had achieved its object. Gordon was not so sure and told his superiors as much. 'They are holding their fire,' he noted, and he was right. Next morning, the infantry advanced. Gordon reports:

About 3am the French advanced on the Malakoff tower in three columns, and ten minutes after this our signal was given. The Russians then opened with a fire of grape that was terrific. They mowed our men down in dozens, and the trenches, being confined, were crowded with men who foolishly kept in them instead of rushing over the parapet, and, by coming forward in a mass, trusting to some of them at least being able to pass through untouched to the Redan, where, of course, once they arrived, the artillery could not reach them, and every yard nearer would have diminished the effect of the grape by giving it less space for spreading. We could thus have moved up our supports and carried the place. Unfortunately, however, our men dribbled out of the ends of the trenches ten and twenty at a time, and as soon as they appeared they were cleared away.

The assault failed. British casualties were some 1,400 killed and wounded; the French lost some 6,000 and the Russian defenders 4,000.

The failure of the assault, so contemporaries said, broke the heart of the British Commander-in-Chief, Lord Raglan. However much a tragedy in human terms, the death of this Waterloo veteran who absent-mindedly referred to the enemy as 'The French' caused a shuffling of the pack of commanders which, eventually, brought victory to the table.

More successful than the British and French was the small but compact force sent by the King of Savoy-Piedmont-Sardinia. King Victor Emmanuel and his Prime Minister, Cavour, had joined in the Crimean War to get British and French support for their campaign to liberate and unify Italy, and, though unprepared in many ways, the 15,000-strong little army proved unbeatable, and its presence on the battlefields vital. After the failure of the attack on Sebastopol in June, the Russians took heart and put together another army, of 50,000 men, which set out to relieve the city via Tchernaya, to the east. On 16 August the Piedmontese Army under General La Marmora, together with 15,000 French troops, attacked the Russian relief force. La Marmora held his sector of the line, and when the French had first fallen back and then counterattacked, both armies advanced and routed the Russians, who suffered 10,000 casualties.

Encouraged and embarrassed by the Italian and French victory, the British at Sebastopol prepared for a final assault in September. The barrages began. Gordon wrote:

When the 13 inch shell drops, you see timber, men, gabions etc. all fly up in the air as if a mine had exploded. The Redan looks very sickly as we fire platoons of musketry all night to prevent the Russians repairing it, and give them shells all day. The Russians repay us with baskets of shells 5½ inch, twelve at a time, each fired from a big mortar. It requires to be lively to get out of their way.'

There were several proving attacks before the main assault. Once again Gordon reported low morale:

Our men went forward well, losing apparently few, put the ladders in the ditch and mounted on the salient of the Redan, but though they stayed there five minutes or more they did not advance, and tremendous reserves coming up drove them all out. They returned well and without disorder, losing in all one hundred and fifty officers and two thousand four hundred men killed and wounded. We should have carried everything before us if the men had only advanced.

On 8 September the main assault began. The French made a determined effort, regardless of casualties, to take the Malakoff bastion where Admiral Korniloff, the Tsar's C-in-C, had been killed eleven months before; Korniloff had died saying: 'Now, gentlemen, I leave you to defend Sebastopol. Do not surrender it. Tell all how pleasant it is to die when conscience is at rest.'

As the eighth and ninth wore on and defeat was in sight for the Russians, they began to build a bridge of boats over which the survivors escaped; 90,000 had been killed during the siege. The city they left was in ruins – 'the whole town in flames and every now and then a terrific explosion', wrote Gordon. British casualties were as heavy and had it not been for Florence Nightingale, using *The Times* relief fund and other private donations, thousands would have died on their way across the Black Sea to the main hospital at Scutari, or of starvation and exposure in the Barrack Hospital itself. As she wrote to the Minister for War: 'The fact is, I am now clothing the British Army.' However, she cut the mortality rate dramatically, from 42 per cent to 2.2 per cent, and gave men hope. Gordon, like many other officers, probably saw and spoke to her when she made a quick visit to the Crimea itself to have a look at the field hospitals. There she fell foul of the Roman Catholic Reverend Mother Bridgeman, whose nurses staffed the field hospitals, and of the principal medical officer, Sir John Hall, only recently made KCB (Florence Nightingale told Herbert that she supposed the initials meant Knight of the Crimean Burial Grounds). Most of the unwounded officers took the part of Sir John; it was only when they saw what had been done for their wounded men at Scutari that they were converted.

Though Florence Nightingale would not have distinguished Gordon at this time from the thousands of other officers with whom she might have exchanged a few words, they were later to correspond and develop a sympathetic relationship, possibly based on their mutual contempt for bureaucracy and concern for practical matters. After his death she wrote of 'the triumph of failure, the triumph of the Cross. . . . With him all is well.' She took an active interest in the Gordon Home for Destitute Boys, and in 1887 wrote to a friend, 'Ask them to tea. The roughest boys first.' Gordon would have approved of that.

A happy encounter for Gordon at this time was with a cheerful young officer interpreter, Romolo Gessi, attached to the Piedmontese forces but much in demand everywhere because he spoke fluent English, French, Italian, Russian and Romanian. This polyglot had been born on a British boat plying between Malta and Ravenna (his father's birthplace), and, as his father was also

working for the British Ambassador in Constantinople, was reg-
istered as a British subject. Romolo's mother was an Armenian,
born Elisabeta Carabeti, of Romanian descent. He was just under
two years older than Gordon, and on the death in 1842 of his father,
by then British Consul in Bucharest, he went to the military
academies at Wiener-Neustadt near Vienna and Halle in Germany.
At the age of eighteen in 1849 he had joined Garibaldi in the
defence of the 'Roman Republic', and had then gone back to his
widowed mother in Bucharest. Five years later, at the outbreak of
the Crimean War, he had volunteered to serve with the British
Army, but there were difficulties – 'Because I was born on a boat to
an Armenian mother they could not make up their minds what
colour I should be.' The King of Piedmont took him on instead and
he was, in theory, a captain in the Bersaglieri.

Gessi and Gordon rode about the battlefields and explored the
now deserted Sebastopol. There was not much left after 'the last of
the old sieges,' Gordon observed, 'and as for plunder there is
literally nothing but rubbish and fleas; the Russians have carried
off everything else. They left their pictures in the churches, which
form consequently the only spoil, and one which I do not care
about buying.' Though Gordon may not actually have been looking
for plunder – he did not care for 'souvenirs' – Gessi was less
squeamish and put together a valuable collection of icons.

When he was not on duty blowing up the docks at Sebastopol,
Gordon would go with Gessi to interpret at various inquiries held
into administrative chaos. There was the warm clothing loaded into
a ship by mistake underneath ammunition boxes; the cargo could
not be discharged in the small and overcrowded Balaclava harbour,
and ship, ammunition and clothing had been lost in a storm while
the authorities debated what to do about berthing it. Then there
was a large consignment of coffee which had been similarly loaded
by mistake, and went to and fro across the Black Sea for a month. It
was something of a shock for Gordon, as was the uninhibited way
Gessi scrounged all sorts of food, drink and clothing for the coming
winter with no regard at all for the legitimate owner or supply
regulations. These lessons in 'living off the land' were to come in
useful to a different Gordon in later years.

Gessi was a great contrast to Drew, with whom Gordon still
corresponded. Nobody could describe him as a devout Christian,
though he was nominally a Roman Catholic, but he lacked Drew's
sanctimoniousness and had a strong feeling for justice, especially
social justice. This appealed to Charlie Gordon, who was also
attracted by the man-of-the-world air which his contemporary wore

so well. But above all Romolo Gessi was a dreamer, and span words around Charlie Gordon like a spider spinning a web. They spent hours sitting in the autumn sunshine at the abandoned North Fort at Sebastopol ('It is a tumbledown affair and we should have attacked on that side,' wrote Gordon in his customary matter-of-fact way), talking about the future. Dreaming had not been encouraged at Taunton, at Woolwich, or in the Gordon home, and dreaming aloud was for poets, not for soldiers. Gessi's candid assessment of himself, his prospects, his weaknesses and limitations had an almost religious quality about it.

During the winter, Gessi vanished to Constantinople to interpret for a whole series of courts martial and civil inquiries, and Gordon was left very much on his own. In March 1856 he wrote: 'We do not, generally speaking, like the thought of peace until after another campaign. I expect to remain abroad for three or four years which individually I would sooner spend in war than peace. There is something indescribably exciting in the former.' Gessi was back in April, and during that month and early May they rode the battlefields again, and, as peace had been declared in March, pushed on along the south coast of the Crimean peninsula and saw the great cathedrals and palaces standing there, untouched by war. Gordon was horrified to hear his revolutionary-minded friend say that cathedrals and palaces were prime targets; in Italy, the rich and the upper clergy would be swept away when Garibaldi struck again. However, something of this romantic, socialist brigandage must have lodged in Gordon's heart.

On 18 May 1856 Gordon, acting captain, was posted to the frontier to be drawn between Russia and the Romanian principalities of Moldavia and Wallachia. The Treaty of Paris of 1856, which put an end to the Crimean War, offered guarantees not only to Piedmont in its struggle to liberate and unify Italy but also to the Romanian principalities, which were to become, in 1859, the Kingdom of Romania, finally guaranteed in its independence in 1878. Gessi was delighted to hear of the posting, and as he had decided to go home on leave to Bucharest, introduced the young Englishman to the gaiety and corruption of life along the Danube. By all accounts Gordon enjoyed the home life of the Gessis. Romolo's mother, like any other Latin mother, did her best to find some young female relative who might be a possible bride for him, but as she had not yet married off her own son she was not optimistic. In the end, though she never gave up hope, she just fed the two young men well and passed on her prejudices and hopes for the future of the new Romania. As Gordon travelled between

Bucharest and the north-east frontier, which he was supposed to help to draw, he had the best of all possible opportunities to test out her feelings, which were anti-semitic and anti-Russian. He realized that there was a great deal of difference between town and country, far more than in England. He met peasants for the first time, and learned to understand them, and this, too, was useful to him in later years. He wrote: 'The Jews swarm in the towns. The doctors, priests, shopkeepers and mechanics are Germans, Greeks, Armenians and Jews.' The peasants in Bessarabia (northern Moldavia) spoke Romanian and the Russian they had had to learn during the years of occupation. They had, like all Romanians, lived for centuries as an island of Latin people, descendants of the Roman legionaries who had intermarried with the native Dacians. They had been surrounded and oppressed by Slavs, Magyars, Turks, then Slavs again, for so long that, though they liked the idea of being members of a Romanian nation state, they neither believed it could last for long nor trusted the townspeople who would go on taxing them, lending them money at impossible rates and taking their young girls off to the brothels.

There were no permanent army camps in Bessarabia, so with Gessi as interpreter Gordon lived where he could in the villages. He saw the continuing intrigue by Russian agents, already murmuring against 'the Turks and the Jews', and soon realized that however skilfully he drew a frontier it would only be a line on a map and the Russians would soon be back. However, he enjoyed his work and his time off. He learned to drink tsuica, a fierce plum brandy, and to eat a variety of spicy foods he had never met before; he liked the tsuica but not the local wine or food.

In March 1857 Gessi told him he would have to return to Italy or lose his temporary commission in the Piedmontese Army. There were great things afoot. He could not give an address but he would be rejoining Garibaldi as soon as he could, and he knew that there would soon be new campaigns, which would last for as long as the pro-Piedmontese feelings generated at the Treaty of Paris discussions lasted. The next battles would be fought against the Austro-Hungarians who occupied Lombardy and the Veneto; then the Bourbons in Naples and the south; then the Pope. If Charles was bored when his service in the Balkans was over, why not join him in Italy? He would keep in touch.

Young Charles Gordon was very sad to lose the best friend he had ever had, but he was not yet ready to become a soldier of fortune.

After an affectionate farewell the two men parted, and Gordon reported to the British Embassy in Constantinople for a further assignment: he was now on the Foreign Office List and the Army did not seem anxious to reclaim him. Most young men would have been delighted at the thought of a leave to be spent in Constantinople in the spring. The climate is at its best, the harbour at the Golden Horn as colourful as the fruit and spices in the market in front of Yeni Cami. And he was an officer in a victorious army, with all that that means in terms of opportunities for pleasure, licit and illicit. But Gordon, who took little interest in a place except from a military viewpoint, and in any case judged it by its people rather than for its architecture, landscape or atmosphere, noticed neither markets nor minarets. Rather baldly, he wrote, 'We arrived at Constantinople at three o'clock, and I must say I was rather disappointed with the view. The city is much lower than I expected, and the finest buildings I saw were the hospital at Scutari, the Seraglio and the Russian Embassy.' He hated the city, the native inhabitants and especially the British expatriates. He could well understand why Marco Gessi, Romolo's father, had been happy to move to Bucharest. He found Lord Stratford de Redcliffe as stupid as his preference for building a church rather than buying bandages for wounded soldiers had suggested. The British Ambassador questioned the young man closely about Bessarabia, and Gordon reported that 'he wished that we had held out for the whole of Bessarabia, when it would have been worth having'. He asked whom the Romanians would like to have as king when the union of the two provinces was proclaimed, and when Gordon said they would like to have a Romanian he was told that it was out of the question – some German princeling would get the throne, some distant connection of Queen Victoria. There was much more questioning, of the sort which reveals that the questioner knows little or nothing about the subject and is not keen to learn, and many invitations to receptions and balls in the British and French diplomatic community and Turkish society. After the simple domestic gaiety of the Gessis' home, Gordon found these affairs oppressive and distasteful; he was always timid and anxious to shun society, and what he saw and heard in Constantinople put him off 'dinners and feasting' for life.

Fortunately, there were interesting people to meet for the short time he determined to stay in Constantinople. Three men in particular, two Italian and one French, were distinguished members of his own profession. Luigi Negrelli, born in Austro-Hungarian occupied north-east Italy, had made a career as a railway engineer. After building the Limnat bridge in Zurich at the age of thirty-three he had been invited to build the Zurich railway system, then the Basle–Baden railway. In 1849 he had been appointed Austro-Hungarian High Commissioner for Lombardy and the Veneto, in charge of building the railway network there, but his principal interest since 1837 had been the digging of a canal between the Red Sea and the Mediterranean. He had also tried to interest people in a canal between the Danube and the Rhine, but the Suez Canal was his great passion, and he had discovered that the Red Sea and the Mediterranean shared the same level so that locks would not be needed. When Gordon met him, he had been appointed Inspector General of the Suez Canal project by the Khedive of Egypt, who governed that country, a Turkish possession, in the name of the Sultan. Negrelli's friend Pietro Paleocapa was an early convert and work done by him in 1856, including a detailed survey, had led to the shifting of the exit point on the Red Sea several kilometres to its present position at Port Said. With them in Constantinople was Ferdinand De Lesseps, who had been French Consul in Cairo from 1831 to 1838, during the period when Negrelli was launching the idea. He had immediately responded with enthusiasm and it was in fact his genius for organization and fund raising which made the Suez Canal a reality. A year after the Constantinople meeting Negrelli was dead, and De Lesseps was the man who got the Canal dug; Negrelli's widow and eight children received five founder's shares.

Gordon had received from Gessi something of a political education on that frontier where the Turkish, Russian and Austro-Hungarian Empires met, but he had no idea of the complexities of international, in particular Byzantine and Levantine, politics, especially where money was concerned. He found it difficult to understand Ottoman feudalism, the farming out of an empire to anybody who would rule it and send the Emperor money at regular intervals. It was all so different from the subtleties of French and British imperialism. The various khedives, pashas, beys and viceroys did not have to be Ottoman Turks, only good administrators and above all good revenue gatherers. The Phanariot Greeks (so called because they lived around the lighthouse in Constantinople harbour) had ruled the Balkans for centuries. Much of North Africa was Turkish in name only, ruled by native Egyptians, Armenians and an assortment of European beys and pashas. The three engineers were at Court to make sure that concessions they had wrung from the Khedive of Egypt would be ratified by the Sublime Porte (the Sultan), which would in some way guarantee that the Khedive kept his word. It was all a question of knowing whom to bribe and how much to bribe him with.

Gordon was fascinated by all this, but more interested in the technical and historical background to Negrelli's project. The dying man told him that the idea had first been bandied about two thousand years before Christ. Thirteen hundred years before Christ a canal had in fact been dug which linked the Great Bitter Lake with a branch of the Nile delta; it had been perfected by Darius, King of Persia, eight centuries later. But it was only a small cut, and had silted up by the time the Romans conquered Egypt. The Emperor Trajan had had it dug out again, but after the Roman withdrawal it had silted up again and was finally closed by the Caliph of the newly Muslim Egypt in AD776. Gordon was intrigued by the casual way Negrelli talked of 'opening it up again and adding a bit from the Bitter Lakes to the Red Sea', though this involved digging a trench about 100 miles long, an average of 100 yards across and 50 feet deep. Luigi Negrelli talked as if he were putting in a few tons of potatoes. The Constantinople lobbying was eventually successful and the three engineers left, De Lesseps for Egypt, Negrelli for Vienna and Paleocapa for Milan.

At the beginning of May Gordon was posted to the Russo–Turkish frontier in Asia Minor, or rather he was posted to the region to redraw the frontier. He went slowly along the Black Sea coast via Sinope – so he could see the masts and wrecks of the Turkish fleet, sunk in 1853 – to Trebizond and then inland to Erzerum. The name Trebizond had just become known in England as the titular archdiocese of Dr Errington, the leader of the Old Catholics, recently appointed by the new Cardinal Archbishop of Westminster, Wiseman; Gordon was to hear a great deal about the turmoil in the Anglican Church and the Roman Catholic revival when he went home for Christmas. Meanwhile, he had been given another amusing companion to guide and protect him. This half-Turkish, half-Kurdish major, who insisted on being called Robert, was a brisk and competent bandit. He had been given neither funds nor supplies by the government in Constantinople, so he just helped himself to whatever he needed. One of his favourite sources of income was the caravans on their way from Persia; he would stop them, levy tolls of his own devising and take horses and mules in lieu if the party refused to pay. Robert was always armed to the teeth, night and day, and just as well, but he was an expert in finding the only inhabitable house or lonely inn in the trackless semi-desert. Charles Gordon wrote home: 'The inhabitants are very poor and in a primitive condition. They sleep in houses which serve as stables and dwelling places at the same time.'

For the next six months, even though, as he wrote, 'there is no such thing as a wheeled carriage to be seen', he covered a great deal of ground. As his companion told him, it was necessary to talk to the chiefs of each region separately, if possible pretending that the region they were in was the one they preferred and would treat preferentially; in this way they would avoid trouble and be well fed. In June they conferred with the Armenians, and he found time to visit the ancient capital, Ani, then a ruined tumble of roofless churches and palaces. In August he was in Kurdistan. He liked the Kurds, a silent, strong race of mountaineers, and he climbed with some of them to the first summit of Mount Ararat, on which Noah is supposed to have landed with the Ark after the Flood.

It was at Mount Ararat that he conceived his plan to follow in the footsteps of other Christian cartographers and map the world of Judaism and Christianity. He had not then read Ptolemy's *Geographica* or seen the maps drawn by the Bishop of Seville, Isidore, in the sixth century, or by Beatus in the eighth, but he had heard of them from Drew; when he got home he would see what he could find. Meanwhile, the important thing was to get the scheme clear in his mind and not be deterred by the difficulties; cheerful persistence, like Negrelli's, was what he ordered for himself. He was not sure quite where to begin, but in the end decided that the obvious place was Genesis and the location of the Garden of Eden; this would require very careful study of the Bible (a copy of which never left him) and constant reference to wherever he was in the world that had a biblical connection. As he looked down 16,000 feet on to Armenia and Georgia, then towards the south, the invisible Persia and Palestine, he became quite excited and began a task which was to last to the end of his life. Years later, in 1883, he was to recall this expedition and write:

> I was never satisfied with Mount Ararat being the site of the Ark's resting-place. For the Ark of Noah was the Church, and nothing in Scripture seemed to denote that Armenia had anything particular to do with Israel. I think the Ark rested on Mount Moriah, and thus was connected with Jerusalem, and the Altar of Noah was the Rock. I feel this is very interesting; to me Mount Ararat never was the true site. Do you remember how I went, or nearly went up it? My name is on it now; Corporal Fisher RE left it there in a bottle.

In August, he had to go to Lazistan, 'the people of which State supply the Constantinople Turks with slaves whom they kidnap from the Gourelians who are on the Russian side . . . in eighteen months, sixty-two people have been kidnapped, sixteen killed and twenty or thirty wounded on the part of the Gourelians'. He was horrified by the extent of the slave trade which went on literally under his nose, and even more horrified when he realized that nobody cared. He sent messages to the British Embassy, and even urged his sister to get in touch with the Anti-Slavery Society. The Embassy ignored his protests, and when he insisted he was told he must be tired so could have four months' leave at home. When he got back he would 'see things in another light'.

He was not sorry to trundle back to Constantinople and take ship for England. He spent the winter of 1857–8 with his parents and enjoyed seeing old friends, including Drew. His mother and sister Augusta were quite excited about his plan to make a portfolio of religious maps and suggested that he join the Royal Geographical Society. They knew that his colonel was a member and would certainly put him up for membership – he was proposed by Colonel Simmons on 8 February 1858 and elected fourteen days later – and at the Society's headquarters he would find all sorts of medieval and earlier maps. Anyway they would tell him where to find what he was looking for.

When he showed the family his drawings of Trebizond, he raised a religious floodgate. The Protestant fundamentalism which had caused his ancestors to side with the Hanoverians instead of the Stewarts was still alive in the two women. They had been horrified when Pope Pius IX had divided the whole of England into diocese, as if he had the right to draw religious maps. What about the Reformation? Cromwell? The civil war of 1688–9? The bloody battles in the Highlands of Scotland? What right did this Italian have to pretend there was any place for Popery in England, Scotland or Wales? From Romolo Gessi Charles had learned a great deal about the declining power of the Papacy and its imminent temporal eclipse. He told his mother and sister that in a few years an Italian king would have his capital in Rome and the Pope would just be a bishop like any other (this was Gessi's simple Garibaldino creed), saying mass and ordaining the clergy. Augusta did not believe this, and anyway Italy was not England. There was now a Cardinal Archbishop of Westminster at the head of an English Roman Catholic Church with its own bishops and diocese, just as if Henry VIII had never existed. This was an exaggeration, but Charles could see what was worrying Augusta.

Rumour had it that the Queen was 'surprisingly sympathetic to the Irish Roman Catholics on the grounds that, as Albert had pointed out, being in the majority in Ireland they could hardly be described as Dissenters'. Manning and Newman had gone over to Rome. It was very worrying. Mrs Gordon urged her son to read the Bible every day and stop his ears against temptation.

Cracks were appearing in the hitherto firm social structure, too. The whole family had gone up to London on 21 May 1856, where the Queen had presented a special Crimean service medal 'personally and with no distinction between officers and men. . . . The rough hand of the brave and honest private soldier came for the first time in contact with that of their Sovereign and their Queen.' It was a rare breaking of social barriers, to be followed by the creation of a medal inscribed 'For Valour', the Victoria Cross, to be awarded to all ranks. This was thought to be dangerously democratic.

The debate went on in the Gordon household throughout the winter and Charles was really quite pleased to pack for his return to Armenia in March. He had half hoped to be sent out to India to help put down the Indian Mutiny, which had taken public opinion harder than the machinations of the Pope. Queen Victoria was only echoing popular feeling when she said she was '*so* distressed by the horrors committed on the poor ladies' which made her blood run cold. She was more distressed than she had been by the sight of her wounded Crimean veterans ('I feel so much for them and am so fond of my dear soldiers', but at least in the Crimea there had been 'glory and honourable warfare and there the poor women and children were safe'). Gordon was still only an acting captain looking for possible quick promotion, and there might be fighting in India, but he did not care to argue with his superiors and set off in good heart for Constantinople.

Rather than go overland from there to the Russo–Turkish border, he decided to go through the Black Sea, via Odessa. When the boat made a call at Sebastopol to refuel he had a whole day in which to visit the places of his baptism of fire. He wrote:

> The grass has overgrown the place where the camp stood that it was with difficulty I found my hut. The graveyards are well cared for, but covered with grass. The Russian works and our trenches have subsided into insignificant heaps, and give no idea of their original size. I thought we had dug up every root, but at present small oak bushes about fifteen inches high are springing up everywhere, and in five years more the ground will be scarcely known again.

Back on the Russo–Turkish border, he found that Robert had been joined by a Russian officer, Colonel Khleb. His two companions quarrelled all the time over the merits and demerits of the Russian and Turkish peasants at their disposal and over the 'seriousness' of the work in hand. Throughout June and July Gordon attempted to keep the two men as far apart as possible, and avoid racially mixed gangs. He also had to ensure that both Turk and Russian had accommodation of the same (wretched) standard, and that food and wine (he found them deplorable) were available in the same quantities to both. He wrote home on 17 August 1858: 'I am pretty tired of my post as peacemaker, for which I am not naturally well adapted.'

The quarrels over the 'seriousness' of the work involved Gordon as well. The first thing he had noticed on his return from England was that the cairns of stones and timber tripods which he had carefully erected the previous autumn had been knocked down or removed by the local inhabitants. In the woods, this meant that he had to start again trying to draw a frontier line in accordance with the rather vague instructions given him in Constantinople. In open country it meant building cairns by day and setting sentries by night. This amused his Turkish-Kurdish companion, who could not see why he was so concerned; the whole point of a frontier was that it should be inaccurately marked, to guarantee work in the future for both smugglers and customs officers. Colonel Khleb was frankly cynical and said in confidence that the Russian government planned to take back every square metre lost, every *verst* displaced, so the whole enterprise was foolish and why did they not do something more interesting? Gordon wrote: 'My work consists chiefly in . . . [matters] such as finding out the pyramids we placed last year, and which the inhabitants have carefully destroyed . . . and in generally keeping the two others from squabbling.'

He did, however, accept a suggestion from Colonel Khleb that as the summer drew in and autumn appeared they should go hunting wolves, 'something you cannot do in England'. It was not hunting as an English Master of Foxhounds would have known it. Khleb's way was to climb the mountains until he came to snow, and there pitch camp with plentiful supplies of vodka and a sort of savoury pancake. At the snowline ('Wolves never come below it'), he would tether a goat and wait until a small pack approached it. Then he would blaze away with half a dozen assorted rifles and sporting guns, killing as many wolves as possible. Next day he would repeat the process, while his four peasants skinned the bag and stretched out the pelts to dry. Eventually Gordon joined in this effortless exercise and was promised a wolfskin coat as a souvenir.

At the beginning of November, they came down to the plateau and surveyed their frontier. Several cairns had already been moved or had disappeared. Gordon wrote frankly to his family and to his superiors that 'I am quite in the dark as to how my mission has been fulfilled, but it is really immaterial to me, for I will not accept other work of such an anomalous nature.' He packed his few belongings, said goodbye to his companions and set off for Constantinople, via Kars and Ardahan, at what he had come to know was really the best time of year. The first rains had refreshed the land, the frosts had not yet stripped the trees and he passed 'scenery the finest I ever saw' on his way along the Black Sea coast.

In Constantinople he made his report in person to the British Ambassador, and declined inumerable invitations to dinner. His Excellency was rather amused by the fact that Gordon seemed to be worried about the usefulness of his mission. Everybody knew that the mission had been pointless, a complete waste of time in any real sense. The point had been to send somebody to seem to be doing something to implement the decisions of the statesmen who had signed the Treaty of Paris. As it was a boring and uncomfortable task it had been given to a junior officer. No senior officer would have accepted it. Gordon ought to have realized that the very fact that he had been sent on his own, with nobody to supervise him, was not *prima facie* evidence of trust or admiration for his professional competence, but merely so that, if he liked, he could just show the flag, drink vodka and hunt wolves as often as it took his fancy to do so. This sort of bland, though often effective, diplomacy was completely alien to Gordon's character and to the 'codes' he had been taught at home. He felt a little guilty at having enjoyed some of it, and resolved never again to get mixed up in such intrigues. The irony was that he was to spend much of the rest of his life in morasses of much worse intrigue.

In Constantinople he met Ferdinand De Lesseps again. De Lesseps told him of Negrelli's death, explaining that he was now President of the Suez Canal Company and that there would always be openings in its service for brilliant young men. Somehow, the offer startled Charles. He continued to muse over it on his way back to England. What a strange world it was into which he had been plunged for four years. At Chatham and Pembroke Dock, everything had seemed so simple. Once through the Academy he had assumed he would follow his father, his grandfather and his great-grandfather in a career in the British Regular Army. He had grown up in the belief that there was nothing else in store for him. He had been trained for that and for nothing else. It had not seemed unusual to him, even if his father's overweening ambition had appeared a little excessive. And yet, here in the Middle East, among the shards of the Ottoman Empire, nobody seemed to have a career for which he had been trained. Both men and women from all over the world seemed to turn up at the Sublime Porte, and if they found favour with the Sultan they might well be given a post of some responsibility – a regiment to command, for instance, or an area as large as the British Isles to govern. Salaries were apparently enormous. The temptations of the flesh were multifarious. Was this perhaps the natural site for Hell on his map of the world?

When he got back to England, he found he had been appointed captain and 2nd Adjutant at Chatham, though he was received with some suspicion by his commanding officer. What had he been doing since the end of the war? He had the Crimea War medal and clasp, but what was that Turkish war medal and why had he been made a member of the French Legion of Honour? It was thought to be too much glory for a young officer, and he was made to work hard to expunge his guilt.

On leave, he would talk only to his sister Augusta, who found him in some ways disappointing. An amateur watercolourist, she had hoped for more detailed descriptions than she had had in his letters concerning all the exotic places he had visited. Was the Danube really blue? No, he said, it was muddy and clogged, and difficult to get more than two barges abreast down at any one time. Sinope, Trebizond – what romantic names. He said he had only counted the masts of the sunken Turkish fleet. Yes, the beaches of the Crimean peninsula and the Black Sea in general were, in normal times, glistening with white sand, but their brother Henry had covered some of them with surplus stores, and on his own voyages Charles had been so seasick that he had rarely been on deck. He was willing to talk at length about the people, his new friend Gessi, and his strange companions on the frontier survey, but for Augusta they all seemed to suffer from grave moral weaknesses.

There were even more deplorable undertones to be caught while her brother was speaking. He talked a lot about his adventures, and hinted that life with the Royal Engineers at Chatham was unbearably dull. He said to her: 'I am resolved never to lead a sedentary life for longer than is absolutely necessary.' And he had no intention of marrying, as he wrote to Gessi who was preparing again for war.

FOUR

Chinese Gordon

'I am glad to say that this disease has brought me back to my Saviour, and I trust in future to be a better Christian than I have been hitherto.'
Gordon to Augusta, from Tientsin, China, in 1860 while recovering from smallpox.

The loss of the American colonies in 1776 enraged every right-thinking Englishman. Boswell records that during a conversation about a religious book Samuel Johnson 'made a sudden transition to [a subject] upon which he was a violent aggressor; for he said, "I am willing to love all mankind, except an American": and his inflammable corruption bursting into horrid fire, he breathed out threatenings and slaughter; calling them, "Rascals – Robbers – Pirates;" and exclaiming, he'd "burn and destroy them".' What Johnson was wrathful about, however, was not the imminent dissolution of a British Empire. The word 'British' was only just coming into general use, after the Union of England with Scotland in 1707, and the term 'Empire' was seldom used at all to refer to British settlements and trading stations overseas. The word 'colony' was used vaguely, to describe an outlying province. It was only when the American 'colonists' revolted and proclaimed their independence that some British statesmen became aware of an imperial mission. French aid to the Americans certainly concentrated the attention of successive British governments on a French threat, real or imaginary, to other overseas interests, particularly in the Far East. That threat focused on the fact that the French certainly saw themselves as successors to the Romans, and their extra-metroplitan possessions as an Empire. Napoleon tried to add the Holy Roman Empire to his own, without lasting success.

It all happened more slowly in Britain than in France. The first purpose-built Colonial Office was only inaugurated in 1875 and it was not until the following year that Queen Victoria was proclaimed Empress of India; in her biography of the Queen, Dorothy Marshall suggests that even then she wanted the title for personal reasons – her eldest daughter Vicky had married the heir to the newly proclaimed Emperor of Germany.

The cornerstone of what was to become the British Empire was a vast area of the Indian subcontinent leased by the British Crown to the East India Company, in much the same way that a laird might rent out a grouse shoot in Scotland. The fact that this particular grouse shoot did not belong to the British Crown was a common oversight. Treaties had been signed with local notables, especially in north-east India, and these were interpreted as giving the Crown the right to dispose of what was commercially advantageous. In return for a commercial monopoly, the East India Company paid 'rent', in the form of taxes, and defended its own interests in partnership with the British Crown – which meant raising its own private army. The Company recruited its own officers and administrators, though by the end of the eighteenth century British governments had begun to take a direct interest in military and political affairs, if only due to the French and, to a much lesser extent, Portuguese presence in India, and the Dutch in what is now Indonesia.

When, in 1780, the East India Company was told to look even further east for an expansion of its and the British government's interests, it did not hesitate. Exploratory voyages were made to the Malayan peninsula and north-east to where the French were already settled in 'Indo-China'. Further north still lay the Celestial Empire. Marco Polo had spoken highly of its trading potential centuries before, but his native Republic of Venice had long since declined and ceased to be a world power. British ships now anchored at various south China ports and began to trade with willing local merchants.

China was a natural market for British manufacturers, but Britain was a long way away. Easier to procure, in Burma and India, was opium, and in 1787 the first cargoes from Calcutta were offloaded at the Pearl River delta. Soon a regular shuttle service operated between Calcutta and Canton. In exchange for the opium, Chinese silks and teabricks went to India for reshipment to Europe. By the end of 1790 British ships had pushed up the coast as far as the port for Tientsin and Peking, the Celestial Imperial capital, and the volume of trade was considerable.

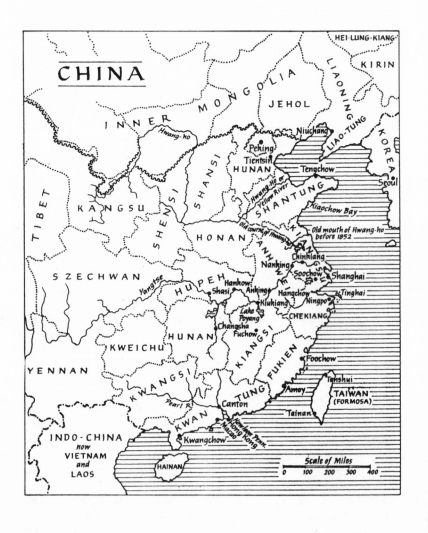

It was this volume of trade which caused the British government of the day to take a direct interest, as it had done before in the case of India. Lord Macartney, whose praise for the *Life of Samuel Johnson* Boswell noted in his Advertisement to the second edition, was sent out to China on what Boswell calls a 'magnificent, yet dangerous embassy'. It was taken for granted that the Celestial Emperor would welcome the appointment of a British ambassador. It is doubtful that the Emperor had ever heard of Great Britain, and if he had, and had known that it was one of the most powerful nations in the world, he would not have admitted it. He divided the population of the world into two – Chinese and barbarians. Barbarians he put up with as long as they traded with him and his subjects and paid their taxes, but he would rather have as little to do with them as possible. He sent a minor Court official to receive Macartney at Tientsin and escort him to the capital. Macartney was deeply hurt when, on asking an English-speaking official in the escort what the words on the banner above his barge meant, he was told: 'Red Barbarian Bearing Tribute'.

This was not a good beginning for Macartney and it was a foolish gesture on the part of the Celestial Emperor. By the end of 1793 Macartney had formulated a set of 'Minimum Demands' on the part of His Britannic Majesty. Among them were the stationing of a diplomat in Peking, with easy access to the Emperor, to look after British interests in general and mercantile interests in particular; free trading rights in Ningpo, Tinghai and Tientsin; the cession of an island or two in the Chusan group where British merchants could reside; the right to build customs-free warehouses and a reduction of the tax on goods transhipped from Portuguese-held Macao to Canton. The Emperor refused these demands and Macartney recommended a declaration of war. However by this time Great Britain had embarked on what became the Napoleonic Wars and it was not until 1816, after Macartney's death, that a fact-finding commission was sent out from London.

The 1816 commission found that none of the pre-war reports of China's potential as a 'trading partner' had been exaggerated. The country was vast, rich, poorly administered and economically backward. The Emperor was an absolute monarch, his country divided into provinces each ruled by a viceroy; some of the viceroys were members of the Manchu ruling family, others were local warlords. The peasant majority worked the land and paid taxes in money and kind to the viceroys, who in their turn paid taxes to the Emperor. The system differed from Norman French feudalism only in that some social mobility was possible, from the peasant class to the bureaucracy, by public, open examination, but there was no school in which bureaucrats were trained; it was enough to be a bureaucrat, a scholar, an official. To prevent the rise of a wealthy class outside the feudal system and the bureaucracy, strict laws governed the growth of any enterprise, industrial or commercial. There were hundreds of thousands of small workshops engaged in smelting iron, making teabricks, firing porcelain, weaving silk, crafting furniture and so on, but everywhere government offices known as *yamen* enforced restrictions on the size of any enterprise and its commercial expansion; it was illegal to own more than 100 looms, and a tax of 50 silver taels was collected for every loom in operation (a peasant could hope to earn a tael a week); the number of teabricks made, the number and type of cup and chair, all were strictly regulated and heavily taxed. Yet somehow a myriad enterprises flourished and, because internal demand was poor, had a surplus to export.

By some oversight there was no import tax on opium, and this may have encouraged the trade. By 1833 when Gordon was born 30 million taels of silver were being exported in exchange for opium alone, not to mention goods to a similar value. The Emperor of the day, Tao Kuang, became aware of the drain on his economy and ordered an official, Lin Tse-Hsu, to stop or limit the opium trade. In the spring of 1839 Lin arrived in Canton and ordered the British Trading Superintendent, Captain Elliott, to surrender all his stocks of opium. Elliott refused, so Lin retaliated by besieging the British in their warehouses, and, when he had starved them into surrender in June he burnt 20,000 chests of opium on the beach at Bocca Tigris. A month later a British sailor killed a Chinese spying on the British fleet offshore. Elliott refused to turn the sailor over to the Chinese authorities and called on two warships flying the British flag to fire on Chinese war junks moored on the Pearl River, just to reassert British authority after the Bocca Tigris 'disaster'. Lin then fermented riots in Canton and several British warehouses were burnt down. Elliott withdrew the British merchant fleet and its two attendant warships to Tinghai, where they were joined in June 1840 by a British fleet. War was declared on Imperial China when an ultimatum was ignored. More ships joined the British fleet and a force of marines was sent to take Chinkiang and Nanking. As the marines were about to enter Nanking, Chi Shan, the viceroy of Chihli, advised the Emperor to come to terms with the British to avoid certain defeat. As a result a treaty was signed at Nanking on 29 August 1842 which put an end to what became known as the First Opium War.

The Nanking Treaty established Great Britain as the premier trading nation in China. The ports of Canton, Fuchow, Amoy, Ningpo and Shanghai were opened permanently to British subjects for trade and residence. Hong Kong was ceded to Britain as a colony, and British nationals everywhere were to be subject only to British law even when in conflict with local Chinese. Tariffs were to be fixed by a committee on which the British were to enjoy a permanent majority, and the Emperor promised to pay an indemnity of 21 million silver taels for the burning of the chest of opium in 1839.

When the terms of the treaty became generally known, the United States and France sent ambassadors to Peking, feigning sympathy and demanding similiar privileges. Under the Treaty of Whampoa the French government lent the Emperor the money to pay the indemnity, in return for trading concessions and the right to send Catholic missionaries to China. The United States received the same concessions and the right to send Methodist missionaries.

The three Unequal Treaties, as they were called, angered Chinese of every station in life. At Court, scholars speculated on the origin of this humiliation at the hands of the barbarians. Wei Yuan thought the answer to China's impotence lay in a profound study of the way in which Europeans and Americans lived and worked, and published *The History and Geography of Foreign Countries (Hai Kuo Tu Chih)* as a primer in which he summarized the progress made in industry and commerce abroad. Other scholars pointed to the lessons of China's own history. There had been thirty-two dynasties. A new dynasty had always taken the place of the old after a great national humiliation. The common people, who had neither the time nor the education for speculation, took the matter into their own hands. The five cities in which the British now enjoyed extra territorial rights were the scenes of rioting and sabotage between 1842 and 1845; this was largely ineffective and only gave the British, as leaders of the international community, an excuse to form a private army with which to police the concessions.

The most important protests against the Unequal Treaties came from the peasants. American Methodist missionaries arrived in large numbers in the provinces of Kiangsu, Chekiang, Kiangsi, Hunan and Kwangtung to preach the brotherhood of man and salvation by Jesus Christ. Since they flavoured their preaching with anti-British sentiment they soon became very popular. These missionaries were very shrewd: they opened schools and hospitals but, realizing the extent of local pride and the degree to which it had been hurt, encouraged the formation of native religious groups not necessarily bearing the name 'Methodist'. The most important of these groups were the Heaven and Earth Society (Tien Ti Hui) and the Society For The Worship of God (Shang Ti Hui).

In 1849 there was a rice famine in Hunan Province. Li Yuan-Fa, leader of the Heaven and Earth Society in the provincial capital, Chang-Sha, decided that this was a sign from God that the time had come to proclaim a New Kingdom and depose the un-Christian Manchu. Li mobilized his followers and, singing hymns and beating bamboo sticks, and armed only with swords and sharpened poles, quickly subdued the whole province. The viceroy fled to Peking, and the revolt soon spread to neighbouring Kwangtung. The leader of the Society for the Worship of God, Hung Hsiu-Chan, called a mass meeting at Chintien to which he preached conversion and revolution. Tens of thousands of his followers marched to join their brothers in Hunan and, after eighteen months of fighting and defeating the Imperial armies, the two societies amalgamated to proclaim on 11 January 1851 the Heavenly Kingdom of Great Peace (Tai Ping Tien Kuo), after which the uprising became known as the Tai Ping Rebellion.

Hung Hsiu-Chan assumed the leadership of the rebels and had himself crowned Heavenly King. Hung was a former schoolmaster in a Kwangtung village not far from Canton, and he had been cured of some form of gastro-enteritis by Methodist medical missionaries. They had converted him to their brand of Christianity and for a time he had worked with them as a lay preacher – for some reason he was told he could not be ordained. He fell ill again and this time had a vision in which it was revealed to him that he was the reincarnation of Jesus Christ's younger brother; this was authority enough with which to start preaching on his own account, and by the time the Heavenly Kingdom was proclaimed he had a reputation throughout southern China. During 1852 and 1853 the Kingdom spread; the old city of Nanking fell in 1853 and Hung declared that this was to be the capital of the Heavenly Kingdom, where revelations would be made – in the meantime a wholesale slaughter of some 25,000 Imperial soldiers and officials took place. When the revelations came it transpired that the whole Holy Family would settle in Nanking, including a wife of Jesus, several sisters and cousins, John the Baptist and his wife. To help increase the numbers of the faithful, polygamy was encouraged; the Heavenly King himself had thirty wives and innumerable concubines. However even with these distractions Hung carried on preaching his gospel and conquering more and more provinces of the Manchu

Celestial Empire. The British were at first amused, then alarmed. Their principal settlements, at Shanghai and Canton, were both threatened and Shanghai was occupied on and off for a year.

The British Minister in Peking, George Bonham, was at first deceived by the faintly musical comedy air which hung about the Heavenly Kingdom of Great Peace – the bizarre names of the sects, the Chinese versions of Methodist favourite hymns and the megalomania of Hung, the Heavenly King. But there was nothing insubstantial about it all. The Imperial armies were defeated again and again. The whole of the Yangtse was in their hands and the improvised government caused the land to be worked, the rice to be weeded and cropped, and houses to be built – not to mention chapels. The Celestial Emperor confessed to Bonham that he would be quite pleased if the rebels contented themselves with what they had already won. There were no loyal troops who could take back the provinces lost. Intrigued by this, Bonham persuaded the government in London that it was worth establishing some sort of diplomatic relations with Nanking, if this could be done without repercussions in Peking. The British government was very willing to ally itself with any strong administration which might pose a threat, however vague, to Tsarist Russia at its oriental back door; the Crimean War broke out shortly after Bonham left Peking for Nanking in February 1854. Bonham, who travelled with his French and American colleagues De Bourboulon and McLane, was received with great kindness but firmness. The Unequal Treaties would not be ratified in the territory under Hung's control. This posed a problem for Bonham, a humane man, who was very impressed by the freedom given to women in the Kingdom, including the end of bride purchase and the binding of young girls' feet, which he particularly detested. Life in the Kingdom was more acceptable to men and women with western standards of behaviour, and yet opium trading, on which the wealth of British merchants was based, was banned, whereas it was legal in the feudal, backward, cruel Empire.

In May 1854 an army of the Heavenly Kingdom under Lin Feng-Hsiang crossed the Yangtse and started a march on the Imperial capital, Peking. In five months Lin 'liberated' the provinces of Anhwei, Honan, Shansi and Chihli. Tientsin, only 100 miles from Peking, fell on 2 October. The Imperial Court panicked and was evacuated to Jehol. On 5 November plans were made to march on Peking itself. However, by granting irreversible privileges to warlords in provinces that were still free the Celestial Emperor managed to save his capital. The Heavenly Army retreated to Lienchin; the garrison left in Tientsin, with only black beans to eat, fought and died there.

The Imperial counter-offensive was led by a Hunanese warlord, Tseng Kuo-Fan. He had lost his land, peasants and concubines during the first uprisings and had a personal grudge against Hung Hsia-Chang, whom he had helped through the Open Examinations many years before. He set up his camp at Lake Poyang, a large expanse of water on the northern border of Hunan, drilled his troops there and commandeered a fleet of junks with which to form a navy. His first efforts did not meet with much success. The Heavenly Army, camped on the opposite side of the lake, frightened the crews of the junks by beating gongs and singing hymns as the junks negotiated the waterway between the Yangtse and the lake, then fired flaming arrows into their sails, destroying a quarter of the fleet. During the winter of 1855–6 there was something of a stalemate, but at least a large number of troops from the Heavenly Kingdom were occupied in holding down Tseng's embryo army and navy.

In October 1856 a Chinese junk, laden with opium and flying the British flag, was boarded by the civil authorities while it was lying at anchor in the Pearl River. The cargo was confiscated and the crew imprisoned. The British Consul demanded restitution, compensation and the release of the crew. When the local viceroy refused, the Consul called in some warships from the British Far Eastern Fleet, providentially paying a courtesy call. Canton was bombarded, taken, and put under British military government. In December 1857, when reparations still seemed unlikely, a regiment of Royal Marines was put ashore. In June 1858, hearing that the Far Eastern Fleet was sailing to bombard Tientsin, the Emperor hurriedly concluded a Treaty of Peace and Friendship. He gave the British seven more duty-free ports – Niuchang, Tengchow, Tainan, Tanshui, Hangkow and Chingkiang; Nanking was to be 'British', too, if they could retrieve it. The Royal Navy had the right to station warships in any of these ports, free of harassment, and could sail into the interior along the main river arteries if and when it chose. The Emperor swore eternal friendship to the British Crown and promised to pay an indemnity of 4 million taels of silver. So ended the Second Opium War.

When Hung Hsia-Chang heard of the terms of this treaty, he assumed that it had been concluded in desperation, in fear of further offensives by his armies. Immediately he gave word to advance. One army demolished the Imperial camp at Chiangpei and started a move towards the south bank of the Yellow River.

Another of Hung's armies captured Hangkow, annihilating the last Imperial forces between the Heavenly Kingdom and the coast.

Perhaps Hung did not know that Hangkow was now 'British'. In any event the fall of the port gave the British the excuse to intervene for the first time in the Chinese civil war. Large numbers of British troops had been shipped out to India in 1857 to quell the Mutiny, and Lord Canning, Governor-General and later first Viceroy, was anxious to get them off the Indian subcontinent and make a lasting peace with the defeated natives. The Chinese Emperor was offered, in exchange for the addition of Tientsin to the list of 'British' ports, such troops and officers as would be needed to stiffen up the resistance offered by the demoralized Imperial Chinese forces. The Emperor agreed, and shortly afterwards British troops began to arrive at all of the treaty ports. The news of these arrivals heartened Tseng Kuo-Fan, and as the 'stiffened' Imperial Army started to move south at the end of 1859, pushing the Northern Heavenly Army steadily back towards the shore of the Yangtse, along a broad front from Anking to Nanking, Tseng began to move from the west. His navy sailed along the Yangtse towards Anking and his troops attacked the Heavenly Kingdom's garrison along the Hunan–Kiangsi border, where he was joined by Li Hung-Chang, the Anhwei warlord who had also been charged by the Emperor – in return for special privileges – with the repression of the Heavenly Kingdom.

What saved the Heavenly Kingdom from defeat in 1859 was a foolish act by the Celestial Emperor, or rather by three of his generals, hurt by the humiliating treaty which had ended the Second Opium War. Four British diplomats had arrived in Peking to collect the indemnity of 4 million taels of silver. They seem to have been ill chosen for the task, and managed to offend everybody at Court, including the Dowager Empress. They were arrested, imprisoned and tortured to death, on charges of lèse majesté and much else, including the theft of priceless ceramics. However much they may have deserved their fate, the death of the diplomats provoked an immediate declaration of war by Great Britain, which, in the person of Lord Elgin, decided to wreak revenge or enact justice.

At this point in the country's confused history Charles George Gordon and a number of other Crimean War veterans arrived in China. After a short visit to Canton, which he found disappointing, he landed at Shanghai on 17 September 1860. For many centuries a substantial walled city and port, in the last two decades it had grown into a cosmopolitan sprawl with a population of 300,000. On the left bank of the River Huang-Ho in the Yangtse estuary, was the Bund, a street of foreign banks and business houses which controlled the commercial life of the city. The foreign communities vied with each other to build splendid churches, clubs and mansions, and the prosperity which came from international trade touched the lives of the native Chinese, many of whom worked for the British, French, Americans and Germans.

The recent attacks by the Army of the Heavenly Kingdom had done relatively little damage. The walls were being repaired swiftly, and Gordon remarked on the skill and effort which went into it, though baskets full of rebels' heads swung above the workmen. There was none of the torpor he had found in the Balkans and the Middle East. As great a contrast, he noticed, was the civility, courtesy and urbanity of the Chinese, notwithstanding a decade of civil war and several decades of European exploitation. He was not allowed to stay long in Shanghai this time, but was posted north to where the British troops and British-officered Indian levies were making the declaration of war a harsh reality. He did not see action there, however. The Imperial armies outside Peking had been defeated and the famous wooden Taku Forts destroyed. Because of the non-payment of the indemnity agreed in June 1858, Lord Elgin had given instructions that it was to be collected in kind.

Gordon reported to the newly arrived officer-in-charge, Lieutenant-General Staveley, CB, Commander-in-Chief, Madras, and father-in-law of his brother Henry. After some pleasantries, he was told he would be employed making inventories of the contents of the Celestial Emperor's Summer Palace. He was driven slowly through the Chinese city to the south to the great Tartar Peking (Khanbalig), built by Kubla Khan's Golden Horde, and wondered why the Emperor had chosen to defend the western approaches instead of this impregnable square of 20 miles of high walls, with their eighteen narrow gates. Inside the outer square was an inner square of government offices, also walled, and inside that again the walled Forbidden City with its seven little lakes and purple stone. But even more impressive, 8 miles to the north-west, were the park, gardens and buildings of the Yuen Ming Yuen itself, the Summer Palace. As a contemporary of Gordon's described it:

> Here, amid an expanse covering twelve square miles, with a background of wooded hills, all the ingenious diversities and embellishments of Chinese architectural and horticultural art had been

exhausted to produce a terrestrial paradise; lakes, rivulets, cascades, pagodas, rocks, open spaces, and woodlands formed a varied setting to the numerous palaces of marble, porcelain, and cedar wood which in turn surrounded the central residence of the Emperor.

The Summer Palace was known as 'the garden of perpetual brightness', he was told by his Chinese interpreter, and the Emperor sought refuge in it from the harsh realities of the modern world. This particular Emperor had tried to come to grips with that world, even creating a Ministry of Foreign Affairs instead of the 'Office for the Management of Barbarians' which was all there was until 1842. It had been to no avail. Civil war and foreign war had broken his heart. Barbarians were not only at the gate but inside the gates. The French had got to the Summer Palace first, to what one of them said was 'a sort of Versailles, but bigger, though with small windows'. They had not been overawed by the sight, but had apparently gone berserk, smashing the porcelain tiles on the towers and the multicoloured wooden shingles on the other roofs. Gordon was horrified at what he saw, as he sat in the small pagoda allotted to him, drinking tea out of a tin cup and writing home:

> You will scarcely conceive the magnificence of this residence or the tremendous devastation the French have committed . . . smashing everything in a most wanton way. The throne room was lined with ebony, carved in a marvellous way. There were huge mirrors of all shapes and kinds, clocks, watches, musical boxes with puppets on them, magnificent china of every description, heaps and heaps of silks of all colours, embroidery and in a word as much splendour as you would see at Windsor. . . .

Though Lytton Strachey is bitter about 'the destruction of the Summer Palace at Peking – the act by which Lord Elgin, in the name of European civilization, took vengeance on the barbarism of the East', everything that could be saved had been saved. Elgin had given orders to this effect and what was eventually blown up was the seat of government, as a warning to the Emperor not to misbehave again. Gordon and other Royal Engineers physically organized the reprisal, though he regretted it; however, as the organized destruction would cost the Emperor the equivalent of £4 million to repair, the lesson was salutary.

After Peking, Gordon was posted for eighteen months to Tientsin, erecting and repairing barrack buildings; it was boring work, relieved only by a single visit to the Great Wall 200 miles to the north-west. In the summer of 1862 he returned to Shanghai, again impressed by the industry and manners of the local people; he now set to work to learn Mandarin Chinese. He was less impressed, however, by his fellow Europeans. There was a handful of more or less respectable diplomats and professional soldiers like himself, but the majority were adventurers, either trading unscrupulously or hiring themselves out as mercenaries. The merchants employed most of the mercenaries, who were appointed as officers and NCOs to 'stiffen up' the regular army in the province, commanded by Li Hung-chang, in whose hands all military and civil authority was vested. This 'inner army', with loyalties first and foremost to European and American interests, was commanded by Europeans or Americans. Shortly after Gordon arrived the American commander, Ward, was killed and replaced by another American, Burgevine.

Gordon had seen dissolution and decadence in south-east Europe and Asia Minor, but he was not prepared for Shanghai. The few traditionally wealthy Chinese families offered an example of discretion, though they bought and sold women openly and even 'free' women were thought of only as objects of pleasure; within six months of settling down in Shanghai in his own establishment Gordon had been offered, as gifts, several young girls, with vivid descriptions of their usual and unusual talents; this only increased, if possible, his horror of intimacy with the opposite sex.

The rich Europeans showed no discretion at all. Middle-class Yorkshire and Lancashire textile merchants enjoyed an opulence which would have been denied them, for both social and economic reasons, in mid-nineteenth-century England. A Mr Featherstone of Bradford had converted an abandoned temple to his private use, and lived there in style with over a hundred concubines, occasionally trading a few with the civil and military Chinese for jade and porcelain. Many British merchants had spent years in India and imported what they had found there to their liking – the multiplicity of servants, the heavy drinking, even Indian food. Occasionally a merchant acquired a taste for silk and porcelain, and many famous collections were put together at this time.

There was little danger of Gordon being vulgarly ostentatious or sybaritic. A British corporal and five Chinese servants made up his household. He rose before any of them and prayed for an hour before performing his curious ritual of 'tasting the water' – every evening he had several gallons of water boiled to cool during the night, and he drank copious draughts of it during the day. He soon acquired a taste for Chinese food and for rice wine. He also drank a little whisky and brandy, and French wine when he was given some, so it is difficult to know where the story originated that he was a teetotaller; he mixed socially with American Methodists, but not all of them were strictly teetotal either. (And, of course, other commentators have contended that he went to the opposite extreme and was an alcoholic.)

In parenthesis, it is interesting to note just how many American Methodists seem to have flocked to Shanghai, and the extent to which they earned the sympathy of the Chinese. Promising Chinese boys were often sent to the United States to finish their education. One such boy was Soong Yao-Ju, born in Shanghai in 1861 and sent to Boston (where he had relatives who kept a shop) and then to the Methodist Trinity College at Durham, North Carolina; Soong's daughters were to become perhaps the most remarkable sisters of the twentieth century – Ching-Ling, who became Madame Sun Yat-Sen, Mei-Ling, who became Madame Chiang Kai-Shek, and Ai-Ling who became a Wall Street millionairess in her own right.

After the daily water tasting Gordon would inspect his household, lining up the staff like a maître d'hôtel to make sure their fingernails were clean; then he would be off to inspect the Royal Engineers squadron of which he was second-in-command. The squadron was employed in building forts and rebuilding the city walls, in addition to making the British residential concession area more secure and attending to the plumbing. There was plenty to do. The soldiers of the Heavenly Kingdom were never far away; like Scottish Highland clansmen, they tended to go home after each battle, attend to domestic affairs and hide the loot, then return to the front, so it was very difficult to estimate the strength of the Heavenly Armies opposed to the garrisons in Shanghai. Mercenaries in the employ of Heavenly King Hung had put together a very efficient set of batteries of artillery; as manpower was not a problem, the batteries were highly mobile and would suddenly be there at dawn, shelling the city, and then be gone next day before reprisals could be planned.

Most of the physical effort involved in the building and rebuilding was done by the Chinese under British supervision. Gordon admired their ingenuity: they worked hard with their heads as well as with their hands, and when some essential material was lacking they quickly improvised to good effect. He got on well with his workers, who were intrigued by this slim, trim officer who spoke to them in their own language, albeit haltingly, and never seemed to be armed with anything more lethal than a short walking cane with a curved handle.

In his off-duty hours Gordon studied, prayed, drank tea with

Methodists and puzzled over the doctrines preached in the Heavenly Kingdom of Great Peace. He did not do anything to arouse resentment in his brother officers – he attended the mess, was polite and even amusing at table, conscientious and not a prig – but his mind was always working at the problem central to his life. What was God's intention? His own intention was quite clear – to serve God; but in what way? Did the Evangelicals at home and abroad have the solution to this problem? Men of his class had little contact with English Methodists, and he shared Queen Victoria's mistrust of the Anglo-Catholic Tractarians, most of whom were of his class. He had found no answer to his questions among the native Scots Presbyterians, nor, after three centuries, did they seem to be able to answer their own questions. Anyway, he was not a bigot and most of the Scots Presbyterians were – at least, those whom he had met. Did Methodism have a genuine international appeal? The Wesleys seemed to have spread their doctrines widely and these rebels, whatever was true or not true about the indulgence of their leader, appeared to have imbibed these doctrines. What *was* the answer? What he liked about the Methodists in Shanghai was that when they had any doubts they turned to action – building schools, hospitals and churches. This was something he could understand. And yet. And yet. Something was wrong somewhere. They did not seem to enjoy their destiny, God's Providence. Moses, St Paul, St Augustine – his favourite authors at that time – all seemed to *enjoy* the certainty with which they faced each new day's labours.

As Gordon built and rebuilt and wrestled with his conscience, Tseng Kuo-Fan slowly strengthened his Hunanese army. At the beginning of 1862 he attacked the army of the Heavenly Kingdom stationed along the Hunan–Kiangsi border and destroyed it. He then reordered his fleet of junks and sailed up the Yangtse to take Anking. The next objective was to be Nanking, the Heavenly Kingdom's capital, but this would obviously be no easy redoubt to storm. Tseng conferred with Li Hung-Chang. Li was to be given the task of moving towards Nanking due west overland, and he would move along the Yangtse to meet Li's armies at the gates of the city. It seemed simple enough. Tseng had the soldiers, the fleet and the initiative along the River Yangtse. Li had the support of the British, French and Americans at the head of a multinational force which had been given the name 'Ever Victorious Army', more in hope than sincerity, by the Celestial Emperor in Peking. Both men agreed that the joint campaign should begin in the spring of 1863.

When Li Hung-Chang returned to Shanghai, having committed himself to this joint enterprise, he realized that he had probably been too precipitate. It was clear enough to most people that the Heavenly Kingdom of Great Peace would only last as long as King Hung himself. No potential successors had emerged from Hung's 'Divine' entourage. But Hung was very much alive, and though the armies of the Kingdom had been sometimes successful and sometimes not, they were still the same indiarubber, unquantifiable force they had always been. Victory was what had been promised by God. Defeat was what they had always known before the proclamation of the Kingdom, and was probably due to their own sinfulness anyway. There would be another day, Hung would have another vision.

Li Hung-Chang spent the winter of 1862–3 wondering whether or not he had done the right thing, praying that some thunderbolt or a heavy piece of loose masonry would fall on Hung's head. As the winter drew to a close, he realized that, reluctantly , he would have to do something. If Tseng moved on his own, and defeated the armies of the Heavenly Kingdom, that would guarantee power, privilege and prosperity to the Tseng family for a generation or two, but where would it leave the Lis?

Gloomily, Li reviewed his troops and conferred with the British, French and American civil leaders and military commanders. The Emperor had promised unlimited funds to spend on the 'inner army', but how was this money to be spent? And who would command the army? The American Burgevine had been dismissed for striking a Court official; he had been succeeded by a British Royal Marines officer named Holland, but Holland had been ignominiously defeated on 22 February 1863 while trying to take the city of Taitsan. The Americans had no other names to put forward. The French had been warned not to get too involved. Perhaps the British Consul-General or senior British officer could suggest somebody? The British Consul-General knew only one British officer who had no enemies in the international community. He had few friends but he was much respected. He spoke French, which pleased the French; the French officers with whom he had served in the Crimean War had thought well of him, and with the award of the Legion of Honour this had become official opinion. Again, he was respected in the American community and the influential Methodists spoke well of him. It also so happened that the SBO, Major-General Staveley was the father-in-law of the brother of the man in question, Major Charles George Gordon. And this Gordon's father was a major-general, too, so obviously enjoyed the esteem of the War Office in London. It seemed there could be no better choice.

Li Hung-Chang knew Gordon quite well already. He was a little afraid of him because he was said to be incorruptible, but this was not a moment for moralizing or demoralizing. On 24 March 1863 he offered Gordon the command of the Ever Victorious Army, Chang-Sheng-Chume, with the prospect of joint command of the regular Chinese forces who would join the foreigners in the campaign against the rebels. Gordon accepted with alacrity, and after the water tasting on 26 March reviewed the Ever Victorious Army in Shanghai. Li Hung-Chang watched that first parade and noted: 'I could not but be pleased at the manner in which his commands were obeyed.'

The Ever Victorious did not make much of a show on parade that day. There were smartly uniformed French, American and British ex-regulars. There were Indian troops in the house regalia of their masters at home. And there was an assortment of mercenaries in uniforms designed by themselves, many of them slung about with bandoliers like the Hollywood version of a Mexican bandit. The first thing to do was to get them into some sort of dress which would be easily recognized in battle. Gordon conferred with the British, French and American quartermasters, and with representatives of the merchants. In the end he compromised, prescribing for everyone British wellington boots, French trousers and American tunics. Where the commissaries lacked sufficient trousers and tunics, the textile merchants supplied the cloth with which Chinese tailors ran them up virtually overnight. Within forty-eight hours he had his troops properly dressed and began to drill them.

The men did not take very kindly to the new regime at first – more than 200 deserted in the first week. The officers resented the early start to the day, the men the marching and counter-marching. But it was soon obvious to them all that at last they had a competent commander, and on his competence their lives would depend. In order to site new fortifications, he had surveyed most of the Yangtse delta with its innumerable waterways. If the armies of the Heavenly Kingdom were effective because they were mobile, then he would be mobile, too. He took a leaf out of Tseng's book and commandeered a fleet of junks, as well as a score of steam boats including pleasure craft belonging to the European community. He had made maps of the whole area, from Shanghai to Soochow, to Hangchow, to Tinghai, and soon every officer had his portfolio with Gordon's comments written neatly in the margins of the maps. His idea was to avoid the traditional advance along a broad front.

He would select a single target, ideally one which could be attacked by land or water, and raid it. By choosing the targets carefully, he could soon accumulate a stock of garrison towns which would control movement anywhere in the delta.

The first sortie of what General Staveley called rather disparagingly 'Charles' New Model Army' was on 9 April, against the town of Chanzu. It was not a particularly important town, and the troops of the Heavenly Army stationed there did not expect an attack. They were also deceived by the flotilla of brightly lit steam launches, which they took to be Europeans on some sort of jaunt. Singing on board further confused them. A total lack of stealth seemed almost offensive and a few rounds were fired over the heads of the 'pleasure seekers'. However, simultaneously 500 of Gordon's men approached the town by land and scaled the walls just before dawn. By midday on 10 April the town had fallen, with little loss of life on either side.

This first victory raised morale and inspired confidence in all concerned. The 'New Model Army' took to its drill and manoeuvres with cheerful resignation, if not zeal. In Shanghai itself, hospitals for the wounded in actions to come were organized in the best traditions of Florence Nightingale whom Gordon admired. Much later, in 1880, Gordon was to write: 'I gained the hearts of my soldiers (who would do anything for me) not by my justice etc, but by looking after them when sick and continually visiting the hospitals.' He spent most of his locally paid salary buying medicines and blankets and shamed the European ladies into forming their own units of auxiliaries. More immediately appealing were his efforts to improve the food and lodging of his men, though many resented his attempts to move them out of the houses where they lived with their Chinese girls and into barracks where there was a military curfew. But the Major was brisk and businesslike and shared comforts and discomforts alike with the men.

On 29 April Gordon led the attack on Taitsan, a fortified town which was strategically important and had to be taken to avenge Holland's defeat. Using the ample waterways, he brought up 12-pounder howitzers and two 32-pounders and battered the west wall until he had opened a breach in it. The first assault failed and Gordon lost his best junior commander, Captain Bannon, but after another barrage the next assault succeeded. As the prisoners and the booty were inventoried, Gordon found to his horror that much of the enemy's arms and ammunition were British, which meant that somebody was selling them illegally, and that there were British deserters in the Heavenly Army. He noted later:

Two men of the Thirty First Regiment were on the breach at Taitsan; one was killed, the other, struck by a shell splinter, was taken prisoner. 'Mr Gordon, Mr Gordon, you will not let me be killed!'. 'Take him down to the river and shoot him!', – and aside – 'put him in my boat, let the doctor attend him, and send him down to Shanghai'. His name was Hargreaves, and I daresay he exists at present.

Gordon's bravery under fire and his magnanimity excited admiration on both sides, but his insistence that his troops should not loot the towns they captured provoked a mutiny on 4 May. He was not insensitive to the fact that they had been engaged on low pay on the understanding that they would help themselves to anything movable after a victory, but he put down the mutiny with great ferocity. While he was reforming the Army he told Li Hung-Chang and the European merchants that they would be well advised to make up the men's pay to an extent which would make pillage unattractive.

A month later he attacked Quinsan and Chunyi, 'key to an intricate system of lake and canal'. He refurbished his little navy, now with an iron-sheeted flagship, the *Hyson*, commanded by a roaring Irishman called Davidson. After a reconnaissance on the *Hyson*, Gordon found a way to attack along the canal which was the only escape route to Soochow, and won another great victory. Li Hung-Chang wrote in his diary: 'It is a direct blessing from Heaven, the coming of this British Gordon. . . . He is superior in manner and bearing to any of the foreigners who I have come into contact with, and does not show outwardly that conceit which makes most of them repugnant in my sight.' Though desertions continued even after the Ever Victorious Army had begun to live up to its name, there were now more volunteers, even from among prisoners of war: 'They went to fight their old friends about a week after they joined me and did pretty well.' Large bonuses were paid to those who had not deserted, substantial payments were made to new recruits, and decorations were invented for officers. Of the latter, a reporter wrote: 'The officers of his force were brave men enough, but not always ready to fight their desperate antagonists. Gordon, in his mild way, would take one or other of these by the arm and lead him into the thick of the fire.' The decorations rewarded courage, direct or indirect.

Two months later Li Hung-Chang went with Gordon on the campaign to free Kapu and Wukiang. It was late July and very hot, but somehow the Army was urged on to do incredible things, even inspiring the Imperial Chinese regulars who normally rested during the summer. Li wrote: 'What a sight for tired eyes! What an elixir for a heavy heart to see this Englishman fight. . . . If there is anything I admire nearly as much as the superb scholarship of Tseng Kuo-Fan it is the military qualities of this fine officer. He is a glorious fellow.' Burgevine got short shrift when he tried to regain command of the Ever Victorious, and was next heard of in the service of the Heavenly Kingdom, Gordon's adversary at Wukiang.

There was trouble again while the troops were being prepared for a late autumn attack on Soochow, the most difficult project to date; various emperors throughout history had failed to breach its 12 miles of walls, and its 'Venetian splendour' (a canal flowed beside every street) and prompted the Emperor Kangi to dismount from his horse and proceed on foot 'in order not to injure the magnificent silks and embroidered tapestries which the inhabitants had laid along the ground'. The soldiers in Gordon's Army wanted to be paid before battles, especially difficult ones; the Chinese wanted pay afterwards, perhaps in the hope that fatal casualties would lighten the load. Gordon complained bitterly, and won the argument. As Li wrote: 'With his many faults, his pride, his temper and his never-ending demand for money, Gordon is a noble man and in spite of all I have said . . . I will ever think most highly of him.'

Li knew that the days of the Heavenly Kingdom of Great Peace were numbered. But Tseng Kuo-Fan, the scholar general whom he so admired, was also winning battles and there would be a race between the two forces to be in at the death, at the taking of the Heavenly capital, Nanking. Li tried to hint at the political importance of haste in victory, but Gordon was not interested in politics.

At the beginning of October Tseng was moving up the Yangtse towards Nanking, and Gordon decided that the moment was propitious for an advance; Tseng would draw off some of the troops in the fortified towns to the west of Soochow. Gordon's Ever Victorious Army was addressed briskly by its commander and one by one the circle of forts and fortified towns around Soochow fell – Wanti, Liku, Walunchao, Fuchukei. Gordon was as concerned as Li to win the war and not just battles, and he felt that the time had come to try to negotiate a surrender. He was partly motivated by the knowledge, passed on to him by Heavenly Kingdom deserters, that there were thirty, maybe forty, Princes or Wangs of the Kingdom in Soochow; the City Governor, Prince Moh, would fight to the death, but his second-in-command, Prince Lar, had declared that in return for great sins the Kingdom was due to experience a series of disasters and, as these were divinely inspired, there seemed to be no point in resisting them. With Li Hung-Chang's approval, Gordon opened negotiations with the Princes and shortly afterwards received a sack which contained, he was told, the head of Prince Moh. Next day he had an emissary from Prince Lar with whom he negotiated the surrender of Soochow, on the understanding that there would be no 'butchery'. On this understanding, Prince Lar opened the city gates; Gordon led in his Ever Victorious Army and began, as usual, to see to their food and quarters and find medicines for the sick and wounded. His men settled, Gordon went to see what was happening elsewhere in the city where Li's other armies were. To his horror he found scenes of bloodshed certainly approaching 'butchery', though many of the deaths of leaders of the Heavenly Kingdom were certainly taking place at the hands of their discontented and disappointed followers. Meeting his colleague, the Chinese General Ching, he asked for an explanation and was told that things had got a bit out of hand – his men would soon restore order. When asked where he could find Prince Lar, Ching referred him to Li Hung-Chang. When Li and Gordon met, there was 'a tempest', as a witness put it. Gordon had discovered that all the Princes of the Heavenly Kingdom had been decapitated and their heads already sent to the Emperor in Peking. He was furious, accused Li of betraying his trust, and threatened to report him to the Emperor and to the European and American authorities in Shanghai; there had already been articles in the British and American Press accusing the Chinese and Ever Victorious armies of atrocities, and even a demand for Gordon's recall. With difficulty Gordon was placated, but, as Li records, he was back two days later. 'in his angriest mood'.

Over Christmas, which he spent with his men in Soochow, Gordon calmed down, realizing that Li had been placed in an impossible position. The Emperor in Peking certainly expected the Princes of the Heavenly Kingdom to be killed; after all, they had committed high treason against him and the Manchu Dynasty, and the punishment for high treason everywhere in the world was death. Indeed, the Emperor was very grateful to Gordon for what he assumed had been his part in the capture and execution of his enemies. He struck a commemorative medal for his general, and told Li to hand it over together with 10,000 taels of silver. But, as Li records: 'He refused the 10,000 taels which I had ready for him, and, with an oath, said that he did not want the Throne's medal. This is showing the greatest disrespect.'

On New Year's Day 1864 Gordon received a personal letter from the Emperor, repeating the offer of the medal and his thanks. To this Gordon replied:

> Major Gordon receives the approbation of his Majesty the Emperor with every gratification, but regrets most sincerely that owing to circumstances which have occurred since the capture of Soochow, he is unable to receive any mark of His Majesty the Emperor's recognition, and there begs His Majesty to receive his thanks for the intended kindness, and allow him to decline the same.

Several factors prompted him to take this 'disrespectful' attitude. He felt personally affronted at what Li and Ching had done, even if he appreciated the realpolitik; surely they could have found some way to warn him beforehand, or have insisted that Soochow be taken and not surrendered. Not even Li's public declaration that he personally had ordered the execution of the Princes of the Heavenly Kingdom stopped the flow of articles accusing Gordon of being part and parcel of the conspiracy to destroy physically the (misguided) rebels of the Kingdom. This Gordon took hard, because his mother and father read these accusations in *The Times*, and it was not until the Radical Press began to mount absurd attacks on him that the establishment newspapers in Britain and Europe took his side. Gordon had a great respect for and understanding of how to use the Press, or at least a part of it. He wanted the world to have good if not golden opinions of him. At this time he was taking an interest in the Jewish Talmud and in the Chashid, a sort of anti-clerical, fundamentalist movement founded by Israel ben Eliezer (Baal Shem Tov), a man described to him by the Lithuanian merchant in Shanghai as the Jewish Wesley. The Chasidim seemed to Gordon to resemble, too, the founders of the Heavenly Kingdom, with their dislike of priests and taste for song and dance in worship. The Chasidim believed that great and mysterious powers were given not to rabbis, but to upright, honest and honourable men who by their example would encourage others to be upright, honest and honourable; Gordon saw himself as one of these *tzaddiks*, and the behaviour of his Chinese allies and colleagues brought him into disrepute, above all in the eyes of his fellow-countrymen at home.

Nevertheless, when his third attempt to resign command of the Ever Victorious Army failed, he got on with the job in hand. He restarted training for his men and recruited a personal bodyguard of Chinese and Indian soldiers, after having been warned that an attempt would be made to kill him in the field. When the spring came he set off and quickly reduced Yesing and Liyang, then regrouped the Army and Li's forces for an assault on the better defended Kintang and Waisoo. At Kingtang he was wounded, and it is not clear whether or not the warnings of an attempt on his life had been justified. One version has it that he was shot by an English mercenary fighting in the Heavenly Army, another that the mercenary aimed his rifle but that it was struck from his hand by an officer who had come to believe that Gordon was a holy man. His bodyguard kept very close to him, and his Chinese sergeant had his own, capillary, intelligence service, so it is probable that the wound was received in the 'normal' course of the fighting, which he led in person, encouraging his officers and waving his little walking stick at the enemy. He was more cautious at Waisoo, if only because he was weak from loss of blood; there the local peasants rose to welcome him and his men and massacred the Heavenly Army. Gordon wrote to his mother: 'I do not regret the fate of these rebels. I have no talent for description, but the scenes I have witnessed of misery are something dreadful, and I must say that your wish for me to return [to England] with the work incomplete would not be expressed if you saw the state of these people.' By this time he had given up hope of persuading Li that the time for bloodshed, massacres and revenge was past, and though he was horrified by the sight of peasants cutting flesh from corpses on the battlefield to take home to eat, he hardened his stomach if not his heart and got on with 'the work'.

The survivors of the Heavenly Kingdom's troops at Kintang and Waisoo managed to reach Changchow, which had a large, well-trained garrison of 20,000–25,000. Tseng Kuo-Fan had been besieging the city for several weeks without success, and he was intrigued to meet Gordon, this now almost legendary figure who waved a magic wand at the enemy and caused walls to fall down in the manner of Joshua. The united armies took Changchow in the middle of June 1864, and there remained only the capital of the Heavenly Kingdom, Nanking. Gordon knew perfectly well that he would not be welcome at this last battle, and he knew, too, that the scenes of savagery would outdo anything he had seen up to now. He had done his bit, even 'elevating the [English] national character in the eyes of the Chinese', as the Consul-General put it. It was time to go. He handed over command of the Ever Victorious Army in Shanghai and officially returned to his unit, promoted Lieutenant-Colonel (acting colonel). To placate the Emperor, he was sent to Peking to report on his campaigns and to suggest how to reorganize the Imperial armies; he was there when Nanking fell in July.

Gordon enjoyed his short stay in Peking, if only because he was able to see the Summer Palace partly rebuilt and so salve his conscience when he recalled his demolition work in 1860. He also had treatment from practitioners of traditional Chinese medicine, to whose skill he always attributed the fact that he was never troubled by his Kintang wounds in later life. He was lionized by the Dowager Empress, Tzu Hsi, who wrote to Queen Victoria extolling his virtues. He was promoted to the equivalent of field-marshal in the Imperial Army and was photographed wearing the yellow cape, ceremonial sword and tassels befitting that rank; he was also presented with the peacock's feather, the highest order given by the Manchu Dynasty, and a large gold medal struck to commemorate his successes and service to the Imperial Crown, but again refused money, determined to leave China a poor *tzaddik* just as he had arrived.

On his return to Shanghai he reviewed the Ever Victorious Army for the last time, and bade a tearful goodbye to his bodyguard. He somewhat reluctantly attended a number of farewell parties given for him by the European community, and joyfully toured the Yangtse delta on his 'flagship', the former pleasure steamer *Hyson*.

As he boarded the boat for home, he heard that he was to be made a Companion of the Order of the Bath. He was more interested to read about Garibaldi, a man after his own heart, also on his way to London (to drum up support for the next part of the campaign to rid Italy of foreign powers). In a way it was typical of Gordon that, instead of dwelling on what had been two triumphal years, taking a thirty-year-old captain out of obscurity into the pages of the history of several great nations, he turned his face towards the future, not as a hero but as a man in search of heroes. Reading a small collection of Garibaldi's writings, given to him by the Italian Consul, he did not watch the coast of China fade away, but pondered on lines such as: 'I am a man who hates all tyranny being profoundly convinced that in it lies all original sin and the corruption of the human race . . . but I am also convinced of the necessity of an honest, temporary dictatorship in those nations like France, Italy and Spain which are victims of Byzantism . . .' and on other sentiments expressed by the self-contradictory Garibaldi, Republican friend of monarchs, nationalist and socialist, Believer and Unbeliever, the pacifist who wrote, during his Latin American campaigns: '*La guerra es la verdadera vida del hombre*' (war is the natural life for a man). Gordon was shortly to meet again one of Garibaldi's officers, Romolo Gessi, who had promised to be on the quayside to meet him.

FIVE

Ragged Boys and Others

*'How far better to be allowed to be kind to a little Scrub
than to govern the greatest kingdoms.'*

Gordon, 1869

On the slow voyage back to Britain, 'Chinese' Gordon as he was
now to be known, realized what it meant to be lionized, and
acquired a chronic distaste for the physical presence of 'fuss'. He
did not, and had not, resented the applause of his troops, nor even
the bibulous farewell of the Irish captain of the *Hyson*, Davidson;
he had avoided the diplomatic and business community in Shanghai; he had had tea with the American Methodists; he had done his
duty by going to Peking and being photographed in his Court dress
as a mandarin. But the behaviour of the widows returning to
England from India, and the mixture of envy and admiration of
colonels twice his age, embarrassed him. Luckily, from Shanghai to
the Indian ports his ship was half empty and he had discovered all
the bolt holes.

When he reached Southampton he found the house at 5 Rockstone Place, where his mother and father and an assortment of
brothers and sisters were waiting for him, besieged by journalists.
He did not like the stories they had written about him in the past,
and he did not like the questions they asked him in person. In
particular, he resented the insinuation that he had come back from
China a very rich man. As he had written to his sister before he left:
'I do not care a jot about my promotion [to lieutenant-colonel] or
what people may say, I know I shall leave China as poor as I

entered it. . . . I did not even want to take the buttons on my mandarin's hat, some of which are worth thirty pounds.' The Press did not believe him when he said, 'I would not take the money [he had been offered by the Emperor] from them in their miserable poverty, and I feel correspondingly comfortable.' Nor did the Press believe him when he said that he had just done his duty, by God and his Sovereign, and did not understand all the 'fuss'. As Sir William Butler put it: 'On the strength of precisely these three things – faith, disregard of money, and straightforward honesty of thought and speech, he was in his lifetime not only without honour in his own country, but was regarded by many of the mandarin and ruling classes of his fellow-countrymen as a madman.' In the meantime he had some sharp things to say about being made a Companion of the Order of the Bath, 'the reward usually reserved for industrious clerks', as Lytton Strachey expressed it. His brother Henry had been made CB in 1857 for superintending the embarkation of surplus stores and clothing at the end of the Crimean War.

Gordon was also rather distressed by the attitude of his father. As Egmont Hake notes in *The Story of Chinese Gordon*:

> He [his father] lived by the 'code of honour': it was the motive of all his actions, and he expected those with whom he dealt to be guided by its precepts. . . . So deeply did General [Henry William] Gordon revere the ideal of the British Officer, and his calling, which he considered the highest and best, that Charles Gordon's acceptance of a foreign command gave him no pleasure; he was proud of his son, but he did not like to think that he was serving among foreigners, and not, as a Gordon should, with the men of his own race and faith.

But his father looked old and ill, and could be affectionately humoured; he had never been further than the Eastern Mediterranean and had rather strange ideas about 'foreigners' even there.

To Charles George Gordon's great relief there was one foreigner who had been laying in wait for him almost as assiduously as the British Press. Romolo Gessi had been left behind in England by Garibaldi, and charged with recruiting his friend, if he could, for the next part of his programme for the unification of Italy, the forthcoming campaign against the Austro-Hungarians in the Tyrol. Gessi had introduced himself to the family, and Mrs Gordon and Augusta preferred him to Gordon's other friend, Drew. After ten years of letters and tracts, and a proposal of marriage to Augusta, Drew had not been seen or heard from for a couple of years, and was presumably sulking somewhere. With his 'charm of a bandit',

Romolo Gessi beguiled all the Gordon females he met, as well as the proprietress of a tavern in Southampton where he was staying.

There was never really any likelihood of Charles going back to Italy with Gessi, even if his father had not been harping on the undesirability of serving among foreigners. Anyway, Garibaldi's principal devotees in England were those very romantic young ladies and male Radicals whom Gordon disliked as much as his father did. On Gessi's own admission, only about 1 per cent of the population of Italy was actually concerned with what Garibaldi was trying to achieve; the vast majority did not care – '*Francia o Spagna, purche si magna*' (France or Spain, as long as we eat), as he said in his dialect, was still most people's attitude. The idea of the Tyrolean expedition was intriguing, but it smacked of brigandage with the brigands pocketing the proceeds.

With Gessi gone in April 1865, life became rather depressing. Gordon was not at ease with his sick father, and did not like being, as he put it, 'aide de camp to mother'. He therefore asked the War Office for a new appointment, but the War Office did not know quite what to do with him. A certain amount of envy was felt at the hero's rapid promotion and present publicity, even if the hero did not exploit the publicity as others would have done. The ideal thing would be a posting to a place sufficiently far from London for the publicity to fade away in the absence of its subject, but near enough just in case the government needed some physical evidence of an active and successful foreign policy. In the end the War Office came up with the ideal posting – Royal Engineer Officer-in-Command at Gravesend, where he would be responsible for the construction and reconstruction of the forts for the defence of the Thames.

During the Middle Ages it had occurred to a succession of kings that something ought to be done to guard the approach by water to the capital. Apart from a system of warning beacons, nothing was done until 1380, when a piratical French raid resulted in Gravesend being sacked and burnt down; somebody had forgotten to supply the beacons with wood, and attempts to light them with damp straw caused the death by suffocation of two townsmen. This contretemps resulted in the building of a castle at Cooling and the fortification of East Tilbury; in 1539 a start was made to the fortification of Gravesend. Two blockhouses were built there which crossed their fire with one at Tilbury; there were two more blockhouses at Higham and East Tilbury. The idea was that an intricate system of crossfire would deter all invaders and protect the Gravesend–Tilbury ferry route; in addition to the guns in the blockhouses, other batteries were set up on the bank of the river.

The new defence system was alerted not against the French, but against the Dutch. In 1588, when England was under threat of invasion from The Netherlands – troops under the Duke of Parma, to be transported by the Invincible Armada – the estuary was swarming with soldiers. An Italian military engineer, Gianibelli, built a boom and a bridge of boats between the Gravesend and Tilbury blockhouses, because the other three had fallen into disuse. But the Armada proved not to be invincible and the Gravesend and Tilbury blockhouses were abandoned, to be hurriedly repaired when the Dutch appeared in the Thames and Medway in 1667. Again they were abandoned after the Treaty of Breda, and by 1730 were in such a poor condition that during a storm part of the Gravesend emplacement, including the soldiers' lavatory, collapsed into the Thames. There was another French invasion scare in 1778 and New Tavern Fort was built, a moated earthwork with gun emplacements on top of it; an artillery barracks, Old Milton Chantry, was built nearby. The new fort saw no action during the Napoleonic Wars, though it was rearmed and by 1846 was the only one left in action to crossfire with Tilbury.

Gordon was appointed on 1 September 1865, during a new French invasion scare. The uncertain relations between Britain and France while they had been allies in the Crimean War had deteriorated, especially since a plot to assassinate Napoleon III was found to have been concocted in England. The new RE Commandant was supposed to bring the whole area into a state of alert preparedness and the *Gravesend Reporter*, which could not believe that the town was to have such a famous, albeit temporary, inhabitant, told its readers that they could sleep safe in their beds. Before Gordon could get down to work, however, he was summoned urgently back to Southampton, where his father died on 19 September.

It was a sad beginning to what was anyway a useless project. As Sir William Butler wrote: 'Some twelve millions sterling was spent upon these constructions (circles of defensive works of the most costly description) . . . and when the works were finished it was found that, being built in the middle of a transition period in the science of defence, they were already three parts obsolete.' Gordon protested, but he knew that once the political decision had been taken there was nothing for it but to get on with the work. After a delay while new batteries were built at Shornmead, Cliffe, Allhallows and East Tilbury, he got on with remodelling New Tavern Fort. Victor Smith of the Kent Defence Research Group has summed up the remodelling which:

involved no change to the basic 1778 plan. The work involved the construction of brick emplacements, on site of the old ones, for 10 heavy rifled muzzle-loading guns with a range of four miles. Seven of the emplacements were provided with thick wrought-iron shields for additional protection. Extensive magazines under the emplacements supplied the guns with shell and cartridge via ammunition lifts. The magazine complex was illuminated by candle lamps placed behind glass for safety.

There was not really much for Gordon to do. He made no original contribution to the design of the fortifications, and as far as siting the guns was concerned, that was the business of his artillery brother officers. His official residence was Fort House, near to Milton church and the medieval chantry (now the artillery barracks). It was a short walk from his house to the fortifications. He would get up at five, have a cold bath and then breakfast, before inspecting his men and going on to confer with the civilian builders and his own subalterns. By mid-morning he would have seen to his own satisfaction that things were going well and the contractors not swindling the government, and after lunch he felt free to do as he pleased, to get to know Gravesend and see if there was anything he could do that was more useful than resiting obsolete guns.

During his first year he was the object of attention of the *Gravesend Reporter*, the respectful city fathers, and mothers who were anxious to marry off this eligible hero to their daughters. The *Gravesend Reporter* remained faithful. The city fathers came to grumble about the expense they were being asked to bear for new lighting to access roads and the refurbishing of the ferry, and protested vigorously when gunnery practice on the new emplacements broke the windows in nearby houses. The mothers and daughters were doomed to disappointment in Gravesend as elsewhere.

What surprised and horrified Gordon was the number of waifs and strays, and elderly poor, for whom no provision seemed to be made. He had seen a great deal of poverty and distress in the Crimea, in the Balkans and in China, but that had been in either time of war or the aftermath of war, deplorable but explicable. Here he was in a prosperous town, further enriched by government contracts, and there seemed to be no official response to the situation. As he had done in Shanghai, he made contact with local religious groups – those, especially the Methodists, with whom he felt most at home. He visited the Whitechapel Mission, forerunner of the Salvation Army, founded the year before his appointment by William Booth, and discussed the Gravesend problem with him.

Booth, however, was at that time attacking the twin evils of drink and prostitution to the exclusion of most other things, and Gordon was not a teetotaller and frightened of all women, fallen or still upright. He met in Gravesend various members of the Religious Tract Society, which believed in the spiritual reclamation of the poor, but did little to feed or clothe them. It was through the Society that he felt impelled to write some tracts of his own, which contained a message halfway between the harsh words of an Old Testament prophet and morals drawn from travellers' tales and his own adventures on two continents. The Nonconformists who agreed to correct his English, which was muscular but not always grammatical, were a Mr and Mrs Freese, with whom he kept in touch for many years after he left Gravesend. They were a practical couple, and suggested to Colonel Gordon that as he had no expenses – his official residence was kept up by the War Office, he had only one civilian servant, a cook-housekeeper, and he could eat in the mess when he liked – he could, perhaps, spend some money on providing the poor with food, and the young poor with clothing and education as well.

The idea apppealed to the Colonel and he looked for ways to put it into practice. Fort House was a large, half-timbered pile with eight or nine bedrooms and several reception rooms, and the gardens were extensive (the house was destroyed by bombs in 1944 but the gardens are now the public Fort Gardens). During the summer of 1866 he decided to hold a number of garden parties for the elderly poor; he was expected to entertain anyway, and by inviting the poor he was sure to keep away polite society. His sister Augusta was only half convinced that the garden parties were a good thing, but she offered her advice on what to serve; unfortunately her tastes ran to jellies and dainty cakes. The more experienced Mrs Freese said that as that particular summer afternoon was almost certainly the only one which many of the guests would enjoy in pleasant surroundings and with abundant free food, the fare should be substantial – suet and tapioca puddings, beef sandwiches and watered beer. Furthermore, they should be encouraged to take home what they could not eat. Mrs Freese herself packed what was left at the end of each garden party and sent each guest home with enough food for the week. These were very successful occasions, and twenty of them, with thirty guests at a time, managed to lighten the lives of 600 old people that summer. Gordon was careful to keep a record of names and addresses and during the following autumn and winter would visit the wretched homes of those who excited his greatest pity and sympathy and bring them broth and coals.

During one of the garden parties, an old woman remarked on how pleasant the gardens were, and how she missed having a garden herself; she had been brought up in the countryside and had come to Gravesend with her husband, now dead. She lived in a one-room attic by herself and only had a pot of ferns to remind her that greenery existed. Gordon was very moved by this and gave orders that during 1867 two-thirds of the gardens were to be divided up into allotments to which the poor could have access to grow vegetables to eat, while the rest of the gardens were to be kept open at all times to all comers.

It was more difficult to decide what to do for the waifs and strays. They could not read his tracts, he discovered, and this prompted him to offer his services as an unpaid member of staff at the local Ragged School; there was no free, compulsory elementary education in England and schools of this type were run by various Christian denominations and paid for by general subscription. Gordon's offer was accepted, and he taught geography and arithmetic for years at the school. He also invited the boys to Fort House and put them up for several days at a time, sending them away well fed, with new clothes and boots.

His physical appearance at this time was attractive. He was not tall, but he had a pleasant face under thick brown hair; his mouth was firm, though he had a slight lisp still, and his blue-grey eyes fixed the attention of listeners just as he fixed his attention on them. Sir Gerald Graham wrote:

> His eyes would appear to double in size as his talk would race galloping along, full of similes and parables leading to his subject, so that you saw the picture he painted. He was the most interesting talker. . . . He was so merry and playful in the garden at Gravesend, with his ducks on which he used to turn the hose. There was the Duchess of —— who waddled her tail, and young Prince ——, who held his head so high. How the old lady ducks put their heads together and gossiped till he would souse them again with another douche from the hose. Each duck had a name, and under Gordon's amusing talk, represented some human frailty or weakness.

The combination of ingenuousness, good humour and authority was irresistible and the boys, some of whom came to steal, stayed to learn. By the autumn of 1867 he had so many followers that he opened a night school of his own, to which the best of the boys at the Ragged School came, and he paid a young schoolteacher to help him with the subjects in which he was weakest. His aim was to give at least some of the boys a good enough education for them to be able to get jobs, on land or sea, and do something with their own lives. 'How far better', he said, 'to be allowed to be kind to a little Scrub than to govern the greatest kingdoms.' He did not call them scrubs to their faces but Wangs, after the Princes of the Heavenly Kingdom of Great Peace, and boasted of the success of those whom he had placed, especially at sea. Graham reports: 'In his sitting-room Gordon had a big chart of the world, with pins stuck in it, marking the probable positions of the different ships in which his 'Wangs' were sailing. He thus followed them in his thoughts, and was able to point out their whereabouts to their friends when they came to inquire about them.'

This activity was remarkable, not so much in itself but for the scale on which it took place, and the genuinely disinterested charity, faith and good works of which it was a rare example. During a period of almost five years, Gordon devoted over thirty hours a week to comforting the sick and the poor and educating the young. It has been estimated that over five hundred boys were taught by him and over two hundred found jobs afterwards; these are figures larger than the roll of many grammar schools of the day. It is difficult to know just how much he spent. He had had the inscriptions in English and Chinese erased from the large gold medal given to him on his departure by the Chinese Emperor, and sent it as a gift to the Coventry relief fund shortly after his arrival, but he is known to have sold virtually everything else other than a few trinkets which he gave to his mother and his sister. What is known is that he was buying boots from a wholesaler in London, in the end by the gross, and that he had a Whitechapel tailor make up some hundreds of suits, including a few mock military uniforms for his favourites. The otherwise unused rooms at Fort House looked like a quartermaster's store, with shelves on which were piled serviceable underwear, socks and shorts. His orderly, Bates, taught the boys how to polish boots, which, it was said, was the only thing they did not enjoy.

Though he was regarded at times with suspicion and envy by other men and organizations with charitable missions, in the main he managed to avoid antagonizing them. Perhaps this was because, as Sir William Butler noted, there was:

No gloomy faith, no exalted sense of self-confidence, no mocking of the belief of others, no separation of his sense of God from the everyday work to which his hand has to be put; no leaving of religion at the church door as a garb to be put on going in and taken off going out; but a faith which was a living, moving, genial reality. . . . The essential principle of Gordon's good work was its simplicity, as it must be the essential principle of good work.

Various denominations tried to 'nobble' him, but he would never declare himself Evangelical, Methodist, Baptist or anything else, and his mother was horrified to hear that he enjoyed cordial relations with two Catholic priests in the area, and even went to mass from time to time.

The city fathers were always puzzled by the behaviour of a man who should have been one of Gravesend's leading citizens, but who never turned up at civic balls and seldom accepted invitations to the Mayor's Parlour. When he did appear among the aldermen it was with 'wild schemes' for organizing the merchants and professional people into a sort of private, municipal Poor Law Commission, and once he proposed a penny rate to build an old people's home. However, he was always civil and received the Mayor at Fort House several times, and really nobody could complain.

A man who spent so much time and money on adolescent and even younger boys would have been the subject of inquiries by investigative journalists in the twentieth century, but there was never a breath of scandal. It was probably the very openness and directness of everything he did which dispelled suspicion in this direction. As Sir Gerald Graham wrote:

> Wonderfully rapid in seeing the motives of others – for an honest man it was surprising how he could so readily see the crabbed lines of life – he understood and saw through all diplomacy, but he knew the shortest way to the end was by the straightest line. He had one motive only – the right; and his prayers or his nature saved him from selfishness, ambition, and the hundred other subjects that blind men to their end.

Fred Plaut, a London psychiatrist, writing in *Encounter*, June–July 1982, expressed his opinion that 'it seems obvious that he [Gordon] was more homo than hetero-sexual [but it] is improbable that he was ever a practising homosexual; in a man who lived so much in the public eye and had many enemies, this could hardly have escaped notice'. Nearly a hundred years after Gordon's death, Plaut's conclusion sums up all the speculation that went on during Gordon's life and after his death.

But who were the enemies of this man who was so good that nobody wanted it to be true? Oddly enough, for a man who brought honour to the profession of arms, they were mostly brother officers on active service or working as hacks in the War Office. Some of those who had been at Woolwich with him, and knew of the backterming for 'bullying', thought he ought not to have been commissioned at all. Those who had not managed to get to the Crimea resented the quick promotion and even the fact that he had been awarded the Legion of Honour (fifth class). Not to speak, of course, of the lotus land along the Danube in which he was supposed to have spent two years, and the real lotus land where he became the equivalent of a field-marshal at the age of thirty. Now here he was, not yet forty and about to be made up to full colonel for all they knew (his promotion came in 1872), because a new diplomatic posting was in the offing. His own subalterns and brother officers in other arms and services at Gravesend resented not only his fame (they certainly could not complain that he was exploiting that) but also the fact that he seldom went to the mess, did not lead the social life expected of an officer and a gentleman and preferred the company of poor boys to theirs and that of their marriageable sisters.

The old men in the War Office were already tired of the polite inquiries about Gordon's health which they met with at all their (angry) meetings with the French and (cordial) negotiations with the Chinese. Obviously Gravesend was not far enough away from the centre of events. Even the Turkish and Russian Ambassadors sometimes mentioned his name. It was unfair. Gordon was upsetting the ruling clique of the Army just as he was upsetting the Army List with his accelerated promotions and foreign honours and appointments.

In the end, they decided to send him to a place where he would quickly acquire even more foreign honours and appointments. The work of the Commission of Demarcation or Russo–Turkish Boundary Commission on which Gordon had served in 1856–8 had ended. Jobs had to be found for the unemployed Commissioners and new men had to be brought in to discuss, among other things, the international right to navigation along the Danube. The delta had to be mapped; it was so vast that nobody was quite sure to whom the north and south belonged. Gordon was not only renowned as a mapmaker but had been there before and would know some of the people, especially the Romanians among whom he would have to live if appointed. It was certainly far away from both London and Paris and it was generally agreed between the War Office and the Foreign Office that Gordon should be appointed Commissioner for carrying out the arrangements respecting the navigation of the Danube, and Her Majesty's Vice-Consul in the Delta of the

Danube to reside at Galatz [Galaţi]'. So it was published in the Foreign Office List, and on 15 November 1871 the appointment was made.

Gordon had mixed feelings about leaving Gravesend. The work had been boring, a waste of time and a waste of millions of pounds of taxpayers' money. For his part, he had tried to minimize the waste and leave behind an improved version of fortifications designed at the time of the American War of Independence, though he knew the guns he had housed would never be fired in anger – never at all if the Mayor of Gravesend had his way. He would not miss his brother officers, with whom he had had so little contact socially that he was probably unaware of their hostility; he knew his senior officers disliked him because in their hierarchy he was still only a captain of engineers (RE) though already a lieutenant-colonel in the Army List and next year to be full colonel.

His old people and his 'Wangs' were another matter. On the one hand, like all teachers and preachers he needed a break from the routine, even if only be become a better teacher and preacher. He was not particularly worried about the fate of his 'street arabs' who were at least as wily and expert in the arts of survival as the Arabs he would have to deal with for most of the rest of his life. Those who wanted to keep in touch would do so. The old, however, were another problem. They were often sick and poorly housed, and he had got into the habit of awarding them 'pensions' out of his own pay, often pretending to them that the money came from official sources. Who would look after them now? His friends, the Freeses, assured him that his example had been an inspiration to them all, and that when he had gone they would undertake to see that no recipient of his help went uncomforted; Mrs Freese later confessed to a friend that 'in a way it had been a *relief* to see the Colonel leave them *for a time* because his example had been so *exhausting* and sometimes in our inadequacy *humiliating*'. The city fathers presented him with an address, and the *Gravesend Reporter*, which had become a little bored with his faith and good works, wished him a safe journey and a speedy journey with many laurels to add to his own and to those of the town.

During a month's leave at Southampton before he left, Gordon experienced some tiring scenes with his mother, who since his father's death had become emotionally more dependent on him than on any of his brothers. His sister Augusta, too, was tearful but told him that, in Butler's words, 'if the Lord had called him, then, of course, he should answer that call', and though, like the *Gravesend Reporter*, she was uncertain about the precise whereabouts of Galaţi, and thought after Vienna that the Danube flowed into the Mediterranean, she felt that at least it would be not so damp as at Gravesend and would remind him of his childhood in Corfu.

In London to buy some map-making instruments, he called in at the Whitehall Place offices of the Royal Geographical Society. He had resigned from the Society in 1866 because they seemed to him to want to take part in the conspiracy to lionize him. He mumbled to the Secretary that he 'hoped to be of service to the Society mapping a region little known', shook hands with a number of clerks, and took his leave.

'Vainglory' or no, it was really the prospect of seeing Romolo Gessi again, after five years of intermittent correspondence, which cheered Gordon on his way to his new post. After presenting himself to the British Ambassador in Constantinople, who would be his superior in the diplomatic mission to the delta, he made for Bucharest and arrived unannounced at the Gessis' home. It was only by chance that he found his old friend there. At the end of the Tyrolean campaign, brought to an end for reasons of state by La Marmora, Gessi had returned to Romania and married a local girl, Maria Purkat. He had tried to settle down as an employee of *Lloyd's Register*, of which his father had been a correspondent for many years. Unfortunately the pay was poor, and Maria was producing children with alarming rapidity. He had to find something more remunerative, and if possible more exciting. He was in Bucharest to raise funds for a new project; with a Romanian partner he intended to buy a mill at Tulcea, equip it with a steam engine and make a fortune as a rural entrepreneur. It seemed an unlikely project to Gordon, but he complimented Gessi on his enterprise and took advantage of his friend's former employment to get an introduction to the local office of *Lloyd's Register*, which was concerned with precisely the sort of navigation, on the Danube and Black Sea, that he was supposed to be controlling.

After a week of home comforts in the Gessi household Gordon left for Galaţi. Gravesend seemed to him wickedly exciting by comparison. Of all the half dozen places called Galaţi in Romania – the name is derived from Gales, a word with the same Celtic origin as Galles, Pay de Galles and Wales – this was perhaps the dreariest. A port since Byzantine times, the only one in Romania to which large vessels had access, it was a huddle of huts and warehouses, with three or four substantial municipal buildings and a small residential quarter where the British and French consulates were to be found. Most of the other Danube Commissioners seemed to have their homes and offices in Bucharest, which was not surprising. When he eventually met them, they did not seem very clear about what they were supposed to be doing. The Chief Commissioner said it was a very delicate business. The Danube flowed through so many countries. In order not to offend the recently independent Romanians and the Turks they had to show an interest in problems of navigation in Serbia and even Austria, without offending either. They were still trying to agree on what should be done, and to be frank had not yet done anything. However, the Danube delta was a naturalist's paradise, and if the British Commissioner cared to explore it in the spring, guides and boats could be found. In the meantime, as winter in the delta was very cold and damp, he suggested that Gordon base himself, too, in Bucharest until at least the following April.

There was nothing to be done, so Gordon did as he was advised and took an apartment in Bucharest where he was able to entertain the Gessi family as they had often entertained him. He amused himself that winter discussing the layout of Romolo's mill and playing with the children. In the second week of February he went to Constantinople to be officially advised of his promotion to full colonel and in late March 1872 he was back in Galaţi. He spent two weeks in the delta, but in spite of the Chief Commissioner's recommendation he took no interest in the birds. It reminded him very much of the Yangtse and he wondered whether or not it could all be made as navigable, and splendid cities like Soochow founded there. He was struck by the fact that downstream from Galaţi stood a town called Cernavoda, which was only about 40 miles from the Black Sea and the port of Constanţa. He went to Cernavoda and Medgidia several times on his way to Tulcea that spring and became more and more convinced that a canal from Cernavoda to Constanţa was a practical possibility. It was certainly a less monumental enterprise than the Suez Canal, to the opening of which he had been invited by De Lesseps in 1869.

Gordon was really quite excited by the prospect of his new canal. After all, it would be within his brief as one responsible for facilitating navigation on the Danube. The big southward bend of the river after Cernavoda, would be avoided and all the work would take place on Romanian rather than Bulgarian territory, no doubt to the delight of the Romanians. At the first plenary session of the Commission, in May 1872, he put the idea to his colleagues. They were horrified. They asked him if he liked Romania. He said he did, and that it was not the first time he had been there. They asked him if he had ever had any dealings with officialdom – even the civil servants who operated the tobacco monopoly. He said that all that sort of thing was taken care of for him by his Romanian friends. They told him that the Romanians were the most byzantine people in old Byzantium; it was impossible to deal with them. They had become worse since the union of the principalities of Wallachia and Moldavia which had taken place just after he had left in 1859. He and they would go mad if anybody suggested to the new government that they tackle such an immense project. They would resent not having thought of it themselves, and they would be pessimistic anyway about the outcome.

In as tactful a way as he could he put all this to Gessi, his Romanian wife and mother, and asked if there were any truth in it. Alas, they said, it was all true. It was even difficult to pay taxes. It was almost impossible to achieve anything. The mill at Tulcea was proving to be not such a bright idea after all. Romolo had even been asked such questions as how much steam would escape from his new engine and why he could not use the millrace and pay taxes as his predecessor had done.

In the end, Gordon ignored the difficulties and drew up a plan for a Danube–Black Sea canal. He pointed out that it would shorten the distance to the Black Sea by 400 kilometres. It did not require much skilled labour. If the money had been found for the Suez Canal, it could be found for this project, too. Being transparently honest, he also calculated and reported to his fellow Commissioners that some 300 million cubic metres of earth would have to be moved, 25 million more than the Suez Canal. However, apart from the commercial advantages, it would probably enable the marshes in the Danube delta to be drained without disturbing the wildlife, and make the new canal the main trunk of a new network of waterways.

The debate went on throughout the winter of 1872 and the spring of 1873. During a visit to Constantinople in November 1872 he tried to interest the British Ambassador, and so the British government, in his project. He also reassured the agents for his bank that his instructions that virtually all of his salary should be sent to Gravesend were correct; of the £2,000 a year he earned as a Danube Commissioner, £1,500 went to carry on feeding and in other ways helping the poor, his 'pensioners'. The bank was reassured, but the Ambassador did not feel he could recommend the British government to interest themselves in this new project; he knew that the government was interested in buying Suez Canal shares (and the list of shareholders is full of British nominees) but did not feel that direct involvement in the actual construction of a new waterway. . . . This refusal irritated Gordon, an engineer, who wrote to his sister that he did not know what would have happened to England if Bridgewater and Stephenson had been bankers – would they have waited until some Frenchman or Italian came to dig their canals and build their railways?

Nevertheless, the visit was not fruitless. At a reception at the British Embassy, he met Nubar Pasha, then sharing power at the Khedive's Court in Cairo with the German Koenig Bey. Nubar Pasha later told Sir William Butler: 'England owes little to her officials; she owes her greatness to men of a different stamp.' He had heard of Gordon's success in China, and remembered him from a meeting with Negrelli and De Lesseps years before. He also knew that he was underemployed and out of his element as a Danube Commissioner, and as he had a roving brief to recruit to the Khedive's service brilliant men of whatever nationality, he hinted to Gordon that when he felt he had done his duty by the Danube there was a challenge up the ancient River Nile which had to be met. Good men were few and far between, exceptional men exceptional. Would the Colonel be attracted by a senior administrative post in Egypt, in the Sudan to be precise? He could choose his own staff, of course. Nubar Pasha had in mind the Governorship of Equatoria, the southernmost region of the Sudan. The post was now held by another Englishman, Sir Samuel Baker, who had told the Khedive that he would like to return to England. There would be no difficulties about the salary. Sir Samuel was getting £10,000 a year. Did that sound like a reasonable sum?

Discontented as he was with his life in Galaţi, relieved as it was only by visits to the Gessis in Bucharest and the mill at Tulcea, Gordon was tempted. However, he told Nubar Pasha he had a project, the sort of idea that the Chief Minister's master would be interested in, a new 'Suez' project on the Danube. He was not making much headway with British, French or Turkish officialdom, but he intended to keep on trying. Maybe Nubar Pasha could have a word with the Turkish government, still nominally suzerain on the Bulgarian bank of the Danube? Anyway, he would think about the offer and let the Minister know.

When he got back to Romania and found life the mixture as before, he decided at the end of the winter to discuss the offer with Romolo Gessi. Gessi was almost desperate. He had not really wanted to be a miller. It had been his wife's idea of a steady, remunerative position, respectable and respected in a peasant community. Now it seemed unlikely, the bureaucracy being what it was, that he would ever get up a head of steam on his new engine and actually get down to the business of grinding corn. Why had his friend kept this marvellous idea secret all winter? Of course he must go and be Governor of Equatoria. And he would need somebody he could trust to look after his troops. Gessi's wife could look after the mill. Did Carlo think the Khedive would be pleased to have him in the Sudan? When was Carlo going to accept the offer, and when could they leave?

By the end of May 1873 Gordon had come to agree with Mrs Freese, who had written to him saying that his time in Galaţi was like Moses's sojourn in the desert, just a prelude to great things. He made one last attempt to convince his fellow Commissioners that his Danube delta canal was a brilliant and practicable idea. He failed. He would have been astonished had he been able to foresee that 110 years later the Romanians would complete his project, along a line which differed very little from the one he had traced. He went to Constantinople again and told the British Ambassador that he felt he was achieving very little either as a Danube Commissioner or as Vice-Consul. He was, in fact, achieving nothing. The Commission had met only three times in plenary session and had taken no decisions, and he had no British subjects at all in Galaţi who could lay claim to his consular services, whatever they were. The British Ambassador tried to reassure him and told him he was making a 'valuable contribution', but did not say to what. He also hinted that many men would be happy to spend a few years in well-paid idleness in that part of the world. It was a chance to cultivate hobbies, to collect icons and other valuable objects with which to decorate a home in England in the future.

Gordon did not find this reply very satisfactory. He wrote to Nubar Pasha asking if his offer were still open, and he wrote to friends in England warning them that he might well be moving on. As Sir William Butler wrote, quoting John Ruskin's lectures on *War* and *The Future of England* given at Woolwich in 1865 and 1869:

Nubar Pasha had soon noted the vast difference that lay between the officer of engineers and any other English official with whom he had ever come in contact. Clearly this rich treasure in soldier-shape, now floating waiflike about Europe was something worth securing. Here was the 'Captain' whose 'good leading' the best thinker of our time [Ruskin] had been vainly asking for England in England. . . .

91

Nubar Pasha replied by return; the offer was still open and would always be open for the Colonel.

After a futile correspondence with the War Office and the Foreign Office Gordon resigned on 18 October 1873, having already accepted Nubar Pasha's offer. He went to Bucharest for a short holiday with the Gessis and told Romolo that he would be delighted to have him in the Khedive's service with him. He, Gordon, planned to take up his appointment in the New Year. They would meet in Cairo, or somewhere up the Nile.

SIX

Gordon of the Nile

'To each is allotted a distinct work, to each a destined goal; to some the seat at the right hand or left of the Saviour.'

Gordon, 1877

After the confirmation of his appointment in September 1873, and the *nihil obstat* of the British Government, Brevet Colonel Gordon was made a general in the Turkish Army. He set to work to find out as much as he could about those parts of the Ottoman Empire that now concerned him, Egypt and the Sudan – in particular Equatorial Sudan, over which he would have dictatorial powers. He had no doubt about his ability to restore order in Equatoria and see that the Khedive of Egypt's writ ran there, just as he had had no doubts about his ability to defeat the armies of the Heavenly Kingdom and restore south China to the Manchus. He was not sure why he had been offered the post of Governor of this ill-charted tract of swamp, forest and scrub-covered mountain, but, as he wrote to his sister: 'For some wise design, God turns events one way or another, whether a man likes it or not, as a man driving a horse turns it to right or left without consideration as to whether the horse likes that way or not. To be happy, a man must be like a wellbroken, willing horse, ready for anything. Events will go as God likes.'

There was, however, some difficulty in getting up-to-date information about the countries straddling the Nile. Egyptians seemed reluctant to say anything, certainly anything pleasant, about the Sudan. There were a few books, mostly in French, and fewer maps. A Scottish explorer, James Bruce, had visited the

Sudan towards the end of the eighteenth century and had reported the existence of ruins of what must have been substantial cities. He had speculated on the origin of the kingdom of Kush, founded about 750 BC and contemporary with Etruria, and there were certainly Assyrian tales of the defeat of a Kushite king, Taharka, who had conquered most of the Nile delta and made his capital at Memphis. After the Assyrian invasion of the valley of the Nile, the Kushites apparently retreated south to an area around Meroe, near the Sixth Cataract, and there flourished until the fourth century AD in what became known as the Sudan. Gordon was intrigued to read that the Queen of Kush (which both the Jews and the Greeks confused with Ethiopia) travelled widely and 'met the apostle Philip on the road which goeth down from Jerusalem to Gaza'. In AD 543 Julian the Monk arrived in the Sudan and found a tiny Christian community there which he called 'Nubia' and expanded into a Christian kingdom, just as John of Ephesus converted Ethiopia at about the same time and reformed its administration. John of Ephesus's voluminous writings include accounts of the inhospitable climate: 'Julian used to take refuge from nine in the morning until four in the afternoon in caves full of water, where he sat undressed except for a linen garment such as people in the country wear.'

When Egypt was over-run by Muslim Arabs the Sudan was cut off from the rest of the Christian world, with the exception of Ethiopia with which it was periodically at war. After the Crusaders sacked Constantinople in 1204 the armies of Islam took revenge wherever they could, and by the end of the thirteenth century they had overwhelmed the most northerly of the three 'Nubian' kingdoms, Nobatia. By the middle of the fifteenth century the other two kingdoms, Mukuria and Alodia, had been conquered and forcibly converted. Resistance to Islam was offered only by the Ethiopians. Travellers' tales from Portugal in the fifteenth century told of a priest-king called Prester John who was supposed to rule over an African Christian kingdom. Portuguese missionaries certainly visited Ethiopia and possibly the Sudan, but the Ethiopians refused to submit to Rome and remained subject to their own Coptic bishops. No further missionary efforts seem to have been made, though Gordon knew that the British Anti-Slavery Society believed that the slave trade had one of its principal headquarters in the Ethiopia-Sudan region and was urging that measures should be taken to stop it.

If the Egyptians spoke ill of these millennary civilizations, then it was also true that nobody spoke well of the descendants of the people of Pharaonic Egypt. Nubar Pasha, the Armenian Chief

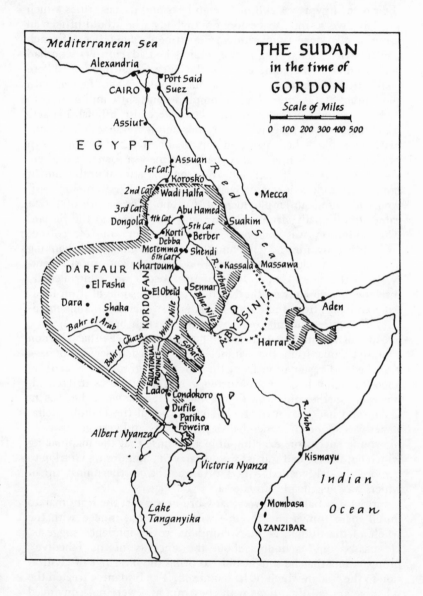

THE SUDAN
in the time of
GORDON

Scale of Miles

0 100 200 300 400 500

Mediterranean Sea

Alexandria

Port Said
Suez

CAIRO

Assiut

E G Y P T

Assuan
1st Cat.
Korosko
2nd Cat.
Wadi Halfa

Red Sea

Mecca

3rd Cat.
Dongola
4th Cat.
Abu Hamed

5th Cat.
Korti
Debba
Berber
Suakim

Metemma
6th Cat.
Shendi

DARFUR
Khartoum
Kassala
Massawa

El Fasha

KORDOFAN
El Obeid
Sennar

Dara
Shaka

Bahr el Arab

Bahr el Ghaza

White Nile

Blue Nile

R. Atbara

A B Y S S I N I A

Aden

Harrar

EQUATORIAL PROVINCE

R. Sobat

Lado
Condokoro
Dufile
Patiko
Foweira

R. Juba

Albert Nyanza

Victoria Nyanza

Kismayu

I n d i a n

Lake
Tanganyika

Mombasa

ZANZIBAR

O c e a n

Minister of the Khedive of Egypt, who had recruited Gordon, was only one of many foreigners who seemed to think of the country as their own. Egypt was full of foreign beys and pashas, titles which the Khedive seemed to bestow on anybody who would officer an army or take over a government department. There were French and Austrian pashas, engineers, soldiers and adventurers who had stayed on after the completion of the Suez Canal in 1869. There were British pashas who had gone out to Egypt when the war with the United States in 1812 had prompted Lancashire mill owners to look for cotton fibres elsewhere. There were also English bankers watching over the Khedive's enormous and increasing debts; some of these bankers had acquired diplomatic status. Gordon's own predecessor, Sir Samuel Baker, had been made a pasha. And there were Germans and Italians left over from the wars of unification at home, including a dozen of Garibaldi's officers, like Romolo Gessi, who had found no employment in Europe. The wealth of Egypt came, traditionally, from the slave and ivory trade in the Sudan, which Gordon was supposed to bring under control, cotton, foodstuffs grown in the delta and the southern hinterland, banking and other invisible exports in the Mediterranean and, most recently, from the Suez Canal. Most of this wealth was controlled by foreigners, who allowed the Khedive to spend some of it on food, wine and girls from the Paris Opera, and so increase his indebtedness to and dependence on British and French banks.

Most of the information about his new provinces that Gordon acquired came from Sir Samuel Baker. Gordon seems to have regretted his resignation from the Royal Geographical Society in 1866, though it had never occurred to him to withdraw it. He had, however, made contact with the Society again while he was in Galaţi and had drawn for them some maps of the Danube delta. Baker was a long-time member of the Society and very generous to his young successor, exacting only a promise that the mapmaking which he, Baker, had started would carry on, and urging Gordon to explore the lake called Albert Nyanza, the northernmost tip of which was just inside Equatoria.

Sir Samuel Baker believed that Gordon was just the right man to do all these things and to cope with Equatoria, indeed with the whole of the Sudan, as his voluminous correspondence suggests. He passed on his doubts about the sincerity of the Khedive's protestations that he sought only to bring the blessings of civilization to the Sudan which he had annexed. The Sudanese treated the Khedive and all Egyptians with contempt and were not convinced that it was in their interests to be ruled by the Khedive, formally a vassal of the Turkish Empire. The Khedive might speak of abolishing the slave trade, but as he pocketed some of the profits it was difficult to believe him. That the Khedive wanted to monopolize the trade in ivory and anything else was true, but Sir Samuel knew from bitter personal experience that Cairo would only come up with a few hundred indifferent Egyptian soldiers and European mercenaries, and little or none of the money with which to pay troops, administrators or anybody else. To be frank, Gordon would have to live off the land and do his best to dispense justice without help from anybody. He recommended the writings of T.H. Huxley, 'a man struggling towards Belief', and in particular a passage from *On the Physical Basis of Life*: 'In itself it is of little moment whether we express the phaenomena of matter in terms of spirit; or the phaenomena of spirit in terms of matter: matter may be regarded as a form of thought, thought may be regarded as a property of matter; each statement has a certain relative truth.' It was up to Gordon to tip the balance in favour of the Spirit by scientific work as sound as it was spectacular. Tax, punish and explore, he thought, should be Gordon's slogan.

The new Governor of Equatoria arrived in Cairo in February 1874. He stayed there for a couple of weeks and was received several times by the Khedive and his ministers. It was soon obvious that what Sir Samuel Baker had said about the Khedive was true. Gordon was given to understand that he could do as he pleased in Equatoria as long as he did not upset his immediate superior, the Governor-General of the Sudan, Ismail Ayub (Yacoob) Pasha, and did not ask for more than the £10,000 a year which had been paid to his predecessor. Gordon told the Khedive that £2,000 a year would be quite sufficient for his own modest needs ('in this way I will show the Court that gold and silver idols are not worshipped all over the world'), that he would pay Ismail Ayub Pasha due respect, and begged leave to depart as soon as possible. The Khedive thought Gordon either a fool or a madman to treat money in this shabby way, and ordered that a boat be got ready to take his new Governor through the Suez Canal and down the Red Sea as soon as possible.

Gordon entertained himself during the journey looking at De Lesseps's work with interest. He had with him the De Lesseps papers and the original schemes proposed by Negrelli and Linant, whose son was to be on his staff. He admired the ingenuity and far-sightedness of the Italian, so many years before the first spade had been sunk, and marvelled at the short-sightedness of the British governments which ignored George Stephenson's recommendation that Negrelli should enter British service. Gordon was more than ever convinced that waterways would rival railways in the future, and that the decline in the fortunes of canals would be reversed. His recent disappointments in Galaţi – his inability to convince the other Danube Commissioners that with a minimum of expenditure a Danube–Black Sea canal would solve many political and economic problems – still rankled. At sundown he ate a plate of rice washed down with brandy and soda and made notes on Negrelli's other great scheme, the linking of Albert Nyanza, Victoria Nyanza and Lake Tanganyika, the great north-east and central African waterway. Victoria Nyanza would be only just outside his jurisdiction and he knew that the Germans in Tanganyika (German East Africa) were surveying the land with open minds about how to link the Indian Ocean with the Great Lake.

Nobody on his boat was interested. His European aides, three English and one German, were not to his liking: they were soldiers of fortune hoping to make fortunes in ivory as a sideline. They were brave but semi-literate, boring and greedy, and he made a mental note to get rid of them as soon as possible.

To Gordon's great delight, a familiar figure came into view as the boat berthed at Suakim on the Red Sea where he was to disembark. It was Romolo Gessi, dressed in the uniform of a major in the Khedive's army. He had left the mill and the interminable quarrels with the tax collectors at Tulcea to his wife Maria, and had set off in November 1873 as soon as he had received news of the confirmation of his friend's appointment. Not wanting to be entirely dependent, at the age of forty-two, on a foreigner, even if a close friend, he had obtained a letter of introduction from Garibaldi to the Egyptian government and had been commissioned on the spot. Garibaldi was embarrassed at having been unable to procure Gessi a commission in the new Italian Regular Army, especially since a close friend of both Gordon and Gessi, Oreste Baratier, later Governor of Eritrea, had got a commission in the Bersaglieri.

Major Gessi reported that his task was to patrol the Red Sea between Suakim and Massawa, checking the movement of slaves and ivory. It was not a bad life. He had friends in Eritrea and Somalia who were colonizing 'in an amateurish way, not like you English', and these friends were always up and down the Red Sea. Since the opening of the Suez Canal, Italian officers going home on leave always stopped off at Suakim for dinner and other delights and brought delicacies from home on their return. Gessi did not mention that he provided them with local girls, nor that he had started an affaire of his own with an Italian widow, Marianna. However, he was now a 'veteran' of three months and maybe his experience could be useful to the Colonel. If the Colonel needed him in the Sudan, they had worked together before. . . . It was only a matter of a quick exchange of signals with Cairo to have Romolo Gessi transferred to service in Equatoria.

One of the things which immediately intrigued Gordon about his old friend was the way he mounted a camel and rode it as to the manner born. Gessi told him that it was exactly like riding a horse, 'except that you had to beat the camel over the head to stop it twisting round to bite you'. A day after disembarkation at Suakim, Gordon mounted a camel for the first time and rode it all the way to Berber, the town just after the Fifth Cataract. At Berber he took a steam-powered barge which reminded him of the *Hyson*, and with his staff and baggage made his way to the Sixth Cataract and Khartoum. As he rode into Khartoum on 13 March on his camel, Gessi at his side, he was met by the Governor-General, a brass band and a battalion-strength guard of honour. There was also an uncertain salvo from the local artillery. An American on the Egyptian General Staff, General R.E. Colston, known as Colston Bey, recorded his own first impressions of the city built by Mehemet Ali:

> The European colony is small and continually changing; for Khartoum is a perfect graveyard for Europeans, and in the rainy season for natives also, the mortality then averaging from thirty to forty a day, which means three thousand to four thousand for the season . . . [but] Khartoum is the commercial center of the Soudan trade, amounting altogether to sixty-five million dollars a year and carried on by one thousand European and three thousand Egyptian commerical houses. . . . I learned that the city contained three thousand and sixty houses . . . the houses belonging to rich merchants being very spacious and comfortable. There are large bazaars, in which a much greater variety of European and Asiatic goods are found than would be expected in such distant regions . . . and a brisk trade is carried on in cattle, horses, camels, asses and sheep, as well as grain, fruit and other agricultural produce. . . .

The next seven days were given over to feasting and briefing. Ismail Ayub Pasha seemed very vague both about his subordinate Governor's duties and about the situation in Equatoria. Gessi, who had been there twice, explained that in order to understand what was going on and why, it was essential to think of Equatoria as part of Central Africa and not as an appendage of Egypt. Cairo was far

enough from Constantinople for Egypt to be a genuinely auton-
omous province of the Ottoman Empire. Gondokoro, the capital
and northernmost of the fortified towns in Equatoria, was as far
from Khartoum as Khartoum was from Cairo, and that was further
than from Cairo to Constantinople. When the Khedive had said
that Gordon must 'do as you think best' he had expressed an honest
opinion. The 300 soldiers at Gondokoro would be the only
Egyptians Gordon would see. He would have Ethiopians as neighbours to the east, negroes to the south and west (in what are now
Chad, the Central African Republic, Uganda and Zaire). There
were all sorts of Europeans on more or less official missions
everywhere – French, German, Belgian, British and Italian, even
some Portuguese – checking each other's claims to vast territories
and reinforcing missionaries of one denomination or another. The
most stable community was one to the south, the Kingdom of
Buganda, discovered by J.H. Speke in 1862 and ruled by the
Kabaka of the Baganda. Speke had reported to the Anti-Slavery
Society that the Kabaka strongly disapproved of slavery, and was
worried by the increasing numbers of Arab slave traders penetrating the kingdom and bribing his feudal aristocracy, which held its
land from the Kabaka in return for raising troops for defence and
levying taxes on legitimate trade. Other British explorers and
missionaries had reported that the situation had not improved, and
the Kabaka would certainly be glad to know that Gordon was in
Equatoria. As far as the French and Italians were concerned, they
were interested in the Horn of Africa. There were rumours that
King Leopold II of the Belgians had his eye (though as a private
individual) on the Congo, claimed by the Portuguese, and that
there were Germans everywhere south of Buganda. Finally, several
important slave routes passed through Equatoria, two of them with
outlets at Suakim and Massawa.

Had Gordon been another sort of man, he might have enjoyed
the feasting which accompanied the briefing. The Governor-
General had put himself out to impress the newcomer with his
hospitality. There seemed to be an infinity of things to eat and
drink, and whereas on the first two evenings the entertainment
consisted of music and readings from the Koran, by the end of the
third the tone had degenerated from the classical to the lewd. A sort
of ballet in which soldiers re-enacted the liberation of naked female
slaves sent most of the guests into erotic hysteria. The Austrian
Slatin Pasha joined the dancers after his second bottle of Islamically
illegal wine, and the Governor-General seemed to be about to
follow him. At this point Gordon got up and left in horror, locking

himself into his quarters until the following day. Ruffled feathers were smoothed by Gessi, who suggested they give a 'respectable feast' of their own, to show their apppreciation of their well-meaning host's intentions. Gordon thought this was a good idea, so he took several Sudanese servants and went into the local markets where he bought scores of cheap plates and drinking vessels. Nobody had told him that Sir Samuel Baker had left behind for him chests full of china and glass, table linen, sheets and several cases of French and Italian wines. There was a moment of tension when Gordon, who had acquired a taste for roast pork in China, suggested that as many of the guests would be non-Muslims it might make one acceptable dish. When this suggestion was gently rejected by his aides, he took his revenge by preparing a 'typical English sweetmeat' instead of the sticky sweets beloved of his chief guest. 'Tapioca pudding is as good a thing to serve for dinner as anything', he said, and made forty of them with his own hands.

On the eighth day news came that the *sudd*, the mass of floating vegetation which periodically blocked the way to the Upper Nile, had broken and the river was now clear for a thousand miles and more to Gondokoro. Ismail Ayub Pasha and Gordon parted with a great show of courtesies, though without regret. The Governor-General assured the new Governor of his constant support, insisted that he take with him the china, glass and linen, and said he hoped to see him later in the year.

The Equatoria party steamed slowly down the White Nile where Gordon was intrigued by the wildlife – storks, monkeys and hippopotami. On 26 March as he passed the island of Abba (on which the future Mahdi was living) he wrote to Augusta:

Last night, we were going along slowly in the moonlight and I was thinking of you all, and of the expeditions and Nubar and Co., when all of a sudden from a large bush came peals of laughter. I felt put out, but it turned out to be birds, who laughed at us from bushes for some time in a very rude way. They are a species of stork, and seemed in capital spirits, and highly amused at anybody thinking of going to Gondokoro with the hope of doing anything.

In fact, when he arrived in Gondokoro on 16 April he found things even worse than he had feared. It was not just the climate: ('No one can conceive of the misery of these lands, heat and mosquitoes day and night all the year round'). During the interregnum since Sir Samuel Baker's departure, military discipline had been lost in the fumes of the whisky, gin and rum which the

Egyptian soldiers had taken in bribes from Arab slave traders. None of the garrisons had been paid for months and there was a brisk market in negro girls and cattle sold to defray expenses. After making sure that his staff and baggage were proceeding slowly up the Nile from Berber, Gordon left Gessi in charge in Gondokoro to try to restore some sort of order, and went back to Khartoum to protest that, however self-sufficient he might become, he could not start his rule with an empty treasury, mutinous garrisons at Gondokoro and Fatiko and no supplies. He was very sharp with Ismail Ayub Pasha: 'I think I have crushed him, told him he told *stories*. It was undiplomatic of me but it did the Governor-General good,' he wrote, and left with several chests full of Maria Theresa silver dollars (thalers), acceptable as currency anywhere.

Back in Gondokoro in May, he held a council of war with Gessi and Linant. There was no disagreement. His Egyptian soldiers and officials were useless. Some of the Arabs were of better quality, but suspected of being in league with the slave traders. The best troops, though few in number, were the local Sudanese levies who since childhood had been 'raised on looting and cattle lifting'. It was decided to 'make a clean sweep without letting them feel the bristles of the broom'. On the northern border of Equatoria a new fort would be built; Fort Sobat would be garrisoned by Egyptians who, in theory, would feel closer to home and so enjoy higher morale. They could also be disciplined, if necessary, from Kordofan. Gessi would go to Bahr-el-Ghazal to reconnoitre and take whatever steps he thought fit. When possible Gondokoro, 'stinking with sin', would be abandoned for Lado. Other forts would be built in a chain south to the border with Buganda, and the Sudanese troops who would be recruited to man them would be well paid and well trained. Freed slaves would be offered short-term service in the garrisons and would supply valuable local intelligence.

Having separated the Egyptian goats from the Arab and Sudanese sheep, fixed new rates of pay and conditions of service, and delivered homilies to all and sundry, Gordon decided that it was high time the spiritual life of his territory was renewed. He let it be known that he was a believer, and that he expected all his soldiers and subjects to be believers, too. He did not specify what or whom should be the object of belief, but for a start ordered all his troops to build at their posts mosques, churches or temples according to their traditions. All religious festivals would be observed – Muslim, Christian and others. There would be public celebrations at Christmas, Easter and during the month of Ramadan, starting at Christmas 1874.

This attention to the spiritual life of the region was politically inspired as well as in keeping with Gordon's own beliefs. Throughout the Muslim Middle East and Africa there was talk of the coming of a Prophet. He would come from the east. He would have flashing eyes and a devout manner. He would be of the family of the Prophet Mohammed. Some Christians and pagans had caught the fervour, too, and were waiting for a New Coming, maybe a return to earth of St Peter via Jerusalem; this was to be unfortunate for the young Anglican Bishop of Buganda, Hannington, who was suspected of being a rival claimant and therefore murdered by King Mwanga when he approached his new diocese from the east, over the Kenya Highlands. In the Sudan, the word passed round that maybe Gordon himself was the new Prophet. He was *engleza* and so Christian and Protestant, never without his Holy Book, but he ordered the building of mosques and kept the holy days that the Koran prescribed. He certainly had flashing eyes and a devout manner. He could certainly unite all men who were not sinners. And he had come from 'far away'. What more proof was needed? One day he would reveal himself.

If the devout thought he might be holy, the Egyptian garrison of the new Fort Sobat hoped he would remain a distant devil in Lado or Gondokoro. Having built the fort, they had settled down under the able commercial direction of their commander to organize the slave trade in their own interests, in addition to levying legitimate taxes on the trade in ivory. They had the bright idea of sending down the Nile a boatload of Somali girls, much appreciated for their golden skin, as a present for the Khedive's Court. It was unfortunate that most of the girls were syphilitic. Gordon received complaints from Cairo and from a slave trader called Abu Said, who resented the competition from the authorities; grateful for all early and accurate information, Gordon took Abu Said on his staff (he had met him in Cairo) until the Governor-General forced him to dismiss the man because he was also an ivory poacher. Setting aside the new training programme for his Sudanese levies, Gordon set off with seventy men on camels – the badge of the Royal Engineers was embroidered on each saddle cloth – and soon arrived at Fort Sobat to hold a court of inquiry. He quickly built a military prison on the banks of the River Sobat and gaoled all the junior officers. The commander and two other senior officers were sent down the Nile, accused of theft from the Khedive; mutiny would have been treated lightly but theft was serious. He demoted and promoted several NCOs, replacing the officers with his own men, and returned to Lado having made a deep impression on all concerned.

He also made an impression on a Captain Burnaby of the Royal Horse Guards, an amateur explorer making his way up the Nile. The captain records:

> The number of things he had to settle and arrange would have been enough to turn the head of any ordinary mortal, but the Colonel went steadily ahead, giving out one order after another, administering justice to the natives, censuring or praising the officials, ordering punishment here and reward there, all this through an Egyptian interpreter, who gravely rendered every word of Gordon's French into Arabic.

Gordon enjoyed it all once he had got used to the heat and the mosquitoes. He wrote to Augusta: 'I prefer it infinitely to going out to dinner in England, the people here have not a strip to cover them but you do not see them grunting and groaning all day long as you see scores and scores in England, with their wretched dinner parties and attempts at gaiety where all is hollow and miserable.'

Having settled matters in the north of his dominion, he decided it was time to show himself in the south. He proposed to build a number of new forts as he went along, make himself personally known to and feared by his officials, and recruit for his army. He also wanted to make himself visible to the French. As long ago as 1854, Napoleon III had sanctioned a large-scale expedition against the Toucouleur and Bambara tribes, devout Muslims waging a holy war against the French in west Central Africa. With the support of Christian Wolof tribesmen, General Louis Faidherbe had slowly pushed back the frontiers of Islam and consolidated French influence in vast areas as far as Lake Chad. The French military were building forts while Catholic missionaries were putting up churches or converting mosques in the grasslands on the southern borders of the Sahara, too close to the Sudan for the Governor's liking. He would call Gessi's attention to this. And then there was the promise he had made to Sir Samuel Baker and the Royal Geographical Society to map the largely unexplored Albert Nyanza and its water sources.

Gordon set off with a large baggage train including three steam-powered barges which could be taken to pieces and portaged round the Seventh Cataract. There were several smaller craft carrying stores and a camel corps escort on shore as the little flotilla left. Once up the Nile at Rageef (Rejaf) rapids, he decided to build his first new fort. It was the end of September and 'the rain is something tremendous; it comes down in such sheets and with such force – a good slope will scarcely carry off the water'. Notwithstanding this extra difficulty, the fort was built, and though he had no European staff who were not on the sick list he wrote on 23 September 1874:

> I am quite well, and things go on smoothly and I have a conviction that, God willing, I shall do much in this country. The main point is to be just and straightforward, to fear no one and no one's saying, to avoid all tergiversation or twisting, even if you lose by it, and to be *hard to all* of those who do not obey you. All this is not easy to do, but it must be my aim to accomplish it.

The flotilla set off again and, as they progressed, forts were built at Bedden, Kerri, Dufile, Moogie, Patiko and Foweira. He stayed long enough to see work started on them all – he was architect and engineer – leaving behind detailed plans, including always an area for religious devotions very much in the twentieth-century ecumenical style.

It was not an easy journey, nor did it pass unobserved by the Arab slave traders. The party was attacked several times and at Moogie Gordon lost forty men and Linant, a good officer who had insisted on staying with the expedition even though he was sick. After Moogie, Gordon formed a personal bodyguard as he had done in China, this time of Niam tribesmen. He caught some Arabs and Sudanese stealing stores and selling them to itinerant tribesmen: 'They are cowardly, lying, effeminate brutes, these Arabs and Sudanese, without any good point about them.' Several times he sent his resignation down the Nile with unflattering references to this 'twopenny halfpenny nation, for whom it is not worth while to stay a day in these countries'. A day later another letter would follow, withdrawing the resignation, and everybody would heave a sigh of relief.

After dealing with all these unanticipated problems, the impassability of the Seventh Cataract, which he had known about in advance, proved too much and Gordon fell into a deep depression. However, on the third day he heard a cheerful and familiar voice outside his tent. Gessi had arrived, 'just in case I am needed'. Gessi not only had a cheerful disposition but was a brilliant organizer, and he managed to take everything to pieces which could be taken to pieces – boats, machinery and artillery – and shift it all overland to be reassembled beyond the Cataract, an operation which took two months.

To Augusta, Gordon admitted that alone he could not have coped:

> I am really quite exhausted – more mentally than physically. It has been a fearful day; one *nugger* [flat-bottomed boat] nearly sank. It is the violent eddies that are so terrible. The slightest faltering in the haulers would be fatal. Your brother prays the *nuggers* up as he used to do the troops when they wavered in the breaches in China, but often and often the ropes break and it all has to be done over again. However, I feel sure that we shall have fully made known to us the mystery of these matters.

Gessi made light of the work, intriguing Gordon with the story of how great slabs of marble had been moved from Lake Maggiore to Milan along a canal, the Naviglio Grande, on which his ancestors had worked – one of these ancestors was supposed to have designed the Via Arena Lock, the model for all those built since the fifteenth century. Gessi's father had wanted to be an engineer, but the Industrial Revolution was slow to come to Italy and he had ended up in business and then in the British Consular Service, as Gordon knew. Romolo wanted to do something his father, Marco, had been unable to do – perform some great engineering feat. He had never believed in the political possibility of the Danube–Black Sea canal, but here things were different. Gordon was Governor – could become Governor-General, if he wanted to, of all the Sudan. Maybe they could raise money, as De Lesseps had done, for new waterways in Central Africa? The money was about. There was the British plan to purchase the 177,642 shares in the Suez Canal owned by the Khedive. Gessi thought this British plan to gain control of the new access to the Indian Ocean an instance of typical English shrewdness; ten thousand Egyptians and a thousand European skilled workers, mostly Italians, had dug the Canal under French direction to an Italian plan – now the British would take it over without ever having lifted a shovel. Gordon, who had a low opinion of all governments, including his own, assured him that the coup had almost certainly been arranged by British businessmen and bankers (Baring, Lange Bros & Co.), who had just been lucky enough to get the approval of a commercially minded Prime Minister, Disraeli. He doubted whether there would be finance forthcoming for a firm, Gordon & Gessi.

However, it was good to have Gessi around and not all his ideas were utopian. Where they differed was in the enjoyment of renown. Gessi was unashamedly ambitious for fame and fortune. Gordon thought, or said he thought, only in terms of duty. Among the famous men whom he regarded with suspicion were all explorers. He had objected to the Royal Geographical Society lionizing those who had only done their duty. He objected to David Livingstone, whose travel books had become bestsellers. He objected even more to H.M. Stanley, the Welsh-born emigrant to America who, since Livingstone's recent death in 1873, seemed to be cashing in on exploration in Africa. Stanley was at that moment, as Gordon knew, not very far away in African terms, mapping and reporting to the Church Missionary Society and others on the advantages to be gained by saturating Buganda with emissaries of one sort or another. The Governor suspected that these emissaries would not be solely concerned with the spiritual welfare of the Baganda, any more than he, Gordon, was solely concerned with the spiritual welfare of the Sudanese: '. . . some philanthropic people write to me about "noble work", "poor blacks" etc. I have, I think, stopped their writing by acknowledging ourselves to be a pillaging horde of brigands and proposing to them that they leave their comfortable homes and come out to their "poor blacks" or to give up their wine and devote the proceeds to sending out *real* missions.' He had half a mind to cross the frontier and go down and beard Stanley in his Bugandan den. In the end, he sent his last British aide, Long, to visit the King of the Baganda on Lake Victoria and see if there were a practicable waterway from the Nile to Buganda; Long did find a waterway, but not a warm welcome – only a broken music box which the Kabaka begged the Governor of Equatoria to repair, having heard that he was an engineer.

There was, however, a promise to be kept to Sir Samuel Baker, and so the party pushed on to the shores of Albert Nyanza, sending a loyal message to Queen Victoria, Albert's widow, when they arrived. Gordon saw to the assembly of the steamer which was to explore the lake, then put the project into Gessi's hands and wished him fame and fortune. As he turned his back on the lake, he wrote:

I wish to give a practical proof of what I think regarding the inordinate praise which is given to an explorer. Now surely Higginbotham did much in getting up the stores; and through the desert what work he must have had! Again, what work – not equal to his – have I not had with these stores. But all this would go for nothing in comparison to the fact of going on the lake. . . . Others sow, and one will reap the results of the labour. Gessi showed me a letter written to him which speaks of the honour and glory of going on the lake – the chaplet of laurels to the great conqueror, etc. It is thus, therefore, that I wish to show palpably that it is a great mistake to draw the false conclusions people do about these things.

On his way back to Lado, inspecting his new forts, he dispensed justice like a Roman consul, with an interlude to celebrate a memorial service to Linant at Moogie. He promoted, demoted, dismissed and appointed as he thought fit. Officials he got rid of and sent down the Nile at the slightest whiff of corruption: 'I make no hesitation about it. *Lettres de cachet* are signed and people are whisked into exile at once with no trial, for trials are a mockery when a man is rich.' He did not endear himself to his officials, but slowly he gave a sense of purpose to his administration. Everyone was treated in the same rough and summary manner, but it was the first justice that had ever been experienced by the population at large. His troops became proud of themselves and of their achievements in keeping order in such a vast territory. He made sure that taxes were paid – no more and no less than had been laid down – and sent large sums of money to an astonished Khedive in Cairo. If he did not send them via the Governor-General in Khartoum it was because he suspected that that worthy would hold back a proportion for his own use, and they had agreed that each should keep his own finances separate, territory by territory. He worked a fourteen-hour day, to the astonishment of Long in particular, and ended it as he had begun it, with readings from the Bible to the picket on guard duty.

Sometimes even Gordon had lapses. Lytton Strachey caused something of a furore with his report that

In his fits of melancholy, he would shut himself up in his tent for days at a time, with a hatchet and a flag placed at the door to indicate that he was not to be disturbed for any reason whatsoever; until at last the cloud would lift, the signals would be removed and the Governor would reappear, brisk and cheerful. During one of these retirements, there was a grave danger of a native attack upon the camp. Colonel Long ventured, after some hesitation, to ignore the flag and the hatchet, and to enter the forbidden tent. He found Gordon seated at a table, on which there were an open Bible and an open bottle of brandy. Long explained the circumstances, but could obtain no answer beyond the abrupt words – "You are the commander of the camp", and was obliged to retire, nonplussed, to deal with the situation as best he could. On the following morning, Gordon, cleanly shaven, and in the full dress uniform of the Royal Engineers, entered Long's hut with his usual tripping step, exclaiming – 'Old fellow, now don't be angry with me. I was very low last night. Let's have a good breakfast – a little b[randy] and s[oda]. Do you feel up to it?'

The anecdote may or may not be based on fact. When Gessi came back, having circumnavigated the lake, he found the Governor in good form and in his memoirs never recorded any excessive consumption of brandy or anything else by his friend and chief.

From April to October 1876 Gordon, Gessi and Long mapped the rest of Equatoria and built some forts, not too visible along the frontier with Ethiopia. As Gordon wrote: 'It is . . . a dead mournful spot, with a heavy damp dew penetrating everywhere. It is as if the Angel Azrael had spread his wings over this land. . . . You have little idea of the silence and solitude. I am sure no one whom God did not support could bear up. It is simply killing. Thank God, I am in good health and rarely low, and then only for a short time.'

Reports of his work, of his unbelievably successful administration and his beautiful maps, had reached the capitals of Europe; especially enthusiastic were the learned societies. The British government showed little or no interest, but the French government was respectful and King Leopold of the Belgians declared that he would give anything to have such a man in his service in Africa. The Khedive could not believe his good luck, and when, at the beginning of December 1876, Gordon arrived with Gessi in Cairo and announced his resignation, there was a Court crisis. Hurriedly, ministerial meetings were called and Gordon was made a Turkish field-marshal, decorated with everything to hand and pleaded with to stay. He had written in his diary:

> When a house gives ominous cracks prior to a fall, one's desire is, like the rats in ships, to leave it, but this proverb is generally used in the sense of 'Having sucked the orange throw away the rind', and I do not like the idea even if the cracks are serious. Why should I fear? Is man more strong than God? Things have come to such a pass in these Mussulman countries that a crisis must soon come about.

Patiently, he tried to explain to the Khedive that he had done all he could, in the terms of his brief. In Equatoria, if the slave trade had not been completely stamped out, it had at least been lessened as a tragic burden the blacks had to carry. ('The slave trade must go on,' he once wrote. 'It is the type of the bringing into subjection of the heathen in us.') A government now existed. Officials and officers had been trained. Forts had been built together with some rudimentary roads. Unfortunately, the rest of the Sudan had not been similarly improved. The Khedive had to make up his mind.

Either the whole of the Sudan, and, ideally, the whole of Egypt, too, had to be reformed, or 'the whole will go under'. To his sister Augusta, Gordon confided in depressed tones, 'I do not feel that I could ever do any more work after this command. It certainly takes the edge off one and adds to one's age.'

The Khedive tried to get round him through Gessi, but bungled the approach. Hearing that Gessi had given up his British nationality in 1860 to please Garibaldi and had become Italian, the Khedive assumed that a third-class Order of Medjedie would be enough as a reward, if accompanied by a small present in cash. Gessi was offended and complained to Gordon, only to observe his friend's shock on hearing that Gessi had 'done this thing, sixteen years ago without telling me'. Gordon brusquely told him that it was a pity he was no longer British, and that nobody who changed his flag as he changed his shirt could expect better treatment. At this Gessi took the next boat back to Italy and swore never to see Egypt, the Sudan or Gordon again.

In compromise, Gordon, who regretted his sharp words to Gessi as soon as he had gone, promised the Khedive that, though he had decided to go to England for Christmas, he would think over matters and 'come back if God guides me to this path'. The Khedive, too, was to think over what Gordon had said and done.

On Christmas Eve Gordon reached London and hurried to Southampton to see his sister (his mother had died in 1873), where he became the reluctant centre of attention again, as he had been on his triumphal return from China. He continued to make sharp remarks about missionaries, but he received civilly some merchants who were interested in his plan to link the three lakes, Albert, Victoria and Tanganyika, and connect them by road, rail or canal to the East African coast; he had, in fact, advised the Khedive to annexe the coastal strip as far as Mombasa. There was also great interest in Zanzibar and some schemes for linking the Congo with the Nile by canal.

There was news, too, from south-east Europe. The Turks had put down a revolt in Christian Orthodox Bulgaria. The Romanians gave overt and covert help to their Bulgarian neighbours, and Prince Milan Obrenovich of Serbia, who had a Romanian fiancée, Natalie Kescu (Keshko), felt he could do no less than declare war on the Turks. The ill-equipped Serbian Army was soon in trouble, and Tsar Alexander II went to the aid of his fellow-Slav Bulgarians and Serbs. Gordon, who disliked all politicians anyway, found Gladstone, in opposition, ridiculous with his suggestion that the

European Powers should 'drive the Turk out of Europe bag and baggage', if only because Turkish presence in Europe was disappearing by natural wastage, and his views were reported in the Press. Gladstone did not like the criticism; in years to come Gordon was to pay for this offence. *The Times*, however, thought Gordon was right and also suggested that, as he was already nominally a Turkish civil servant, he should be recommended to the Sublime Porte as temporary Governor of Bulgaria. Disraeli, anxious to deprive the Tsar of the fruits of victory against the Turks, at first thought it was a good idea, but nothing came of it, in spite of Gordon's warm response. The Khedive of Egypt was anxious to have his best civil servant back as Governor-General of the whole Sudan, and asked Disraeli to use his good offices. The Prime Minister, probably with an eye to increasing British influence in Egypt, which Britain was to take over in 1882, decided to support the Khedive. The Duke of Cambridge and the Prince of Wales (promoted field-marshal in 1875) admired Gordon and had befriended him in spite of his difficult relations with his own senior officers, so were able to persuade him to return to the Sudan. After all, the Duke of Cambridge, the Queen's cousin, was still Commander-in-Chief and Gordon was nominally a serving officer, so there could be no argument. Queen Victoria, who seems to have been an admirer of Gordon since his Chinese days, and liked eccentrics, may also have put in a good word.

Replenishing his medicine chest (Sloan's liniment, Dr Collis Browne's stomach bromide and Warburg's tincture), and with some new mapmaking paraphernalia, Gordon left for his new assignment on 31 January 1877. He had been frustrated in his attempt to meet Disraeli in person and interest him in his great lakes schemes, but he did not despair. There would be time. He had agreed to serve for only three years. He felt refreshed. He had managed to avoid dining out – 'Men think giving dinner is conferring a favour on you. Why not give dinners to those who need them?' He was even eager to return. The Duke had said he was needed. The poor Khedive had said he was needed. Who was he to argue? 'To each is allotted a distinct work, to each a destined goal; to some the seat at the right hand or left of the Saviour.'

SEVEN

King in Khartoum

'I declare if I could stop this [slave] traffic, I would willingly be shot this night. This shows my ardent desire, and yet, strive as I can, I can scarcely see any hope of arresting the evil.'

Gordon, El-Obeid, 31 March 1879

On his way through Cairo, Gordon was received very kindly by the Khedive, who said he was flattered to think that this respected subject of the Empress (Victoria had been proclaimed Empress of India the previous May) could serve him. He was about to conclude a new treaty with Great Britain and a Slave Trade Convention, and he was sure the new Governor-General would help him to observe its terms. The Khedive looked forward to years of efficient administration in the Sudan, and to seeing Gordon, as one of the senior members of his administration, in Cairo from time to time.

What the Khedive did not tell him was that things were not going well in two of the great topographical and political divisions of the Sudan. Gordon had restored law and order in one of the three, the Upper Nile and all that area around known generally as Equatoria, though he might find that even during his short absence, there had been a resurgence of trouble. He would surely find trouble to the east, along the frontier with Ethiopia. Part of the money that the Khedive had received from the sale of his Suez Canal shares had been used to equip an army with which to invade Ethiopia, and this campaign had dragged on, from disaster to disaster. Though the Egyptian Army was equipped with the latest Remington rifles, it was routed by Ethiopian cavalry armed with spears and swords, and hundreds of thousands of pounds in gold sovereigns were taken; the

Ethiopians had never seen a gold sovereign, so they were willing to exchange them for silver dollars, but the booty was still almost beyond their wildest dreams. Fortunately, the King of Ethiopia did not intend to leave the mountains in hot pursuit and anyway had in mind a campaign of his own against Menelik, the King of Shoa. In the third division of the Sudan, the Muslim kingdoms of Darfour and Kordofan, the slave trade which Gordon had dislodged from Equatoria was flourishing and the sheiks were celebrating the defeat of the Khedive a thousand miles away by ignoring his local administration.

The new Governor-General was made *au fait* with all this on his journey from Massawa, where he disembarked on 26 February 1877. He made his plans as he rode by camel from Massawa to Khartoum, where he arrived to a hysterical welcome on 1 May. He was very moved by this tumultuous reception, though his reply to the flowery addresses was laconic: 'With the help of God, I will hold the balance level.' He had a lot to do in his capital. He disbanded the local militia, which had terrorized citizens and shopkeepers alike, and announced that a new rigour would take the place of the soft living of his predecessor. Justice would be done and would be seen to be done. As in Gondokoro, he put at the door of his suite a locked box into which anonymous informers and petitioners could drop their messages; it was an idea he had taken from Gessi, always an admirer of the Venetian Council of Ten and their police work based on information in secret and in quantity. Bribery was officially abolished, though nobody had thought that giving baksheesh to officials to speed a cause was illegal. After a general survey of sewers and the water supply, orders were given to improve them. Public flogging was abolished, too, though Gordon reserved the right to hang murderers and mete out punishment to thieves according to Islamic law, which meant cutting off their hands; this further confirmed the suspicion held by his devotees that he really was the New Prophet. For fifteen days after his official inauguration on 5 May he worked to establish his authority, view his policy and plan its execution. As he wrote: 'With terrific exertion, in two or three years time I may, with God's administration, make a good province – with a good army, and a fair revenue and peace, and an increased trade, – also have suppressed slave-raids, and then I will come home and go to bed and never get up again till noon every day, and never walk more than a mile.'

Having sent a letter to the King of Ethiopia assuring him of his eternal friendship and neutrality in any war with the King of Shoa, Gordon decided to turn his attention first to Darfour and Kordofan. On 19 May he set off for Darfour, 400 miles away, 'on the wonderful camel that flies along faster than the *hygeen* [mythical steed] of the Prophet'. With him rode his camel corps and staff, bearing copies of the Slave Trade Convention in four languages. There was to be a census of slaves, according to sex and country or tribe of origin. Attempts would be made to contact relatives and friends who might help them to resettle at home, though it was seen that there might well be problems, such as wives who had remarried, and land that had been reparcelled. After seven years in Egypt proper, and twelve years in the Sudan, all slaves were to be freed and settled either at home or at the place of release, whichever was more practicable. Gordon had some doubts about the prospects of success: 'When you can get the ink out of the blotting paper which has soaked it up, then slavery will cease in these lands.' There were markets for slaves all over the Middle East, and as long as there was a demand, somebody would make himself responsible for the supply. But something had to be done. Somebody had to make a start.

Crossing the Darfour border on 7 June, he rode on to Fogia, the capital of the province. The local chieftain, the Mudjir, had set lookouts all the way along the border and at the intermediate wells. He was anxious to impress the new Governor-General with his wealth, strength and devotion, and needed advance notice to prepare a fitting reception. Unfortunately for the Mudjir, Gordon and his aide, a Bedouin sheik, were so far ahead of the rest of their party as Fogia came into sight that they were mistaken for scouts. Gordon, in his field-marshal's uniform, and his Bedouin rode past the guards at the gates before warning could be given. Wearing the Khedive's highest decoration, the Grand Cordon de Medjedie, Gordon seated the Mudjir in front of him and harangued him for an hour until the rest of the party arrived, then relaxed and enjoyed the banquet prepared at sunset. Notwithstanding the raggle-taggle appearance of the Governor-General's troops (the best soldiers in Egypt had been called up to fight for Turkey in the Russo-Turkish War in Bulgaria), his arrival was certainly dramatic and represented a good beginning in his attempt to repress the slave trade there.

The campaign was exhausting, simple in design and effective. The whole of Darfour is a desert, but well supplied with wells and oases of varying sizes. There is no other water, so it has always been obvious that any authority which controls the wells controls the entire region and all movement across it. From June until the beginning of October Gordon visited every well and garrisoned those some 40 to 50 miles apart which were large enough to attract slave caravan. Up and down the province, from Omchanga to Dara, to Shaka and El-Fasha, nobody could be quite sure where Gordon was. There is a well-known tale, which has become part of Arab folklore, concerning Suleiman-bin-Zobeir, the son of Zobeir Pasha who had gone off to fight the Russians. Suleiman had declared, rashly, that he would not submit to this mad English infidel, would disregard the new Slave Trade Convention and rule the south of Darfour, in his father's interests only, until he got back from the wars. This threat to Gordon's authority had to be put down, and so he got together a troop and rode to Dara, the principal town in south Darfour. He arrived, as usual, ahead of his troops – 'a single, dirty, redfaced man on a camel, ornamented with flies', as he described himself in a letter to Augusta – and went to his divan or official lodgings. Gordon records how he imposed his authority on Suleiman-bin-Zobeir:

> Dara, September 2d. – No dinner after my long ride, but a quiet night, forgetting my miseries. At dawn I got up, and putting on the golden armour the Khedive gave me, went out to see my troops, and then mounted my horse, and with an escort of my robbers of Bashi-Bazouks, rode out to the camp of the other robbers, three miles off. I was met by the son of Sebehr [Zobeir], a nice-looking lad of twenty-two years, and rode through the robber bands. There were about three thousand of them, – men and boys. I rode to a tent in the camp. The whole body of chiefs were dumbfounded at my coming among them. After a glass of water I went back, telling the son of Sebehr to come with his family to my divan: they all came.

Unable to convince his men that Gordon was not, after all, the New Prophet ('Who but a madman or a saint would ride into the enemy's camp alone?'), Suleiman had no option but to kiss the Governor-General's feet and promise to disband his army and live in peace. 'The Cub', noted Gordon, 'has been tamed. We will see what the lion does when he returns.' It took Suleiman over a year to reassert his authority over his tribesmen.

However, it was one thing to convince the local sheiks that he was determined to suppress or restrict the slave trade, but quite another to find ways of rehabilitating the slaves. The slave traders retaliated at first by just abandoning caravans of unfortunates in the desert, far from the garrisoned wells. Gordon wrote, 'There, of course, it is impossible to find food for them. I declare solemnly that I would give my life to save the sufferings of these people. . . You would have felt sick had you seen them. . . I am a fool, I daresay, but I cannot see the suffering of these people without tears in my eyes.'

Having demoralized Suleiman-bin-Zobeir, Gordon moved next to set up an administration of his own in Zobeir's stronghold, Shaka – 'Shaka is the Cave of Adullam; all murderers, robbers, etc. assembled there, and thence made raids upon the negro tribes for slaves.' By 16 September he had frightened the murderers and robbers to such an extent that they scattered to the four winds. He spilt little blood on that campaign and was glad of it. As he wrote: 'People have little idea how little glorious war is. It is organised murder, pillage and cruelty, and it is seldom that the weight falls on the fighting men; it is the women, children and old people. The Crimea was the exception.'

Not only did he spill little blood, but he earned for himself the respect of all the Darfourians, robbers, murderers and honest men alike. They knew he would never harm a woman or child or desecrate a mosque. His Christianity was a private conviction, not to be imposed on those with a different vision of God. In his letters and diary he was often angry with his fellow-countrymen at home when they urged him to 'convert the heathen' and prepare the way for the arrival of missionaries. He wrote: 'I do not believe in you all. . . . The Christianity of the mass is a vapid, tasteless thing, and of no use to anybody. The people of England care more for their dinners than they do for anything else, and you may depend on it, it is only an active few whom God pushes on to take an interest in the slave question. . . . 'It is very shocking! Will you take some more salmon?'

Gordon missed Romolo Gessi, though he had not forgotten or forgiven him for 'changing his flag'. Were all men as weak and venial? Could he not find another like himself: 'Find me the man, and I will take him as my help, who utterly despises money, name, glory, honour; one who looks to God as the source of good and the controller of evil; one who has a healthy body and energetic spirit, and who looks on death as a release from misery; and if you cannot find him then leave me alone. To carry myself is enough for me – I want no other baggage.' No such paragon was ever found for him, but Gessi was still alive – seeking money, name, honour and glory with his usual lack of success.

On his return to Ravenna at Christmas 1876, however, Gessi had been fêted by the local notables, and the Italian Geographical Society had awarded him its Gold Medal in January 1877 for his 'immense services to exploration in the Egyptian Sudan'. This was really the high point of his career as far as his 'own' country was

Daguerreotype of Charles George Gordon, aged eleven, with his uncle, William Augustus

Fullands School at Taunton in Somerset, a drawing from the school prospectus for 1878. Gordon was sent to Fullands at the age of nine, in 1842

FULLAND'S SCHOOL, TAUNTON, SOMERSETSHIRE.

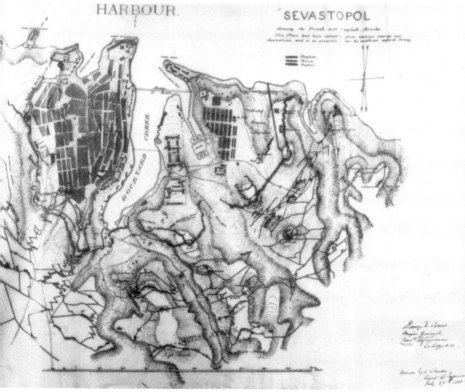

Above: a general view of the ruins of Sebastapol from the Redan, from a photograph taken after the siege in 1855

Below: a map of Sebastapol, showing the French and English attacks, drawn by Lieutenant Gordon in July 1855

A caricature of the Secretary for War as Mis(s) Management, showing up all too clearly the logistic chaos in the Crimea at the outbreak of war in 1854

Romolo Gessi, wearing his Crimea decorations

Charles George Gordon, aged thirty-two

Gordon depicted in the Yellow Cape, Peacock Feather, of the highest order of Mandarin. This portrait was painted in 1864 at the express wish of the Dowager Empress

Map of Shanghai and district, showing the area under the protection of the allied forces, 1862-3, signed by Gordon

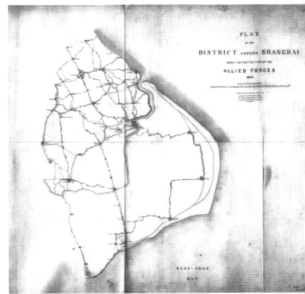

Three pages from Gordon's essay of 26 February 1882, in which he propounded his theory of the location of the Garden of Eden. His little sketch maps refer to his belief that before the Flood there was a great river that flowed from Turkey through Israel and the Gulf of Aden to its delta off the coast of the Seychelles. The third page refers to the *coco de mer* tree (*Lodoicea Seychellarum*), which Gordon identified as the tree of knowledge from the Bible

A photograph of General Gordon, taken in 1880

A photograph of Romolo Gessi, taken in 1877 in Trieste, on his return from the Sudan

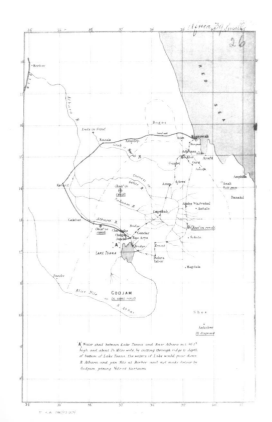

Sketch map of Gordon's journey in Ethiopia, 1880

Gordon's last enemy, the Mahdi

'Too Late': a *Punch* cartoon that still kept alive the hope that Gordon was safe, 5 February 1885

"TOO LATE!"

Telegram, Thursday Morning, Feb. 5.—"Khartoum taken by the MAHDI. General GORDON's fate uncertain."

Gordon's statue that formerly stood in Khartoum

The statue of General Gordon that originally was set up in Trafalgar Square. Now it stands on the Thames Embankment

concerned. When he heard that Gordon had returned to the Sudan as Governor-General, he said to a friend: 'He is like a little king in Khartoum, and I suppose I must forgive and forget and go to him again.' But Gordon had left Cairo for Massawa by the time Gessi got there, and had not answered his old friend's letters and cables – in fact he never received them. Very angry, Gessi went back to Ravenna, determined to organize an expedition of his own to explore the River Sobat and the area around it; the idea was that he would meet Gordon casually somewhere along the way and they would exchange courtesies as equals. He spent all his own money on stores and equipment, and by the beginning of April 1877 was back in Cairo to obtain the necessary permission before setting off. While he was waiting, the warehouse in which he had stored everything caught fire and it was all destroyed. Back he went to Ravenna, in an attempt to convince the city fathers and business-men that it would be worthwhile financing a new expedition, but the rumour had got around that Gessi was unlucky or incompetent or both, and the Comune of Ravenna would only put up a derisory sum which was wholly inadequate to fit out even a modest private enterprise. However, the Italian Geographical Society put him in touch with two other Italians, Cecchi and Chiarini, already in Kaffa and also intent on exploring the Sobat. With this sort of sponsorship some interest was shown by an Italian bank and the Ravenna Chamber of Commerce in 'prospects for trade in the region', and Gessi managed to obtain a further subsidy. He took along with him a friend, Pellegrino Matteucci, and a German photographer, Richard Buchter, but he quarrelled with Buchter before they set off and finally left him behind in Cairo. On 15 December the little expedition reached Khartoum.

Gessi immediately asked where the Governor-General was, only to be told that he had just missed him. He had been in his capital in November and was on his way via Wadi Halfa – to see what the prospects were for continuing the railway line to Dongola – to the frontier with Ethiopia, where he had heard that a hostile army had invaded the Sudan.

The news of the invasion had puzzled Gordon. After the failure of the Khedive's campaigns, his orders were to keep the peace with the King or Negus John (or Johannes as his Dutch adviser had renamed him). There were certainly Ethiopian marauders in the eastern Sudan, commanded by a ras (chief) named Walad-el-Michael, nominally subject to the Negus. Did the Negus know what Walad was doing, or was this banditry rather than invasion? Repeated messages sent to the Negus brought no reply, so Gordon repeated his Dara enterprise, rode alone into the enemy's camp and demanded to know what he was doing across the frontier. Walad-el-Michael was as astonished as Suleiman-bin-Zobeir had been and assumed that the Negus himself must have ordered his return to the Ethiopian capital, using Gordon as an emissary. So he did as he thought he had been bidden to do, and this mistake cost him his head.

On his way back to Khartoum Gordon collected the post and a wad of cables at Shendy on the Nile. One of the cables was from Gessi and this made his good, simple heart leap with joy. Another was from the Khedive: 'Come at once to my assistance. I know no one who can help me so faithfully in the difficult time that is impending.' Gordon rode hard to Khartoum and with difficulty kept his face severe at the reunion with his old friend. Gessi had discovered that, although he had indeed become an Italian citizen, he had not lost his British nationality; the infant Italian state had not worked out a system for renouncing nationalities, as so many 'Italians' were still Austro-Hungarian or Spanish or even held Papal passports. Gordon reproved him for being Machiavellian – 'But, Carlo,' retorted Gessi, 'Machiavelli was an Italian, too, anyway a Florentine' – and said that, with so many flags to which he could swear allegiance, it was perhaps unfair of Gordon to accuse him of 'changing'. It was a happy reunion and gave Gordon the courage to face a trip to Cairo, to see what it was that had so upset the Khedive.

He had mixed feelings about the Khedive. On the one hand, Gordon was his servant: 'I can only feel that I would not desert this government for anything that could be offered me, for it would be indeed cowardly . . . I will use my very life to aid him.' On the other hand the Khedive Ismail, a womanizer and worse, was the very antithesis of 'one who looks to God as the source of good and the controller of evil'. Loyalty to a pledge given won the day, as was to be expected, and a fortnight after receiving the Khedive's cable Gordon was in Cairo.

As the Field-Marshal looked through his letters in Cairo he discovered that the Royal Engineers had promoted him lieutenant-colonel on 1 October 1877, but he had little time to meditate on the bizarre structure of the Army List. He was summoned immediately to the presence of the Khedive, who explained his problem. Egypt had been effectively independent since the days of his illustrious predecessor, Mehemet Ali. Now, as a result of the Congress of

Berlin after the Russo-Turkish War, the last ties of the Ottoman Empire were to be cut as Britain, France and Germany mediated between the Tsar and the Turkish government. But virtual independence had been expensive and *de facto* independence would be even more expensive. It was hard to find honest, independent advisers. He had debts. He did not deny what he described as a certain personal extravagance. He looked at Gordon, who had not had time to change and was still covered with the dust and dirt of the long journey. But dinner was waiting, had been waiting for an hour. Would the Governor-General take the place of honour next to him at table? If so, he would hear much which they could discuss further the next morning.

Gordon did not enjoy that dinner at the Kasr-el-Nousa Palace, though between courses he managed to have a wash and brush-up in a fountain and by the end of the meal was the cynosure of all eyes. The Palace, he wrote, 'is full of lights, mirrors and gentlemen to wait on you', but he was not a man for lights and mirrors. The following morning he heard the real extent of the Khedive's 'problem'. He had no money and nothing to sell since he had disposed of the Suez Canal shares. British and French bankers and what he called 'Jewish moneylenders' no longer believed he could meet from revenue even the interest on his debts. Yet the Governor-General knew that Egypt and the Sudan could be made prosperous. Look at what he, the Governor-General, had done even in Equatoria. Would the Governor-General be President of an independent inquiry into the state of Egypt's finances? The international Debt Commissioners could not be trusted – they wanted the Khedive dissmissed.

For days Gordon shuttled between the Palaces of Abdeen and Kasr-el-Nousa trying to find out the truth. He was not allowed to find out. Sir William Butler sums it up very well:

Looking back on the intrigues that went on during the next few days among the rival foreign diplomats in Cairo, whose one object was to defeat Gordon's proposals and to drive him back to the Sudan, it is difficult to repress a feeling of animosity against the men on whose shoulders must most justly rest the responsibility of having . . . deliberately destroyed the sole chance which the presence of an incorruptibly honest and farseeing man at the head of a Committee on Egyptian Finance would at that time have given to Egypt. Nothing could have been simpler than the main conditions proposed by Gordon; they were these: First, examine what is the real income you derive from all sources of taxation. This inquiry will take some months to complete; meanwhile you must pay the unfortunate officials and employees, many of whom have been left absolutely without their salaries in order to meet the outrageous interest. . . . While you are doing this you must suspend payment of the coming coupon, and finally reduce the interest of the whole debt from seven to four per cent. . . . M. de Lesseps had consented to act as a member of the Committee. . . . If at this time of the year 1878 the world had been searched to find two men of the highest integrity, purest motive and most commanding genius, no better couple could have been discovered than these men, Lesseps and Gordon – the greatest civil and the most celebrated military engineers of their age. Their names were at once a guarantee that their work would have been above suspicion. But, in truth, honest men were not wanted either by the bond-holders of Egypt or by the rival powers who were hankering after her fleshpots. Ismail had summoned to his aid the one man who might have saved his throne and his country, and that man must be got rid of as soon as possible. He was got rid of.

In a way, Gordon was relieved when the Khedive, realizing that nothing could be done, gave him leave to return to Khartoum. 'Opposed on all sides, snubbed by English Government officials, rudely answered by English Ministers, turned into ridicule by the hirelings of the Press in Cairo, and plotted against at the Palace and the Consulates by Pachas, Commissioners, consuls and the whole tribe of Cairene intriguers,' it was good to be on his way back again to where his word was law. He inspected his garrisons at Zeila and Harrar, then wound his way slowly back to Khartoum. Gessi had left to get on with his expedition, which went wrong, and his partner Matteucci eventually gave up all hope of it ever going right and went home to Italy on 4 June 1878. Gessi himself returned to Khartoum and asked Gordon for a job.

Since his return from Cairo, Gordon had been overwhelmed by the backlog of paperwork which had accumulated during his campaigns in Darfour and his skirmish on the Ethiopian frontier. His office staff was largely incompetent, and the Sudan's expenditure during 1877 had been over a quarter of a million pounds in excess of income. He felt as desperate as the Khedive: 'I am at war with nearly everyone in Cairo, and my crest is a thistle. I could justify my rows, for they arise from dishonest officials, undue interfering of consuls etc. Since the long camel rides are at an end I have no nice thoughts.' Gessi's presence was a boon, and he was taken back on the staff.

There were worrying reports of a large-scale revolt in Bahr-el-Ghazal, led by Suleiman-bin-Zobeir, whose father had not been allowed to return from the wars but was for some reason under house arrest in Cairo. The young Suleiman had re-established himself in southern Darfour and the Bahr-el-Ghazal, the area where the headwaters of many rivers converge to form the White Nile. Very ambitious, he was anxious to avenge the discomfiture at Dara. Gordon himself did not feel well enough to lead a campaign against him: 'I was so unwell in my vast, lonely house, quite alone. I used to wander up and down it and think, think for hours. It is a very great comfort to me never to have the least fear of death when I am ill. I declare I never did more work than I did in my brain, uselessly. . . . Imaginary petitions were presented. I gave the answers; but over and over again they came up, till one was almost wild with them.'

There was only one thing to do – send Gessi to put down the revolt. Promoted for the occasion colonel in the Khedive's service, Gessi set aside vague plans for opening an import–export business, said farewell to his mistress Marianna and rode south. The situation was worse than Gordon and he had been told. Suleiman's father, Zobeir Rahama, had established himself in Bahr-el-Ghazal in the late sixties and had become something more than just a successful slave trader and ivory poacher. He was a just man and brave, and soon became a source of justice and ally at arms in both Darfour and Kordofan. Suleiman had inherited the prestige of his father without the human strengths, but the fact that his father was still alive gave him the allegiance of many of the Arabs in all three parts of the region. Again, he had no moral doubts about his father's commercial activities. He had been heard to say that in Central Africa captives in war are either killed and eaten or sold; for a slave there was always the chance of finding a good master in Damascus or Cairo, and this was surely better than ending life in a cooking pot. As for the ivory, his father had never stolen *all* the tusks crossing the lands over which he had ruled – he just levied taxes in kind, as the Khedive did in cash. As for the allegation that he and his father were rebels, they had not tried to interfere with the administration of the Sudan; they just had their own parallel administration, that was all, which they called the Kingdom of Manduga.

Gessi's first needs were for camels and a drastic increase in numbers of troops if he were at first to hold, then to defeat Suleiman-bin-Zobeir in battle. He sent back to Khartoum a request for more funds, but Gordon replied that he would be hard put to it to find £50. He did send 100 men, but suggested that Gessi find ways to feed them off the land and gave him a written authority to levy taxes of his own; he would ask the Khedive to make him a pasha, which would give him greater powers.

Romolo Gessi did more or less what he had seen Gordon do when he first arrived in Equatoria. He held court, punished, rewarded, and recruited slaves who would wait for pay until it was available. He was later accused of stealing ivory and organizing his own caravans destined for Italian communities in north-east Africa, but as they would have had to skirt the foothills of an Ethiopia in arms the accusation seems false and was held to be so. Whatever his methods, the local officials remembered that he had always been a close friend of the man who was now Governor-General, and that was enough for them. They feared Gordon more than they feared young Suleiman-bin-Zobeir.

In Khartoum, Gordon was worried by letters he received from London telling him that Stanley had now entered the service of King Leopold of the Belgians. They had formed a Committee for the Study of the Upper Congo, later renamed the International Congo Association, which the Royal Geographical Society told him was not a truly scientific society but a cover for commercial interests anxious to assume control of the whole of the Congo. The Upper Congo bordered on Equatoria, of whose mineral wealth Gordon had always been convinced. He did not like it. Stanley's Committee had sent out prospectuses calling for mapmaking and exploration in the interests of the natives. Gordon knew of only one man whom he believed had at heart the interests of the natives in Africa, and that was himself. What was the Queen's cousin doing mixed up with the adventurer Stanley? Obviously they planned to annexe the Sudan to the Congo and the whole of East Africa. He wrote to the Foreign Office outlining his fears, but had no reply. He returned to ordinary administration, levying taxes and tolls, promoting and demoting, appointing and dismissing, building roads and putting a new roof on his palace – part of the flat mud roof had fallen into his audience chamber. It was hard, not to say boring work: 'The dullness is insupportable . . . one lacks books; and I scarcely see any one except on business, for I have no associates here. I feel my own weakness, and look to Him who is Almighty, and I leave the issue without inordinate care to Him.'

General R.E. Colston from the General Staff of the Egyptian Army, sent to make a tactful inspection of Gordon's administration for the new regime in Cairo, reported:

He had received the most stringent orders to suppress the slave trade by the sternest exercise of military power . . . but the trade was so interwoven with the ideas and customs of the people that very little effect was produced beyond forcing it to seek concealment by going around the city instead of through it. The Austrian consul, Mr Rossett, a very intelligent gentleman told me that the slave bazaars were closed, it was true; but if anyone wanted one hundred boys or girls, they could be procured quietly, within two hours, at the rate of thirty-five to fifty dollars a head.

Gessi, to whom Gordon sent a hand-drawn Christmas card with a scriptural message, was having a hard time, notwithstanding the two and a half thousand men he now had under arms. He was not a religious man and was not comforted by the words: 'It is difficult for the flesh to accept "Ye are dead, ye have naught to do with the world". How difficult for anyone to be circumcised from the world, to be as indifferent to its pleasures, its sorrows and its comforts as a corpse is! That is to know the Resurrection.' The Nile floods were only just starting to recede, and there were hundreds of corpses floating about. Gessi did not want to think about pleasures, nor even about sorrows and comforts. He thought of Ravenna. However, he was a good soldier, so he trained and retrained his men, fed them and paid them whenever loot fell into his hands. He succeeded in halting the slave trade in his part of the Sudan and he was able to send back reassuring messages about Stanley and his ambitions. Far from seeking to harass Governor-General Gordon in the Sudan, it was the height of both Leopold's and Stanley's ambition to have him in the Congo as Governor-General, resident adviser, anything. The King was using his personal fortune to buy out all other interests, philanthropic or otherwise. He planned to grant concessions to companies which would exploit the country's immense natural resources, and 50 per cent of the shares he would keep for himself. The Belgian officials whom Gessi had met had told him that the King would give anything to have Gordon – and, of course, his friend – in his service. Meanwhile, Gessi wrote, the pacification of the south and south-west was going slowly and he would appreciate a visit when Gordon had time.

In March 1879 Gordon set out to join Gessi. On the twenty-seventh he was at the Kordofan–Darfour border and recorded: 'What a country, with districts as much as two hundred miles long and broad without water. . . . Here the wells are nearly dry. We expected to find water sufficient for the camels, some forty – there is not enough for two. The nearest wells are one and a half days off, and the camels are exhausted. I must go all night and try thus to avoid the heat.' He plodded on, feeling responsible for Gessi, who had been fighting alone for nearly nine months and who had left him cheerful notes at every well.

The news at Shaka was very good. Gessi wrote that he had broken the back of the revolt and was pressing on to capture Suleiman-bin-Zobeir if he could. He would pursue him into Darfour and hoped to rendezvous with Gordon in Dara in late May or June. Meanwhile, would the Governor-General do something about the 25,000 slaves he had freed and recruited for the army? They did not ask for pay, but had to be fed, clothed and armed. He had taken what he needed for the last stages of the campaign and there was not much left.

Gordon spent a month trying to reorder the finances of Shaka and its hinterland. There would be nothing to spare to send to Cairo this year – 'When the nakedness of my troops is partially covered I may talk to you. It is very fortunate that there are only black ladies here for the poor wretches are not clad.' He had doubts about his ability to achieve what he had set out to do without going mad: 'Could I sacrifice my life and remain in Kordofan and Darfour? To die quickly would be to me nothing, but the long crucifixion that a residence in these horrid countries entails appals me. Many will say that it is a worthy cause to die in.' But whenever he had a letter from a particularly stupid bureaucrat in Cairo he would have more doubts, doubts even about whether the region should remain part of Egyptian Sudan. Maybe they would be better off as part of the Congo, some of whose wealth might immediately spill over into Equatoria? Maybe they would be better off independent, or under the sway of Zobeir? He replied sharply to Cairo always, noting: 'I do not care what I say for I feel very confident that the way I could pay these people off best would be to throw up the post, for no-one could keep the incendiary materials of the Sudan quiet until he had been here some years. It is only by hard camel riding that *I* hold my position among the people.'

Having partially clothed some of the freed slaves and sent others home under escort, Gordon set off again to clean up those pockets of resistance which Gessi had told him still remained. The pockets were, however, very few and Gordon noted with pleasure the good condition of the roads and forts, the occasional gallows, the polite, even servile, tax collectors and the absence of ostentation. Gessi's plan had been a simple one. He had divided the territory into 'blocks', which he cleared one at a time; rebels and slave traders had been given exemplary punishments and, he heard, Suleiman

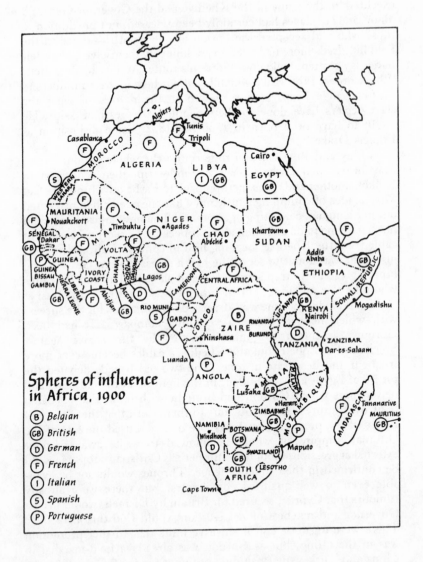

Spheres of influence
in Africa, 1900

- (B) *Belgian*
- (GB) *British*
- (D) *German*
- (F) *French*
- (I) *Italian*
- (S) *Spanish*
- (P) *Portuguese*

Algiers

Casablanca (F) — MOROCCO

Tunis (F)
Tripoli

ALGERIA   LIBYA   Cairo

(S) WESTERN SAHARA   (I) (GB)   EGYPT
                                              (GB)

(F)

MAURITANIA   (F)   NIGER   (F)
Nouakchott   Timbuktu •   Agades   Khartoum (GB)

(F)   M A L I   (F)   CHAD   SUDAN
SÉNÉGAL   VOLTA   Abéché •
Dakar

(GB)   (F)   Addis
(P) GUINEA   Ababa •   (GB)
GUINEA   ETHIOPIA
BISSAU   IVORY GHANA TOGO DAHOMEY   (GB)   (F)
GAMBIA   COAST   Lagos   (GB)   SOMALI REPUBLIC   (I)
(GB) SIERRA LEONE   Accra   CAMEROON CENTRAL AFRICA   Mogadishu
(F)   Abidjan (D)   (F)

RIO MUNI   (D)   UGANDA (GB)
(S)   CONGO   KENYA
GABON   (B)   Nairobi

(F)   ZAIRE   RWANDA
Kinshasa •   BURUNDI   (D)
Luanda •   TANZANIA   Zanzibar
(P)   Dar-es-Salaam
ANGOLA   Z A M B I A
                    Lusaka • (GB)
                    ZIMBABWE   (F)   Tananarive
          • Harare   MOZAMBIQUE   MADAGASCAR   MAURITIUS
NAMIBIA   BOTSWANA   (P)   (GB)
Windhoek •   (GB)   Maputo
(D)   SWAZILAND
          (GB)   LESOTHO
SOUTH
AFRICA
Cape Town •

himself had been told that if he did not give himself up, after disbanding his illegal army, he would eventually be taken and executed 'in the name of the Khedive and the Governor-General'. Thousands of slaves had certainly been released, but in addition to those who had accepted the option of one month's service in the field hundreds more had tried to get home by themselves, and their bones lay scattered all about Gordon's route. At Toashia he noted: 'I have ordered the skulls which lay about here in great numbers to be piled in a heap, as a memento to the natives of what the slave-dealers have done to their people.' Of Gessi he said: 'He ought to have been born in 1560 not 1832. Same disposition as Francis Drake.'

In May and June Gordon rode round the whole region. On 14 May he reached Fasha after a 230-mile trip, then rode west to Kolkol, another 200 miles, getting back to Fasha on 5 June. He had a vague idea of equipping a little navy like the one he had had fitted out in Shanghai, consisting of armoured Thames barges, but he did not have time to do anything about it because he received an urgent cable from the Khedive, begging him to come to Cairo. However, just as he was about to set off he had a message from Gessi asking him to go south to trap a small force of slave traders and Bedouins whom he was pursuing. On 25 June he was reunited with Gessi at Dara and paid him some well-deserved compliments for the success with which he had waged a year-long compaign. It had been Gordon's intention to join Gessi for the final drive against Suleiman-bin-Zobeir, but the Khedive's cables became ever more frequent and desperate in tone. The two old friends debated the future of Egypt and the Sudan, in the light of all the old news and newspapers which Gordon had brought with him. They debated their own futures. It was obvious to them both that the Treaty of Berlin of the previous year had more or less settled the fate of the Ottoman Empire; it would be allowed to waste away without external aggression, though the Emperor's Christian subjects would be confirmed in their independence. Thrones would not be available even to well-qualified commoners, but there were already rumours that Cyprus, secured for Britain by Disraeli, would need a Governor and maybe Colonel Gordon would find this attractive? There were unsubtle and insensitive hints that further promotion was in the offing, but as Gordon was already a field-marshal in China and Turkey 'that bait did not tempt the fish'. Gessi liked the idea of Cyprus, handy for Italy, and saw himself, his dual nationality forgotten, as Deputy Governor. But the dreams were dreams and there was not even going to be a last campaign together.

On 1 July, as the camels for the advance party were being prepared, a cable reached them to the effect that the Khedive Ismail had been deposed and one Tewfik put in his place. Leaving Gessi to carry on, Gordon saddled his camel and rode non-stop to Khartoum. By 21 July he was in his capital, and a month later he was in Cairo.

As was to be expected, his behaviour in Cairo was not that of an indifferent subordinate: 'It pains me what sufferings my poor Khedive Ismail has had to go through,' he wrote, as if Ismail had spent two years fighting slave traders from the back of a camel. But the new Khedive was calm and persuasive. He had taken no part in the dismissal of Ismail. He, too, was a prisoner of British and French bankers. He implored Gordon not to desert him now – had he not put a special train (refused) and a palace at the Governor-General's disposal so that he should be able to rest and decide in comfort? When the appeal of the fleshpots failed, Tewfik played the winning card of the ideal, of the triumph of justice. Gordon thought about it for a week, during which time news came of another threat of invasion from Ethiopia. At the end of the week Gordon had agreed to go to Ethiopia and negotiate a long-term peace with the Negus. When that was done, he would go back to England. He hoped that Tewfik would accept his advice and confirm his appointment of Gessi as Governor in Equatoria. The Khedive said neither yes nor no, but left Gessi with *de facto* powers and gave Gordon extravagant letters of accreditation to the King of Ethiopia.

At the end of September Gordon was on a mule at the foothills of the Kingdom. As he had suspected, negotiations by letter had proved fruitless, as the Negus seldom answered letters from anyone. Gordon was not dismayed and pressed on for five days from the foothills into the blue mountains where Ras Aloula, the frontier warlord, had taken the place of Walad-el-Michael. The meeting with Ras Aloula ended in something of an anti-climax, as neither could speak the language of the other and a sudden downpour drenched both Gordon in his field-marshal's uniform and the ras in his linen and feathers. With what was described as 'studied discourtesy', Gordon was passed on with an escort which took him through spectacular mountain scenery along tracks which were supposed to frighten and exhaust him. The tracks did neither. Gordon was intensely curious about Ethiopia and its ancient Christian civilization – after all, since AD 640 it had been the spiritual capital of Africa. In Cairo he had read an account by

Francisco Alvares, a Portuguese explorer, of strange churches carved out of the living rock, not at ground level but with their roofs just visible on the surface. These churches were at the former capital of Ethiopia, Lalibela, named after the king who had built them. It was in those very remote mountains through which he was being sent, and Gordon blessed Ras Aloula's malice.

The underground churches of Lalibela were every bit as splendid as Alvares had written, the icons fascinating and the engineering and architecture impressive. There was even a church dedicated to St George. The art and architecture showed what had been learnt and put into practice in long centuries of building and rebuilding, Greek, Romanesque and Byzantine, and the sheer ingenuity in solving the engineering problems existing or created by design. Gordon found it stimulating and stayed as long as he could, while his escort was bemused by his enthusiasm.

On 12 October he received a letter from Gessi telling him that the campaign was over, that he had captured Suleiman-bin-Zobeir, tried him and shot him with ten other recalcitrants. It had been a difficult campaign and Gessi deserved not only the praise that he might or might not get in Cairo but also an immediate message approving the execution, just in case the boy's father in Cairo should find friends who would take action, legal or otherwise, against the Italian; the message went off straightaway, as Gordon confirmed in his diary: 'Gessi only obeyed my orders in shooting him.'

Taking up the journey again, he was dragged up and down the banks of the tributaries of the River Tacazzae. It was a thousand feet up and a thousand feet down, and the object of the exercise was to show the Khedive's emissary that any invasion of Ethiopia would be as ill-fated as the last attempt. When he finally reached the capital, he was impressed by all that he had seen and anxious only to be friendly and complimentary to the Negus, who had, after all, referred to him as his 'brother' in their desultory exchange of compliments. He was to be disappointed. Before his reception, a courtier explained that the visit to Lalibela had been a mistake. King John was of the Solomonid dynasty, which had been overthrown by King Lalibela's Zagwe family, which had been in its turn overthrown by the Solomonids in 1270 (the Solomonids claimed descent from King Solomon and the Queen of Sheba). Was this Englishman trying to hint that another palace revolution was due? There was another complication, too. As Gordon recorded later: 'He is of the strictest sect of the Pharisees. He talks like the Old Testament; drunk overnight, he is up at dawn reading the Psalms.

If he were in England he would never miss a prayer meeting, and would have a Bible as big as a portmanteau.' Gordon was received at dawn, with a sermon and a demand that all the lands that Egypt had appropriated – Dongola, Berber, Nubia and Senaar – should be returned to Ethiopia. Then followed an acrimonious debate between the two Bible scholars which went on for several hours, quote against quote, Moses against Malachi. The debates were renewed several times over several days, always at dawn, and by 8 November the biblical tournament was over. It had been as exhilarating as the journey, but had led nowhere. Gordon took his leave and was given a letter to the Khedive, which he opened at the first halt and which read: 'To Mohammed Tewfik: I have received the letters you sent me by that man. I will not make a secret peace with you. If you want peace, ask the sultans of Europe.'

As on the way in, Gordon was taken by the most difficult highways and byways and reached the border on 14 November. As he rested there, looking down at the panorama of the Blue Nile winding its way through the Sudan, he was joined by a troop of the Negus's cavalry who forced him to take the road to Massawa and Cairo rather than the one to Kassala and Khartoum that he had had in mind. He was, in a way, under arrest, but he managed the journey with some dignity and succeeded in cabling ahead from Galabat to have an armed river gunboat and a troop of artillery on show at Massawa for when he arrived under escort. The escort was impressed. He shook hands with their commander and noted: 'Men of stern, simple habits, and utter freedom from bombast, or ordinary uncivilised tinsel and show. It is a race of warriors, hardy, and though utterly undisciplined, religious fanatics.'

He set off down the Nile to Cairo where, as Butler recounts,

His reception at the capital was worse than the mere negative coldness of official displeasure. It is only true to say that every man's hand was against him, the hardest blows coming from his own countrymen. His cipher telegrams to the Khedive he was soon to read in the London papers, with his proposals clipped and changed to suit the objects of the men who were now in power in Cairo. Quick as steam and electricity could carry the warped messages, they were sent to demonstrate to England that this great son of hers was not only inconsistent, disobedient and insubordinate but that he was also mad.

The Khedive was kindness itself and did not think any of these things, but he was a prisoner of the bankers who had put him in

Ismail's place. He waved his arms, turned his palms uppermost and said he could do nothing except give Gordon a medal. Between audiences, Gordon hunted Sir Evelyn Baring, the senior British government official and representative of the London banks, and Nubar Pasha, who had appointed him and now wanted to get rid of him. Baring hid in a bank vault and Nubar Pasha fled to Alexandria, hearing that the Governor-General was challenging all and sundry to duels.

Gordon asked for nothing for himself. He managed to have Gessi promoted general – he was off on a campaign again and had won a great victory at Dem Idris – and recommended that his friend be appointed Governor-General in his stead. This recommendation was ignored. As quickly as they could, the Court found a luxurious passage home for Gordon and on 10 January 1880 he took ship at Alexandria. Everybody in Egypt sighed with relief. They had had enough of this honest Englishman and his friends and hoped that they would never see him again. They were to be disappointed. In the Sudan, his greatest admirers wept. He had not revealed himself as the New Prophet, the Mahdi. Well, another man would. They were not to be disappointed.

EIGHT

Odd Job Man

*'The praise and blame of the world are equally indifferent
to me – you may write of me as if I were dead.'*
Gordon, 1880

As he sailed across the Mediterranean, Gordon confessed to a
fellow passenger that for the first time in his life he felt really tired.
Like many active men, he had always had a dream life in which he
'stayed in bed until eleven eating oysters', but it was nothing to be
taken seriously. Now, suddenly, he realized that he was nearing
fifty and no longer young. A doctor on board suggested that he
should go to Switzerland – Geneva, Lausanne, somewhere along
Lake Geneva; the weather would be fine in February and the nip in
the air a welcome change from the Sudan. There were good hotels
everywhere and, speaking French as well as he did, he could avoid
those patronized by his fellow-countrymen; there would be good
bookshops, too, where he could buy the English papers, and for a
man interested in religion there was much to see and hear in
Geneva.

Gordon took the advice and booked into a smallish hotel in
Lausanne. He was amused to read that the government was taking a
great interest in Africa – South Africa. Two regiments of cavalry,
fourteen battalions of infantry, four batteries of artillery and a host
of irregulars had been sent to crush the Zulu King Cetewayo, who
had had the temerity to defeat another British force at Isandhlwana.
The British heroes of this expedition were being fêted in London,
and the Press was full of it. 'I like Nelson's signal – England expects

duty; now the race is for honours, not honour, and for newspaper praise. . . . The praise and blame of the world are equally indifferent to me – you may write of me as if I were dead.' How far an element of pique had crept into these deprecatory comments it is difficult to say. It is certainly true that, as his brother Henry said, Charles Gordon was largely unknown to the general public (which had long forgotten 'Chinese' Gordon) and the new heroes were lesser men. As Sir William Butler wrote,

> The real African hero, the man who for six years had by his great genius maintained the authority of a weak State over a region as large as Europe and among races whose bravery and power in war we were soon to test to our cost; the man who, sweeping like a whirlwind across immense deserts, had seemingly multiplied his individuality into legions of soldiers; this man whom, it is possible, the future will look upon as the hero of our time and race, was now an unnoticed stranger. . . .

However, the sun did shine on Lake Geneva, the much needed rest was doing him good and he was getting on with his map of Creation. He visited Geneva and talked to divines there. He saw the statues of Calvin and John Knox and drafted a pamphlet on the origins of the Protestant Reformations. In March, somebody in England remembered that he was an African expert if not a popular hero, and he was offered the post of Commander-in-Chief at the Cape. It is not now clear why he refused the offer. Perhaps he was too busy with his Christian cartography. Maybe his dislike of Disraeli and the Conservative government he often accused of 'wanting an Empire on the cheap' prevented him from going to a part of Africa which offered a climate as equable as Switzerland and a view of the continent he had not seen before. Whatever the reason was, he turned it down, and lived to regret the refusal.

When a Liberal government took office in April 1880 he expressed even graver doubts about its commitment to the extension of civilization and justice, as he saw it. Gladstone had campaigned vigorously against British policies in Africa, India and Afghanistan, not to speak of the policing of eastern Europe. Gordon was now afraid of unemployment in an anti-imperial Britain, and in a moment of weakness, as he noted, he accepted the offer of a post as Private Secretary to the new Viceroy of India, Lord Ripon, bidden to reform the corrupt and inefficient administration of that country. He went back to London, ordered a suitable wardrobe and by the beginning of May was en route to Bombay. By the time he was through the Suez Canal and the Red Sea he regretted that decision, too. There was bad news from the Sudan, for one thing. Against his advice, Raoul (Raouf) Pasha had been made Governor-General and Romolo Gessi Governor of Equatoria; though Gessi had been promoted general, and was supposedly in command of all forces in action south of Khartoum, Gordon knew that the two men could never work together, and that sooner or later Raoul Pasha would have his friend on a boat back to Italy or even worse. Off Aden, Gordon wrote: 'I have been an idiot, and took this place with Lord Ripon, who is a kind and considerate master; but I hate India, and how I ever could have taken the post is past my comprehension. The endless sort of quarrels which seem to be going on there by all accounts is enough to sicken one. I shall get out of it as soon as I can.' Soon was to be very soon indeed.

When he reached Bombay, and sat down immediately to a series of briefings by outgoing officials, he realized the full extent of his 'idiocy' and wrote: 'My views were diametrically opposed to those of the official classes, and in the face of the vested interests in India I could not hope to do anything really to the purpose.' The outgoing Viceroy, Lord Lytton, had been given a very simple brief. There were to be no more Indian mutinies. Caesar's maxim, divide and rule, was also his. Muslims were separated from Hindus and Christians, Sikhs from Tamils, Bengalis from Maharastris, whites from Indians of all sorts. A native Indian Civil Service, in fact, existed as a cushion between the British and the mass of the people. Native policemen and tax collectors were given a free hand to enrich themselves and impoverish still further the population at large, with the result that a general officer could say 'There never could be another rebellion in India because the people are too weak from want of food to fight.' Lytton's policies were not concealed by a mask of hypocrisy. There was law and order and those who administered it had got rich, and would certainly do everything possible to keep their wealth intact. There were, no doubt, selfless magistrates and brave soldiers on the North-West Frontier, but Bombay reminded Gordon of nowhere more vividly than Cairo, with its institutionalized corruption and intrigue.

On his fourth day in Bombay he was asked to tell a deputation of Indians that Lord Ripon had read their petition with great interest. It was the right moment. Gordon said to Lord William Beresford: 'Lord Ripon has never read it, and I can't say that sort of thing, so I will resign, and you take in my resignation.' He said he could not tell lies in and about India any more than he could tell lies in or about the Sudan, and had told Lord Lyons, British Ambassador in Paris, as much recently. Sir William Butler, who knew Gordon well

133

at this time, said: 'Gordon's presence in Egypt had been a reproach to a wide class of foreign officials, who regarded that country as a good place for doing English work in and drawing Egyptian money out of it. . . . He would no more have joined the official view of India and its people than he could join with the foreign element in Cairo against the people of Egypt.'

During the latter part of May and into June the telegraph wires hummed as Gordon tried to resign, foreign governments tried to recruit him and the British government would neither give him useful employment nor let him go. The Chinese government, in particular, was very pressing. His former colleague in arms, Li Hung-Chang, was now the leader of a large party in Peking, but was contested by another party which was urging war with Tsarist Russia (on the mistaken assumption that Russia would not fight the Turks and their western European allies in the west and the Chinese in the east simultaneously). Li's telegram read: 'Work, position, conditions, can all be arranged to your satisfaction.'

Gordon decided to go to China, though he was indifferent to status and pay and said as much, but that was not good enough for the War Office and the Foreign Office; he could not have leave until he explained what he was going to China to do and in what capacity. He would not know until he got there, he replied, and he was asking for unpaid leave of absence, anyway, so what did it matter – 'Never mind pay and fear not that I will involve our Government in war.' This was too much for his superiors. If serving officers, even on secondment, behaved in this way the War Office, which was only just getting used to its new name, could not cope. Unpaid leave of absence was refused. Gordon then resigned, or retired (he left it to them to decide) and booked his passage to China. He was at the receiving end of some residual harassment by his Indian governmental colleagues, who made him reimburse his fare from England, and in the end he had to borrow money to pay for his passage, but he was so glad to go that he would have signed anything, never mind a promissory note. As he had heard malicious rumours that he was only leaving because the Chinese were offering him more money, he made a statement to the Press:

My object in going to China is to persuade the Chinese not to go to war with Russia. . . . Whether I succeed or not is not in my hands. I protest, however, at being regarded as one who wishes for war in any country, still less in China. Inclined as I am, with only a small degree of admiration for military exploits, I esteem it a far greater honour to promote peace than to gain any paltry honours in a wretched war.

The Press published his statement, but also raked up old stories about the Ever Victorious Army (had he really turned down the offer of all that money?) and the Sudan (could all those stories about him having enriched himself in the ivory trade be untrue?), which rather detracted from the general effect.

Gordon got to China in July 1880 and received a very cordial reception in Tientsin. Li Hung-Chang told him that no doubt he had not seen in Europe reports of all the aggression by Russia along the frontier, especially in Siberia. There was a good case for going to war. Indeed, he would be frank and say that he would make a profit out of any war because he was in partnership with French armaments manufacturers in Shanghai, Soochow and Nanking. However, he was not sure that the Chinese armies were strong enough or well enough equipped, and he was quite sure that they were not well enough led. Would his old friend, who was, after all, a mandarin, a member of the Imperial bodyguard and so entitled to give advice, be so kind as to state the case for peace to the present government of China? Charles Gordon would and did. After sounding out some British officials whom he knew (Robert Hart, a British government representative, told him that the Nanking arsenal 'was equipped exclusively with imported machinery, small in production and scope and unable to turn out any heavy weapons . . . was badly managed, riddled with corruption and has lost a lot of money'), he soon came to the conclusion that war would be a form of suicide. Within weeks a Tsarist army would be in Peking and would annexe the whole of Manchuria.

At a meeting of the Tsungli-Yamen (in effect, the Imperial Cabinet) Gordon made a brisk review of the situation as he saw it. He had fought the Russians in the Crimea, and though they had formally lost the war they had lost it with honour. They had tried again in 1877–8 and had been frustrated again, not so much by force of arms as by diplomacy. However, diplomacy was an unreliable ally and Britain and France might abandon the Ottoman Empire to its fate, helping themselves to what remained of it, at any time. Freed from its preoccupation with the Turks, and anxious to win a war somewhere to restore lost prestige, Tsarist Russia would certainly put its heart into a war in the Far East. The only negative factor here was the rise of terrorism in Russia itself, with organizations such as Narodnaya Volya (The Will of the People) and Zemlaya Volya (The Will of the Earth), which had culminated in the recent attempt in February 1880 on the life of Tsar Alexander II, but, of course, this itself might make the Tsar and his friends anxious to re-establish themselves. Was China ready to take on these desperate men? He thought not. To be frank, it would be sheer idiocy to fight Russia.

The Chinese Cabinet listened patiently, through their interpreter. They were alarmed when the interpreter dropped his teacup and refused to translate the last sentence. Gordon reached for a Chinese–English dictionary and pointed to the appropriate sign for idiocy. Instead of being offended, the Cabinet, chaired by the Emperor's nominee, Prince Chen, thanked their English fellow-mandarin and took his advice. There was no war with Russia. Back in Tientsin, Li Hung-Chang asked Gordon to settle down and write a treatise on what had to be done to reorganize the Chinese armies, and how they should tackle the Russians if and when the day came when war was inevitable; Gordon completed this task in record time. Unable to avoid a certain amount of feasting, but refusing lavish gifts, Gordon asked only for his passage home and a note to the British government to the effect that his intervention had been 'useful'.

On his way back to England, having averted a major war, Gordon was not surprised to hear that his resignation had been refused and he was back on active service. There were no thanks for his efforts. He cabled from Aden: 'You might have trusted me.' The British government was extremely embarrassed by the whole sequence of events. Civil servants scurried about the corridors of the new, purpose-built Colonial Office, for all the world like the White Rabbit or Red Lenin, both of whom were given to saying 'What is to be done?' What was to be done with this statesman, a field-marshal in the Imperial Armies of Turkey and China, though only a colonel in his own, 'a man who', in Sir William Butler's words, 'knows as much as Gordon knew, who thinks as much as Gordon thought, and who has a disagreeable habit of laying his finger on some . . . sore and saying, without fear, favour or affection the opinion that is in his head'. To Gladstone's government – to any government – he was an embarrassment. He ought to have been made Ambassador in Peking or Constantinople, Director General of Training at the War Office or Commandant at RMA Woolwich. Instead he was sent on indefinite leave.

After a fortnight spent with his sister, with the Rev. H. Barnes of Heavitree in Essex, an Evangelical minister whom he had befriended in Gravesend and with whom he had corresponded ever since, and with the old Sudan hand Sir Samuel Baker, Gordon decided to go on a walking tour of south-west Ireland. It would clear his head, he said, and anyway he was interested in the peasant problem in an industrializing world; the former English peasant was now a millhand and the Highland crofter a collier or emigrant, but there were still peasants, 'the best and truest product of the soil', across the Irish Sea.

Mr Gladstone was always saying that his mission was to pacify Ireland, or words to that effect, but why should Ireland need pacifying? Gordon had known the three old soldiers of the 41st, Hartnady, Kennedy and Pat Mahony, heroes at Sebastopol and the inspiration for some of Kipling's characters, and had had Irish troops under his command in China and even in the Sudan. They were excellent soldiers, but peaceable enough off duty. He said as much to the Irish photographer who took his picture for *Vanity Fair*, and to the artist who drew him at the same time. He would see. He took a couple of sporting guns and set off to walk through Kerry and Connemara.

November 1880 was damp and cold, but he covered hundreds of miles on foot and stayed in a variety of inns and a few hotels. He lived a simple, unaffected life, and went to mass in remote villages. He was entertained in a few great houses. He heard landlords say over the port that the Irish Question could be solved by sending the priests to Rome and the peasants to the United States. He heard the peasants, over porter, say what they thought of Gladstone's Land Act. He was astonished at what he saw, and wrote:

> The state of our fellow countrymen in Longford, Westmeath, Clare, Cork, Cavan and Donegal is worse than that of any people in the world, let alone Europe. I believe that these people are made as we are; that they are patient beyond belief; loyal but at the same time broken-spirited and desperate, living on the verge of starvation in places in which we would not keep our cattle. The Bulgarians, Anatolians, Chinese and Indians are better off than many of them are. The priests alone have any sympathy with their sufferings, and naturally alone have a hold over them. In these days, in common justice, if we endow a Protestant university, why should we not endow a Catholic university in a Catholic country?

These were not proper sentiments for an officer and a gentleman, nor did their publication endear Gordon to the establishment. Worse was to come. He had his own plan with which to 'pacify Ireland'. He saw that no half measures would do, that 'a gulf of antipathy exists between the landlords and tenants of the north-west, west and south of Ireland. He wrote:

My idea is that, through this cause or that it is immaterial to examine, a deadlock has occurred between the present landlords and the tenants, the Government should purchase up the rights of the landlords over the whole or the greater part of Longford, West-meath, Clare, Cork, Cavan and Donegal. The yearly rental of these districts is some four millions. If the Government gave the landlords twenty years purchase, it would cost £80,000,000 which, at three and a half per cent, would give a yearly interest of £2,800,000, of which £2,500,000 could be recovered. The lands would be Crown lands – they would be administered by a Land Commission, which would be supplemented by an Emigration Commission, which might for a short time need £100,000. This would not injure the landlords, and so far as it is an interference with proprietary right, it is as just as the law which forces Lord A. to allow a railway through his park for the public benefit. I would restrain the landlords from any power or control in these Crown Land districts. Poor-law, roads, schools etc. should be under the Land Commission. For the rest of Ireland, I would pass an Act allowing free sale of leases, fair rents, and a Government valuation.'

This inspired plan raised many hackles, if only because of its essential reasonableness. It would probably work. Those Irishmen and women who wanted to stay and farm, after two disastrous harvests, could do so. Those who wanted to emigrate would emigrate. There would be an end to boycotting and riots. It would cost less than freeing the slaves in the West Indies had done – £20,000,000 in 1833 – and were these poor Irish peasants any worse, or better, than slaves? What did the government think?

The government and the opposition were both horrified. Abuse was heaped on poor Gordon, even by his family, and he went into a spiritual retreat at an ecumenical centre run by Evangelicals at Thrapston in Northamptonshire.

It was early in 1881 when he heard the horrific story of the death of his old friend Romolo Gessi. Losing the fight with Raoul Pasha for pre-eminence in the Sudan, Gessi had resigned as Governor of Equatoria rather than be demoted, and on 15 September 1880 had embarked on his boat the *Saphia* to go down the Bahr-el-Ghazal. He had intended to do a little mapping, then join the White Nile and sail downstream. Unfortunately he had chosen the worst possible time of year, and the boat had stuck in the marsh grass and other aquatic weeds. For three months he and 600 men and passengers were alone, without food, far from any mission or fort. When hunger got the better of the living, they ate the dead: 430 of the 600 died. When, by chance, an Austrian friend, Ernst Marno, came on the *Saphia* from the opposite direction, as the rising waters began to make navigation possible again, the scene was beyond description. Gessi was still alive, a cannibal like the other survivors, and Marno's boat the *Bordeen* towed the *Saphia* back to Khartoum, arriving on 25 January 1881. It was from there that Marno wrote to Gordon a discreetly veiled account of the tragedy. By the time Gordon received the letter Gessi was on his way to Suez, where shortly afterwards he died. On 10 May Gordon wrote of Gessi's death to Augusta: 'Gessi Gessi Gessi how I warned him to leave with me when at Towashia how I said "Whether you like it or not, or whether I like it or not, your life is bound up with mine". He knew me to the depths. I almost feared this in one way. However, Gessi, is at rest. It is God's will.'

It is at this point in Charles Gordon's life that the question is sometimes raised, had he become a Catholic, and what did he mean by being a Catholic? There is no record of his ever having been received into the Roman Catholic Church, though he was a friend of Monsignor Sogaro at Khartoum, went to mass with Gessi at various mission churches, and was known to have disapproved of the Public Worship Act of 1874 which was supposed to 'check excessive ritualistic practices in the Established Church of England', because the High Anglicans, Queen Victoria said, were 'Roman Catholics at heart, and very insincere as to their profession of attachment to the Church'. Would the Roman Catholic Church have kept secret such a conversion, at a time when there was a 'mission to England'? It would not be in keeping with Gordon's character to be an Anglo-Catholic, halfway between Rome and Canterbury. And what about the fundamentalist Protestantism of his childhood and youth? During the years at Gravesend he had certainly been an Evangelical Christian, and his own tracts written there and later were not particularly 'Romish'. Maybe his friendship with Gessi and the shock of his death so soon after the experience of Ireland turned Gordon towards Rome. Maybe he was the first of a new generation of ecumenical Christians: a believer but never a bigot, as one of his friends said.

Whatever thoughts were going through his head at Thrapston, he was certainly much involved with his religious mapmaking. The Royal Geographical Society had hoped to mark his return from the Sudan 'by a deputation from our Council on his arrival', and Sir Ernest Ommanney, a Councillor, had written to his friend Sir Henry William Gordon to see what Sir Henry's brother's reaction might be. As might have been expected, he received a reply direct from Charles Gordon to the effect that he wanted no fuss and confirmed his 'antipathy to any sort of public demonstration concerning his actions and merits'. The Society had accepted this well-known attitude as something long-standing – it had been the cause of his resignation in 1866, after all – but managed to persuade him to become an Honorary Corresponding Fellow and by the beginning of 1881 a cordial relationship had been established between him and the Secretary, Bates. He gave the Society a collection of his maps of the Sudan and in return asked for maps of the Middle East and Africa. Poring over these and the Bible, and with the help of a friend, the Rev. D. Berry, he worked out to his own satisfaction the site of the Garden of Eden. He wrote: 'To the Rev. Berry I owe the final thought on the subject of the site of Eden. I had already thought that the two trees [of life and knowledge] were distinguishable at Seychelles.'

Having established to his own satisfaction the site of the Fall, it only remained to get himself there. He cursed himself at the thought that he had turned down the post at the Cape of Good Hope, from where the journey to the Seychelles, in the Indian Ocean some three thousand miles north-east of the Cape, would not be too arduous. Accordingly he cabled the government at the Cape to the effect that he was willing to go out and help to put an end to the Boer rebellion and that of the Basutos; the Dutch were in rebellion against Britain's annexation of the Transvaal without a by-your-leave, and the Basutos were up in arms because of the Native Disarmament Act. The government at the Cape ignored his telegram. Even worse, he got wind of a plot by the War Office either to make him retire (to which he would not have objected) or to give him some insignificant command in a remote part of Australasia. On 4 April 1881 he wrote to a friend at the War Office: 'Now it would be trying to me to go and look after ordinary Royal Engineer duties, so if you could aid me to anything in a very mild way at Cape, or elsewhere (in South Africa) with the mildest of salaries, or even with Lieutenant-Colonel RE's pay, I would be much obliged.' Somehow his friend managed to dissuade the War Office from sending him to Van Diemens Land, and Gordon could write:

> For myself [this] duty was particularly vexatious, for I should certainly have come to dire loggerheads with my obstructive RE chiefs. I claim to sympathise with any who try to stem the effete administration of our rulers. What we want is a man who will

steamhammer all departments to the welfare of our army, and this is therefore why I do not wish to be shunted about, for I believe the time is near when there will be a cry for such a man, and it is then I would like to be active.

Then Gordon had a stroke of luck. In London one day he met an old friend, also an RE colonel, Sir Howard Elphinstone, who was looking very down in the mouth. When asked what was wrong, Elphinstone told Gordon that the War Office had just posted him to command the RE establishment on the Indian Ocean island of Mauritius. Who would want to go to Mauritius, 'a thankless office, with nothing really to be done, and having exile thrown in along with idleness'? Sir Howard would give anyone £800 to take his place, but who would do it even for that fairly substantial sum? 'Elphin, I'm your man!' said Gordon, and they went off straight-away to the War Office to arrange it. The War Office could not believe its good fortune, though they were not surprised to learn that Gordon had refused the £800. The generals did not hesitate, and before Gordon could change his mind they had him on a boat for Mauritius. In mid-May he was already there, 'looking after barrack repairs, and seeing that the drains were in order'.

Having settled in and handed over work on the island to his second-in-command, he set off for the Seychelles, in theory to repair the harbour facilities on Mahé. In fact he went on a tour of the smaller islands to fix the exact site of the Garden of Eden, which he found on the island of Praslin in the Vallée de Mai.

From an eight-page essay dated 26 February 1882, which came to light again recently, it is possible to follow Gordon's reasoning. It began, inevitably, in Genesis 2:

And the Lord God planted a garden eastward in Eden; and there he put the man whom he had formed.

And out of the ground made the Lord God to grow every tree that is pleasant to the sight, and good for food; the tree of life also in the midst of the garden, and the tree of knowledge of good and evil.

And a river went out of Eden to water the garden; and from thence it was parted; and became four heads.

The name of the first is Pishon: that is it which compasseth the whole land of Havilah, where there is gold;

And the gold of that land is good: there is bdellium and onyx stone.

And the name of the second river is Gihon; the same it is that compasseth the whole land of Ethiopia.

And the name of the third river is Hiddekel; that is it which goeth

141

toward the east of Assyria. And the fourth river is Euphrates. . . .

And the Lord God commanded the man, saying, Of every tree of the garden thou mayest freely eat;

But of the tree of the knowledge of good and evil, thou shalt not eat of it; for in the day that thou eatest thereof thou shalt surely die.

For Gordon the Bible was a clear and factual account of how things had been done and why. He looked at his maps of Africa and the Middle East. It was what he had already thought at Thrapston. The four rivers were not a delta, but were obviously four tributaries of one great river which flowed before the Flood: '. . . in no instance in this world do we find four rivers flowing out of one river, while there are many instances of four rivers flowing into one,' he wrote, thus dismissing previous theories that the Eden river had branched into four. What were these four tributaries? The Bible had given a clear indication in two cases: the Euphrates still flows through Iraq to the Persian Gulf and the Hiddekel is the Tigris, which does the same – Gordon had seen where they rose in Turkey. There was a problem, however, with the Pishon and the Gihon. Other religious cartographers had thought the Gihon must be the Nile 'that compasseth the whole land of Ethiopia', and the Pishon would be the Indus or the Ganges. But 'in Genesis II, verse 13, Gihon is said to encompass the land of Cush [Kush]. Cush was the son of Nimrod and Nimrod was of Assyria [Gordon was in error here: Cush was the father of Nimrod]'. Some time before the Flood, then, there must have been a river which flowed from Turkey south across present-day Jordan and Israel and into the Red Sea, along the coast of the Sudan (Kush) and into the Gulf of Aden. 'Aden is Eden. Eden was a district, the Garden of Eden was a chosen spot.' That left the Pishon which must be the Nile; the Blue Nile and the Atbara rise in Ethiopia and so do several tributaries of the White Nile. Before the Flood, the Nile flowed into the Red Sea.

That settled the rivers, then. But what happened to the Tigris and Euphrates after they had flowed down the Persian Gulf, and the Gihon and Pishon in the Gulf of Aden? The Bible was not much help here, so Gordon had to speculate on what the map of the watercourses had been before the Flood, which had sealed off the Garden of Eden from the wicked, or rather, created a museum of the Fall. The Flood had been caused by the melting of the icecaps, which tilted the earth on its axis to 23°. The four rivers before the Flood had joined together at Aden and the Great River had flowed towards the Garden down the present-day coasts of Somalia and

Kenya. This watercourse was now 2,600 fathoms deep at its delta, off the coast of the Seychelles; there is, in fact, a basin 2,600 fathoms deep off the Seychelles. So that was it as far as the old watercourse was concerned. However, if the Garden had been deliberately sealed off by God to keep Noah's descendants from going the way of Adam's first progeny, there should be traces of all that lush vegetation, and, above all, there must be the tree of life and the tree of knowledge of good and evil; God would not have moved the latter!

But how would Colonel Gordon in the nineteenth century recognize the descendants or present incarnations of these trees? His knowledge of botany was sketchy and the trees would not be 'conveniently labelled as at Kew'. He wrote to Bates at the Royal Geographical Society, who, by chance, was in correspondence with the Superintendent of the Royal Botanical Gardens at Pample-mousse in Mauritius, a man called Scott. Gordon got in touch with Scott, who was bemused by the request for botanical details of the tree of life and the tree of knowledge of good and evil. How tall would they be? What sort of flowers? Would they be hermaphro-ditic – self-pollinating? Would the leaves be large enough to be mistaken for the fig leaves for which Adam and Eve made themselves aprons, according to Genesis 3? Scott did not know. Nor was he sure that even if the Colonel did find a self-pollinating tree it would have sexual organs resembling human ones. He did not know if he could put the Colonel in touch with the Liverpool doctor who was supposed to have examined a pregnant man. Gordon wanted drawings of everything – the pregnant man, a prehistoric female reproductive system, the sexual organs of flowers which ate flies, and all tropical fruits.

Fortunately for everyone concerned, one day on Praslin Gordon raised his eyes and beheld the *coco de mer* tree (*Lodoicea seychellarum*), wrongly categorized by the French as a coconut or double coconut. Or rather there were two versions of the tree, male and female. And nearby he saw another palm tree (*Artocarpus incisa*), the breadfruit tree. He had found the tree of the knowledge of good and evil and the tree of life – and, to boot, a 3-foot snake nearby, which he shot. He photographed the *coco de mer* and 'its fruit, shaped in the husk like a heart, when opened like a belly with thighs'. It may well be, as Gessi had observed, that to his knowledge 'Carlo has never seen what there is between a woman's legs'. It may well be true, as an RE subaltern recorded, that the Colonel chased female goats all over the island to get a look at their sexual organs. Whatever the truth is, his photograph of the dehusked fruit of the *coco de mer* has a strong resemblance to a fugitive view of a female sexual invitation. And there was more. The tree was not self-pollinating. There were two sorts of *coco de mer*, one obviously made with a pollinating phallus, and the other which bore the tempting fruit; the fruit had been known for centuries – mysterious, of uncertain origin, possibly aphrodisiac – but only recently identified as being native to the Seychelles. And next to it was the breadfruit tree, just as Milton had inaccurately described them:

> *And all amid them stood the Tree of Life*
> *High eminent, blooming Ambrosial Fruit*
> *Of vegetable Gold; and next to Life,*
> *Our Death, the Tree of Knowledge grew fast by,*
> *Knowledge of good, bought dear by knowing ill.*

Except that Milton had not known, could not have known, that there were, as the Bible hinted, two trees of knowledge, one male, one female, one good and one evil. That was what had God meant by saying that 'in the day that thou eatest thereof, thou shalt surely die'. If a man ate of the male tree, he would die. If the woman ate of the female tree, she would die: in one sense like poor Gessi, who had become a cannibal, thinking he could save his life, but had lost it; in another sense like the homosexual which Gordon had always been afraid he might become. He wrote to Augusta that he had 'pretty well settled the site of Eden, of the Garden and the Trees of Knowledge and Life'. He knew now:

> *Of Man's First Disobedience, and the Fruit*
> *Of that Forbidden Tree, whose mortal taste*
> *Brought Death into the World, and all our woe,*
> *With loss of Eden ...*

And there he was like

> *... them who saile*
> *Beyond the Cape of Hope, and now are past*
> *Mozambic, off at Sea North-East windes blow*
> *Sabean Odours from the spicie shoare*
> *Of Arabie ...*

In the almost perfect climate of Mauritius ('This Patmos of idleness') and the Seychelles, Gordon could well understand the Fall. Adam and Eve were tempted by their stomachs and by curiosity. 'They ate and they fell . . . their act was one we commit every moment, as to say forgetting God and trusting self, heedlessness, greediness, forgetfulness. . . . What did Eve think, did she go and study the tree, no, she took and ate to see for herself, she wanted to gratify herself. . . . ' How right he had been to avoid women, marriage and sins even worse than those he had committed, because woman had been the cause of the original sin.

He might have gone on speculating about what had happened after the Fall, about the placing 'at the east of the garden of Eden Cherubims, and a flaming sword, which turned every way, to keep the way of the tree of life' (Genesis 3), about the Flood and after, but he had to end his meditations in the spring of 1882. On 2 April the government of the Cape, in increasing difficulties with the Basutos, replied to Gordon's offer of a year before and asked him if he were still willing to help. In a way relieved. at the prospect of action, he cabled that his offer was still open and took it as an omen that a sailing ship, the *Scotia*, was about to set sail for Cape Town. Putting together his meagre kit, he boarded the *Scotia* on 4 April and for a month was tossed about in the seas off Madagascar, as the autumn storms of the Southern Hemisphere battered the old barque. He was relieved to set foot on dry land again, and go to be briefed as Commandant-General.

The government of the Cape, or, as they now preferred to call themselves, the government at the Cape, suggested that their difficulties had arisen because of a misunderstanding. Knowing that General Gordon had had so much experience with 'natives' all over the world, they were confident that the obstacles of communication could easily be overcome. The General was not so sanguine. He made his own inquiries, having learnt to mistrust all governments.

A Roman Catholic missionary, expelled from Basutoland by the Anglican governments and harassed by the Dutch Reformed Church Boers, explained to the new Commandant-General what the situation really was, and asked to be taken with him. The Basutos, an ancient people bullied by the Zulus and afraid of dilution by Bantu immigrants, had welcomed the offer, made twenty years ago, to become British subjects. Their chiefs and Supreme Chief had rightly judged the British to be the strongest power in southern Africa, and if there were to be a struggle for power wanted to be on the winning side, as they had done centuries before, allying themselves with Zimbabwe against the first Bantu immigration. They had welcomed British administrators, had fed them well and given them women. They had also agreed to pay a hut tax. Under British protection the Basutos had increased and multiplied, as had their taxes. They had been the first to volunteer to work the newly opened diamond mines further south. As money had not been attractive to a people with a prosperous pastoral economy and with few trading stations, it had been agreed between the chiefs and the owners of the diamond mines that the Basuto miners should be paid in guns and ammunition. In 1880, fearful of an alliance between the Basutos and the Boers, the Cape government of the day had passed a Native Disarmament Act, requiring all natives, including the Basutos, to hand in their arms and ammunition. When the Supreme Chief, Masufa, had commented that this was, in effect, asking the Basuto miners to hand back seventeen years' worth of wages in the mines without compensation, he was dubbed subversive and intractable. Two million pounds sterling had been spent on trying to convince him that he was wrong. His well-armed, well-led troops had defeated every expedition sent from the Cape to convince him of the error of his ways.

The Commandant-General, having checked to see if this were the true story, and found that it was, put to the Cape government that it appeared that they were on the side of injustice. They must admit to this and change their ways. They must replace the magistrates who had tried to enforce this unjust law. He, Charles Gordon, would be the just steward who would apologise and try to make a new beginning.

The businessmen at the Cape, who had hoped to reduce Basutoland and make a fortune from its semi-precious stones and prospects for intensive cattle raising, were horrified. They thought they had hired a mercenary, not a missionary.

It is only fair to say that the government at the Cape ignored the protests of the businessmen (thus ensuring its early fall) and urged Gordon to do what he could to make peace with the Basutos. In China and the Sudan he had learnt to be very patient. Pretending to be interested in the countryside he rode up into the Drakensberg Mountains and along the Orange River, finding for himself 'a real winter' at over 10,000 feet. He showed himself to be indifferent to the cold and the rains, and was seen, draped in a sodden blanket, riding up and down the slopes like a native herdsman. In this way he won the confidence of the local people, and in particular of three of the four native chiefs. The fourth, the Supreme Chief Masufa, had his doubts. Gordon telegraphed to the Cape government that

146

he hoped to convince even Masufa of the government's sincerity; the only condition he made was that he should be given time, and that no troops should be sent in to 'rescue' him.

Masufa, who visited his capital, Maseru, only occasionally, was astonished to see this slight, serious emissary arrive without an escort. After a week of probing and querying, familiar to Gordon, a sort of rapport was reached, on the brink of trust. Suddenly, Masufa heard that an 'expeditionary force' was on its way to force him to submit. It says much for both men that, when Gordon denied all knowledge of this treachery, Masufa believed him and let him go. Back in Cape Town, Gordon refused to believe that his wire had not got through, resigned as Commandant-General and was back in England at the beginning of November 1882.

With Gordon, by the same boat, arrived the official complaints and a letter from the Secretary for Native Affairs. General Gordon had been insubordinate. He had disobeyed some orders and ignored others. He had insulted the Governor and stepped on the train of the dress of the Governor's Lady. Gordon's complaint that he had resigned because it was 'impossible to act against natives who I believe are being treated injustly by the defective Government of the Transkei' was dismissed as frivolous. The British government was embarrassed. Gordon had been promoted major-general in the British Army that spring, even though he had been taken off the Active List. He was still a field-marshal in Imperial Turkey and Imperial China. Moreover, the King of the Belgians had sent Queen Victoria a copy of a letter to Gordon which read: 'I now again request you, as you are at liberty, to enter my service. For the moment I have no mission to offer you, but I wish much to have you at my disposal, and to take you from this moment as my counsellor. You can name your own terms. You know the consideration that I have for your great qualities.'

What was to be done with this fellow who upset honest businessmen in the Cape, and as a result honest businessmen at home who supported Gladstone's Liberal government financially and electorally? There was no question of a reprimand for a man admired by statesmen all over the world, not to speak of the Queen-Empress Victoria at home. The sooner he was out of the way, the better. He would not go to join the King of the Belgians if there were no real work to do; foreign potentates had always found it hard to get him to accept a large salary even where and when there was a lot to do. In the end, several of his friends were prevailed upon to suggest that until King Leopold came up with a specific task, the General should go to the Holy Land and complete his mapwork. There was that River Gihon to be traced. There was the exact site of the Crucifixion to be established, not to speak of the Holy Sepulchre. One of Gordon's *bêtes noires*, the Secretary of the Palestine Exploration Society, had published his own theories, calculations and maps – 'wrong, wrong – horribly wrong!' Now was the General's chance to get at the truth.

These were telling arguments and had the desired effect. For most of 1883, wrote Lytton Strachey,

> A solitary English gentleman was to be seen, wandering, with a thick book under his arm, in the neighbourhood of Jerusalem. His unassuming figure, short and slight, with its half-gliding, half-tripping motion, gave him a boyish aspect, which contrasted, oddly but not unpleasantly, with the touch of grey on his hair and whiskers. There was the same contrast – enigmatic and attractive – between the sunburnt brickred complexion – the hue of the seasoned traveller – and the large blue eyes, with their look of almost childish sincerity.

From his modest lodgings he wrote hundreds of letters to Augusta, to his brother Henry, to the Rev. Barnes, and to Dr Schlick, the archaeologist who was looking for the ruins of Satan's domicile, which Gordon fixed, like the Garden of Eden, in the Southern Hemisphere 'at Lat. 31° 74' S, Long. 144° 45' W, close to Bass Isle, south of Otaheite, not far from Pitcairns Isle, where the mutineers of the *Bounty* settled'. As Sir William Butler observed: 'There were many men who spoke of his belief as being "a strange mixture of Mysticism and Measurement." He was not content if he could not give the exact height and breadth of the Deity.' Gordon worried for some time about the physical presence of the Son of Man – 'Being a Man, he must be in some definite place' – and assumed that He must be above the Altar of the Temple, a convenient location because 'all prayer (from whatever part of the globe) must pass by and through Him'. The General had no doubts.

Nobody really believed that he was there only to contest the claims of the Palestine Exploration Society. The French were sure that he was spying, perhaps in areas of the Turkish Empire in which their interest was predominant, such as Syria and the Lebanon. The Germans were convinced that he was recruiting a gang to sabotage the Berlin–Baghdad railway. Certainly he kept in touch with political affairs in the region, and especially in the part he knew best, Egypt and the Sudan.

Just before he left, an Egyptian colonel of peasant origin, Arabi, had led a national revolt against the new Khedive Tewfik and the bankers and businessmen who manipulated him. This was a genuine 'national liberation' movement, perhaps the first of the new imperial era, and was promptly put down by the British Liberal government. Alexandria was bombarded by the British fleet in 1882, and a British army under Lord Wolseley defeated Arabi Pasha at Tel-el-Kebir; Queen Victoria's son, the Duke of Connaught, commanded a Guards battalion and contributed to the victory, she was proud to note in her diary. Others, it must be said, saw the successful British naval and military campaign in a different light. Lieutenant-General Charles P. Stone, an American who was the Khedive's Chief of General Staff, wrote:

> To my astonishment the notice of only twenty-four hours [of the bombardment of Alexandria] was given, and that notice was given late in the afternoon of the 9th of July, after the departure from Cairo of that last train on that day for Alexandria. At the same time the foreign warships and ships of refuge were advised to quit the harbour at noon on the 10th. This barbarous disregard on the part of the British of the lives of citizens of all other nationalities caused me, as well as thousands of others, fearful anxiety, and caused the horrible death of scores of Europeans – French, Germans, Austrians and Italians. . . . All British subjects had been carefully sent away.

The peasant-led revolt was surprising. What was even more surprising was its sequel in the Sudan. The nephew of Gordon's old guide in Darfour ('a very good fellow') had set up camp on the island of Abba in 1881, and proclaimed himself Mahdi, a descendant of the Prophet, who would free Africa from the infidel. He was tall, handsome and remarkably eloquent and had a deep knowledge of the Koran. Born Mohammed Akmed, he was a carpenter's son like Jesus of Nazareth, and while his uncle was acting as guide to the Governor-General of the Sudan he had seen how a strong personality could overcome almost unsurmountable difficulties. The British puppet government in Cairo ignored him for a time, though by the end of 1882 he had won over all the sheiks of Darfour and Kordofan and Egyptian rule in the Sudan was threatened. The assorted pashas in Cairo decided to follow a well-worn path, to raise an army and put it under foreign command; this would have to be English, now, of course. Ten thousand Egyptians were rounded up, many from the gaols to which they had been sent after Tel-el-Kebir (their irons were struck off as they swore loyalty to the new regime), and after a few weeks' training at the Barrage, the large barracks in Cairo, they were sent up the river to Khartoum to be orientated.

In command was an officer named Hicks, a retired British colonel promoted general for the occasion, and he had ten assorted – mostly British – European officers as his staff. What would have been an ideal command for poor Gessi, who knew every square mile of Darfour and Kordofan, was too much for Hicks. With the arms and gold captured at El-Obeid in January 1883 the Mahdi had been able to equip and train not only the followers of the local sheiks, but a whole division of mercenaries from Central Africa, together with his own nucleus of European officers supposedly converted to Islam. When Hicks marched out of Khartoum into Kordofan he thought of himself as a new Gessi, maybe even a new Gordon. Then he was ambushed, and the Mahdi's hordes descended on his pitiable force. He was deafened by the drums, blinded by the red, black and green flags flying everywhere and overwhelmed by the hordes in their white tunics or *jibbehs*, each one bearing its symbolic patch representing sin. On a camel nearby, in his patchless *jibbeh*, the Mahdi himself watched while Hicks and his troops were cut to pieces. It was a black November for Britain and Egypt.

Charles Gordon read of the massacre while he was resting after mapping Golgotha, the place where Christ was crucified. The date of the battle was 5 November. The news reached him on St Martin's Day, the eleventh, as he was leaving the Greek Orthodox church after mass. He was very sad, though sadder for those who had not worn 'the greatcoat of Faith' in the heat of the day. 'I see no-one; my books are enough companionship . . . but He is always with me.' He remembered Hicks, a rather stupid and unpleasant fellow. He wondered what had happened to his own subordinates in the area – the Austrian Slatin, who had taken over from Gessi as Governor in Equatoria, and the eccentric Lupton. Well, it did not concern him. He prepared himself for Advent, noting in a letter to the Rev. Barnes that he still felt sexual temptation, and recalling: 'I wished I was a eunuch at 14. . . . ' This is the only explicit reference to the subject in his correspondence or indeed in records of his conversations with Gessi and other friends, so it is difficult to deduce what prompted these random musings. He decided to go home for St Lucy's Day, 13 December, and stop off in Ravenna on the way to pay his respects to the body of Gessi, for whose homecoming he had paid.

NINE

A Waste of Heroes

> *'I would sooner live like a dervish with the Mahdi than go out to dinner every night in London. . . . Life is a leaden business, and if anyone can lighten it, so much the better . . . but my resolve is never to be taken alive.'*
> Gordon, Khartoum, December 1884

Charles George Gordon arrived in Brussels by train on New Year's Day 1884, and was rather annoyed to find the city still recovering from the previous night's celebrations. He spent the day at a desk in his hotel, writing to friends. He was looking forward to his next mission: 'I have a nice house, with garden and no worries, on the horizon . . . and it seems that the Congo is the route which is quickest to it.' He was toying with the idea of buying a house for himself near Elgin in Scotland, and had several prospectuses to read; he hoped to obtain a further advance from the King of the Belgians to cover the purchase.

Next day he told the King – just back, as Betty Kalen records in *The Mistresses*, from a frolic with the 'uncountable fruity girls that grew on the espaliers of Paris' – that he had already written to the War Office asking for indefinite leave of absence. Given the fact that he was no longer on the Active List, and the close ties between the British and Belgian royal families, he was sure there would be no difficulty. With His Majesty's permission, he would like to go to England for a week or so to put his affairs in order, and leave for the Congo in early February. The King shook his hand warmly and said he was very happy to have such a valorous administrator at last in his service. Gordon had two matters to settle. First, he had the results of his researches in the Holy Land to get off to the printers as well as several tracts, the proofs of which he hoped to correct before leaving. He also had to settle Augusta, now its legal owner, in the house in Southampton. Some legal nicety had cropped up in the transfer of the deeds and he did not want there to be any difficulties for her, now ill, cantankerous and seldom visited by her sisters.

When he arrived in Southampton on 7 January, however, he discovered that the War Office had refused him leave to take up the appointment in the Congo, though without giving any explanation. Angrily, and before he had unpacked, he sat down and wrote a letter of resignation (the nineteenth of his career to date) in which 'Charles George Gordon, Major-General, humbly petitions to be allowed to retire from Her Majesty's service without any claim whatever for pension from Her Majesty's Government. . . . His Majesty King Leopold II has most kindly assured me that His Majesty will compensate any pecuniary loss I may incur in leaving Her Majesty's service.'

What puzzled him was that he had been released from liability for active service in April 1882, and had assumed that the War Office had no further use for him. Things had been going from bad to worse in the Sudan ever since he had left, but he had not been asked for help, or even for advice, so they could not be thinking of sending him out there. He commented sardonically that he was the professional, the expert, and as such undesirable. In a way he was right. The desk officers at the War Office wanted nothing to do with him. There were 'three armies in Cairo, three generals, and naturally three ambitions'.

The Foreign Office, however, though Gordon did not know it, was less hostile. The government, and Prime Minister Gladstone in particular, wanted the whole mess in Egypt and the Sudan cleared up as soon as possible and did not care who got on with it. And things were getting worse. On the same day that Gordon arrived in Southampton, the puppet Egyptian government resigned rather than evacuate the Sudan and leave it to the Mahdi; this was in spite of the fact that the British officer commanding the Egyptian troops in Khartoum had reported that he could not hold out for more than a month. The British Press was waking up to the fact that something was terribly wrong. Would there be another massacre to follow that of General Hicks and his 10,000 Egyptian unfortunates? When was the British government going to do something?

The Foreign Office had been trying to do something ever since the Hicks massacre. It had been suggested at the end of November 1883 that General Gordon, the former Governor-General of the

Sudan, should be sent out, at least to supervise the evacuation of all British nationals. There was a clear British responsibility. Egypt had annexed the Sudan in 1822, and Britain had, *de facto*, annexed Egypt in 1882. The businessmen and bankers in Cairo did not see it this way. They told their leader, Sir Evelyn Baring, now British Consul-General, that Gordon was the last man they wanted. With his mania for honesty and horror of corruption he would ruin everything. Up to now, things had gone according to plan. Without having to dig the Suez Canal, they had got control of it and the trade routes to East Africa and India. Ever-increasing Italian, French and German interest in East Africa looked likely to increase profits even faster than those from vessels bound for India and the Far East. The Sudan? Let the Italians, the French or the Germans have it. They would learn some imperial lessons there. As a wise Italian observer noted later: '*L'inghilterra aveva in fatti favorito il nostro insediamento nel Mar Rosso pe' suoi fini d'equilibrio internazionale e ci considerava dei pupilli*' (England had in fact encouraged our settlement on the Red Sea as furthering her interest in the international balance of power and considered us her protégés). The important thing was that Egypt was now a puppet state, though some of the strings holding the puppets had to be replaced. This would take time, and brooked no interference. When Lord Granville, the Foreign Secretary, had asked Sir Evelyn Baring if Gordon should be sent out to Egypt, he had received a very discouraging reply.

Stead, the editor of the *Pall Mall Gazette*, got wind of this and of Gordon's return to England. He set off for Southampton and found Gordon there, still fuming and unpacking. He was told that the War Office and the Foreign Office were obviously staffed by fools. But much could be done to save the situation. There were good men in England, who knew what had to be done. Sir Samuel Baker and his brother, General Baker, were two; Gordon understood that the General was on his way to Egypt, maybe already there. He said much about corruption in high places, in London and Cairo. On 9 January 1884 this interview appeared in the *Pall Mall Gazette* slightly twisted so as to recommend Gordon himself rather than the Bakers as the saviour. General Gordon was a good man, honest, able, unemployed, probably the only man who knew the place and the people well enough to achieve anything at all. A younger generation might have forgotten what he had achieved against all the odds in China. A mature, responsible readership would soon call this to mind. The next day Lord Granville telegraphed a summary of the interview to Cairo and asked Sir Evelyn Baring again if this were not, perhaps, the moment when, notwithstanding local objections, the expert might be called in. Again Sir Evelyn rejected the suggestion.

Meanwhile, Gordon had signed his deeds and set off for Heavitree in Essex to confer with the Rev. Barnes on his latest tracts (on the sacraments and the Resurrection), and to show him his maps of the Garden of Eden and the Holy Places. Sir Samuel Baker, who lived nearby, called to pay his respects. They talked about the crisis in Egypt and the Sudan, about the interview in the *Pall Mall Gazette* and about what was to be done. Both former Governors of the troubled provinces of Equatoria, over the years they had exchanged views, diametrically opposed to those of the Foreign Office, about the folly of taking an interest in North, West and East Africa and ignoring Central Africa, where the great rivers rose, where the rebel tribes lived, where the slave trade flourished, where immense resources were waiting to be exploited. They reflected on the obtuseness of a British government which had refused Stanley's offer of the Congo on a plate, years before; Leopold was hated not for his avarice or his predilection for girls from the Paris Opera, but because, a better businessman than any in the City, he had seen the potential of Stanley's 'little Empire'.

Sir Samuel Baker extracted a promise from his successor in Equatoria that he would pen his thoughts that very evening and send them over next morning by messenger. They went for a drive together, then parted. Gordon seemed pensive but excited. Lytton Strachey dramatized the events following that parting:

> Late that night, after the Vicar [Barnes] had retired to bed, he was surprised by the door suddenly opening, and by the appearance of his guest swiftly tripping into the room. "You saw me today?" the low voice abruptly questioned. "You mean in the carriage?" [with Baker] replied the startled Mr Barnes. "Yes", came the reply; "you saw *me* – that was *myself* – the self I want to get rid of." There was a sliding movement, the door swung to, and the Vicar found himself alone again.

The letter containing Gordon's thoughts on how the crisis should be tackled was duly sent over to Sir Samuel, who, interpreting his younger friend's intentions, passed it to *The Times*. *The Times* had already received some alarming dispatches from Frank Power, its correspondent in Khartoum, as well as an intimation that it was generally agreed in the Sudan that only Gordon could save the day. On 14 January *The Times* published the letter. Again, the Foreign Office was stirred to action. Lord Granville asked permission of the

Prime Minister to put pressure on Sir Evelyn Baring to accept Gordon as the man of the hour. When Gladstone agreed, reluctantly, Granville put it, untruthfully, to Baring that Gordon was 'ready to go at once to the Sudan . . . to report to Her Majesty's Government on the military situation, and to return without further engagement. He would be under you for instructions and will send letters through you under flying seal.' Sir Evelyn was too realistic to imagine that Gordon would ever accept such a mandate, but he sniffed the sulphur of popular pressure on the government and replied on the sixteenth that 'Gordon would be the best man if he will pledge himself to carry out the policy of withdrawing from the Sudan as quickly as is possible consistent with saving life. He must also understand that he must take his instructions from the British representative in Egypt.' In any event, whoever was sent must know that there was great difficulty and danger, though these would not deter the former Governor-General of the Sudan.

The former Governor-General had left Southampton for Brussels, whether believing that he had shot his bolt or that his absence would make the government's heart grow fonder it is difficult to deduce from his behaviour. In an audience of the King on 16 January he referred to Egypt and the Sudan, but he is reported to have limited himself to saying that all Equatoria should, ideally, be detached from the Sudan and incorporated into the Congo – northern Sudan could be absorbed by Egypt and easily administered from Cairo. The King of the Belgians is said to have assumed that this meant that Gordon would eventually be going to the Congo on his behalf, though he might go via the Sudan on a final reconnaissance for the British government.

What followed next is often vague and contradictory in contemporary accounts. What is known is that at noon on 17 January Gordon received a telegram from Lord Wolseley, the Adjutant-General and a friend, asking him to return to England for consultations. Gordon took a boat as soon as he could and was in London at 6 a.m. the next day; he breakfasted with Wolseley and talked to him for several hours. Then, as Gordon wrote later to the Rev. Barnes:

> At noon, he, Wolseley, came to me and took me to the Ministers. He went in and talked to the Ministers, and came back and said, 'Her Majesty's Government want you to undertake this: the Government are determined to evacuate Soudan, for they will not guarantee future government. Will you go in and do it?'. I said, 'Yes'. He said, 'Go in'. I went in and saw them. They said, 'Did Wolseley tell you

155

our orders?'. I said 'Yes.' I said, "You will not guarantee future government of the Soudan, and you wish me to go up to evacuate now." They said "Yes," and it was over, and I left at 8 p.m. for Calais.

However, this is not all that was said. Sir William Butler, a close friend of one of the politicians present, Lord Hartington, the Minister for War, notes:

There are contradictory accounts existing of this interview. . . . I have heard it stated on very high authority that the mission, as contemplated by the English Ministry, did not extend beyond Suakim, from which place a full report was to be sent by Gordon to the Government, both sides holding themselves perfectly free after that point was reached. I have heard the same high authority declare that Gordon, at starting, had specially stipulated he was not to go by way of Cairo. We know that at Port Said he received the pressing invitation which induced him to change his intention and visit Cairo, but few persons are aware that the English Government knew nothing of the appointment of their officer as Governor-General of the Soudan, or of the change of destination from Suakim to the Nile route, until some days after both had been effected by our Minister in Cairo. When one remembers the enormous issues that were depending upon this mission, and thinks of the blood and treasure afterwards to be poured out, one knows not whether to marvel most at the vagueness in which such colossal results could be initiated, or the strength of the nation which survives such vagueness of direction.

Fortunately, recent research carried out by members of the American University at Cairo has cleared up much of the mystery. As Sir William Butler has written and Lord Hartington said, Gordon left London to report on the military situation. He took only hand luggage and little or no money; he was expected back in a month. 'I go to the Soudan tonight to finish a work,' he wrote on 18 January, 'then to the Congo.'

In Cairo, nobody believed that Gordon would land at Suakim and take a camel into the interior, carrying only a bundle of telegraph forms. The British military authorities were afraid that this forthright and locally experienced soldier would report on their incompetence, as were the Egyptian military authorities, long accustomed to criticism from that source. The Egyptian government's various Austro-Hungarian, French and German advisers had learnt from

their spies in Brussels that Gordon intended to recommend abandoning the southern provinces, which would be annexed by King
Leopold to the Congo, then subdued by Belgian troops and
mercenaries under Gordon's supreme command. The British business community was hostile and suspicious. For all of them, a
General Gordon who, having evacuated British subjects from the
Sudan for the British government, would then become a Belgian
supreme commander with a writ which ran from the Atlantic to the
Red Sea, was a frightening prospect. He might even come to terms
with the Mahdi, leaving him in control of the northern provinces of
the Sudan; after all, both men shared the same fundamentalist,
some said fanatical, views.

What had to be done, everyone agreed in Cairo, was to detach
Gordon from the British government and send him to Khartoum as
an Egyptian civil servant again. He would then, because he was an
honest man, protect Egyptian interests, which meant also British –
business – interests. His loyalties would be to Cairo, not to London
or Brussels. If he came into conflict with the Mahdi, who was very
anti-Egyptian, one of them would be killed. It did not matter much
which one; the other could be dealt with at leisure. It was a very
'sound' plan.

Nobody will ever know just how the Egyptian government and
Sir Evelyn Baring seduced Gordon from his original intention.
Probably it was not very difficult. He had said in his various
interviews with the British Press that he felt that Khartoum should
be held, whatever else was left in the Mahdi's hands; it was a sort of
Shanghai, from which one day a counter-attack could be launched
against the Mahdi, just as the counter-attack on the Heavenly
Kingdom had been launched twenty years before. That may well
have been the starting point of the negotiations, which began
immediately after he had been spirited away from the boat at Port
Said and rushed to Cairo. By the evening of 26 January Gordon had
been convinced that it was unwise to proceed to Suakim, because
the road to Berber was in the hands of the 'rebels'. He had better go
up the Nile to Korosko. His mission had already become quite
different. He wrote to Lord Wolseley:

I leave tonight via Korosko as Governor-General, with the same
instructions [i.e. to evacuate the Sudan] you told me, and as H.M.'s
Ministers did. I go with every confidence and trust in God. . . .
Several ask me, "Do you advise abandonment of the Soudan?" I
answer, "How will you answer these two questions? 1st. Will H.M.'s
Government guarantee future Government of Soudan? 2nd. Will

H.M.'s Government sanction funds from Cairo to go to Soudan to the detriment of the creditors [of the Khedive]?" None can answer these questions in affirmative.

He did not say that the Khedive had asked him to ensure that, after the evacuation of the garrisons, 'proper Government would be established in the Soudan', nor, it must be supposed, did he tell the Khedive that the only 'proper Government' he foresaw in the southern provinces, and maybe more, would be Belgian. He set off, and reached Korosko on 1 February.

At Korosko, Gordon found the garrison in good heart. They seemed unaffected by the gloom cast by the bare hills, burnt by the sun to the colour of cooling lava. The place was, after all, only a day away by boat from the First Cataract, so they felt secure. From Korosko to Abu Hamed was a track through the desert, vast expanses of land, isolated bare ridges and outcrops of volcanic rock, known to the Arabs as Bahr-Bela-Moya, or the Waterless Sea. The whole region as far as Berber seemed at peace; the local tribes were friendly and their sheik, Hussein Pasha Calipha, was officer in command at Berber. Gordon sent gifts to Hussein and received gifts and salaams in return, then rode off along the track through the Waterless Sea, via the oasis at Murat. He enjoyed being on a camel again and noted that the 'cushioned footfall' helped him to think. After six days he was at Abu Hamed. Again he found peace and a garrison in good heart. He wrote: 'All seems hopeful. . . . in a month the whole country will be quiet and the roads open.' He was even optimistic about the Mahdi, though cautious: 'Contagion of that kind cannot be kept out by fortifications and garrisons.' Perhaps there was a diplomatic solution to be found? He told the garrison at Berber that he had come to help the 'infidels' to leave and that in future the whole of the Sudan would be an independent federation of sheikdoms, policed by their own militias. Maybe there would be some foreign guarantor of the federation. They would decide. He urged them to pray for peace.

On 18 February he came in sight of Khartoum. He was glad to see the sprawl of low buildings, the flat-roofed palace which would be his again, and the spires of the two churches. He exchanged his camel for a boat which was waiting for him, and sailed towards the junction of the White and Blue Niles where half the population seemed to be afloat or on the shore to welcome him. They had all suffered under his cruel and incompetent successor and were glad to see him back.

Lytton Strachey, not an immoderate admirer of Gordon, sums it up very well: 'His first acts seemed to show that a new and happy era had begun. Taxes were remitted, the bonds of usurers were destroyed, the victims of Egyptian injustice were set free from the prisons; the immemorial instruments of torture – the stocks and the whips and the branding irons – were broken to pieces in the public square.' As he threw open the prisons on his first day, Gordon addressed the cheering citizens: 'I come without soldiers, but with God on my side, to redress the evils of the Soudan.' *The Times* correspondent wrote home: 'Not a bad day's work.'

Life returned gradually to what it had been during the years of his previous administration. Morning and evening prayers became compulsory for his Egyptian troops, and he held his own services, went to early morning mass at the Italian or Austrian church, and issued a statement to the effect that they all worshipped the same God. After breakfast he would receive petitioners under a banner on which was written in Arabic 'God rules the hearts of all men'. He would hand out rewards and punishments until mid-morning, then tour the city, shops and markets. He would eat a meagre lunch with the troops at the fortifications on the landward side of the city, make plans for the following day with his officers, then return to his palace and his paperwork. He lived in some splendour: his predecessor had spent lavishly to redecorate and refurnish the palace in contrast to the austere Gordon style, and Gordon either did not notice or chose to leave things as they were; the only change he made was to transform the harem into a store for arms and ammunition.

England seemed a long way away. He read with amusement a newspaper report that the Deputy Lord Lieutenant of Pembrokeshire had been heard to say (on reading the headline 'Chinese Gordon for the Soudan'): 'I see the Government have just sent a Chinaman to the Soudan. What can they mean by sending a native of that country to such a place?' Gordon recalled the dreary wastes of Pembrokeshire, relieved only by the company of Drew, and found the wastes of the Upper Nile more attractive.

Over 100 miles away the Mahdi was living in even greater splendour, though in a similar style. He, too, began the day with prayers, some of which he led himself. Then he would sit on a throne outside his silken tent and hand out rewards and punishments. Rewards to the faithful consisted mostly of loot, women of various nationalities, male and female slaves, captured arms and ammunition, horses, camels and gold. Punishments were more drastic than those meted out in the palace in Khartoum. Thieves had their right hands cut off, adulterous men were flogged and adulterous women were stoned to death. Flogging was the usual punishment for drinking alcohol, swearing or disrespect. Blasphemers were hanged, long-haired youths had their heads shaved. All were sinners and their coarse white cotton or linen *jibbehs* bore a coloured patch to remind them of it. Only the Mahdi himself, without sin, was dressed in immaculate white, his turban starched and smelling faintly of rosewater.

The two rivals knew, of course, everything the other was doing. Men left Khartoum every day, swearing they would never have anything to do with the Mahdi, and hastened to report in person on what was happening in the Sudanese capital. Muslim purists, who knew that the Mahdi smoke, drank and fornicated with any woman, married or unmarried, who caught his fancy, found excuses to go to Khartoum to let Gordon's intimates know what was happening in the camp of the Prophet. Both men waited for a word, a conciliatory gesture, a signpost to a road along which they could both travel.

Gordon kept his word to the British government, and evacuated widows, wives, children and men who would not be pressed into what he called euphemistically his Civilian Volunteer Defence Force. They were sent by land across the desert via Abu Hamed, and then down the Nile, arriving, as a Colonel Duncan, MP, said in the House of Commons, 'in an almost perfect state of comfort'. Before they left, they had all volunteered (in the army sense) to give the city of Khartoum 'a scrub up and sweep out'. Two and a half thousand of these 'weaker brethren' were sent out during the first seven weeks after Gordon's arrival. It would have been child's play to keep this escape route open.

As Sir William Butler, then serving in the area, wrote later:

> We held the Nile to Dongola; Korosko was but a day's steaming from the First Cataract; from thence to Abu Hamed the track lay across a desert, which even the Arab cannot permanently live in; put a post of troops at Abu Hamed; hold the single intervening well of Mourat with a small party of loyal Bedouins, and your line of communication is perfect. Assemble one thousand camels at Korosko to follow Gordon with troops and supplies to Abu Hamed; reinforce Berber with another battalion of infantry; hold Abu Hamed with two hundred men, and your work will be done. He will do the rest.

Sir William's advice was good then, and good over half a century later when Wavell was reinforcing his left flank against Marshal Graziani in the Second World War. Had the British government even done just nothing, which was what Gordon expected, a way might have been found to keep the Korosko–Abu Hamed route open. Unfortunately, Sir Samuel Baker had continued to put pressure on the War Office and Foreign Office after Gordon's departure, and his brother, the General, had been authorized – though without proper supplies or reinforcements – to try to open the road from Suakim to the interior. General Baker was ignominiously defeated by the Mahdi's local commander, Osman Digna, who took the fortified towns of Sinkat and Tokar as well. When the news of this defeat reached London the Press let out howls of rage, and the hand of the war party in London and Cairo was immediately strengthened. Sir Gerald Graham, a giant in stature who had met Gordon in Gravesend and been greatly impressed by him, stepped forward and offered to take revenge. He was sent to reinforce Suakim, but sallied forth and won two bloody battles at El-Tab and Tamai, so alienating all the tribes in the area. By so doing he made it impossible for Gordon to hold Abu Hamed and Berber with troops under the command of the local sheiks, who forthwith joined forces with the Mahdi. El-Gordon, said the Mahdi, had obviously come not to send away the infidels and give back independence to the Sudan, but to enslave them all.

Gordon had one more string to his diplomatic bow. Though Gessi had captured and executed Suleiman-bin-Zobeir in July 1879, the boy's father, still under house arrest in Cairo, bore Gordon no ill will. He should be released and sent to reclaim the loyalty of all the tribes in Darfour and Kordofan, the Mahdi's strongholds. It was possible. Old Zobeir was still thought of as a Grand Old Man and the victim only of Egyptian machinations. He would be welcomed home like royalty. What if he *were* a notorious slave trader? Everybody in the Sudan was a slave trader. Gordon asked for Zobeir to be released immediately and sent post haste up the Nile with money, arms and ammunition which would be handed over to him by the Governor-General once they had come to an agreement. Unfortunately, Gordon confided his plan to *The Times* correspondent in Khartoum, who was also the British Consul. This man, Power, was horrified, in both his official capacities. He had heard that Lord Wolseley had put before the Cabinet a proposal that the Sudan be abandoned. What would happen then? Gordon would go to the Congo and leave the Sudan in the hands of this wily old slave trader and the fanatical Mahdi, who between them would usher in a new Dark Age. He sent back to his paper an article couched in these terms, and to the Foreign Office a report. The article immediately aroused the wrath of the

Anti-Slavery Society, and Gladstone was forced to announce in the Commons that Zobeir would not be released and, what is more, Sir Gerald Graham and his troops would be withdrawn. The British government would have nothing to do with any scheme which made it appear to be an agent of aggression or repression.

The British government could not have done anything worse. Aggression and repression had been well known in the Sudan for two thousand years. All the Sudanese asked for was a measure of moderation in both, food and a share of the loot for all. The Mahdi could not believe his luck. Until that point he had been ready to treat with Gordon, maybe to share power, or confine himself to the Arab north Sudan, leaving the Sudanese, Animist, south to go its own way. There is reason to believe that Gordon had even planned a visit to the Mahdi in Kordofan. Now even that would be impossible. Sir Evelyn Baring telegraphed to Lord Granville on 24 March that 'the question now is how to get General Gordon and Colonel Stewart [Gordon's principal aide] away from Khartoum'. Queen Victoria, who was well informed, told Lord Hartington the next day: 'General Gordon is in danger; you are bound to try and save him.'

The biggest obstacle now was General Gordon himself, who had no intention of leaving Khartoum. He was cheerful and confident. He had dealt with foolish governments before – they would see things his way in the end. Since 11 March rebel Arabs had been encamped on the right bank of the Blue Nile, in sight of Khartoum, but there was only desultory firing. The Mahdi had not yet decided either to blockade the city or to attack it; he was busy to the north, besieging Berber. On 8 April Berber surrendered and the cable between Khartoum and Cairo was cut. For Gordon it was almost a relief. There would be no more pointless exchanges with Baring, and Power could not let the cat out of the bag again, poor fellow.

Now he could get on with earthworks, mines, wire entanglements and expeditions of various sort. The situation was not desperate, but there was no time to lose. He had written to his sister that he could go on for quite a time; there was food enough for six months, if they were careful, and there were arms and ammunition a-plenty. With the help of Sheik-el-Mugdi he began to expel disloyal Arabs in his service, and most of the sheiks whom he did not know well. He shot two senior Egyptian officers who had been accused of cowardice by their men. He promoted Nubians and demoted Egyptians as before. As he had the White and Blue Niles on his doorstep, he decided to arm and armour a little fleet of nine paddle steamers and Thames launches, as he had done on the

Yangtse. The fleet was enough of a threat to keep the Nile open for 50 miles, and the sight and sound of it was a great boost to morale.

During his absence, some of his old forts and watchtowers had been allowed to fall into ruins. These works had to be repaired and walls built between them to fortify the whole of the landward side. On the Blue Nile, he fortified Omdurman and threw a temporary bridge from the town to connect it with Khartoum. While he was getting on with all this, he managed to deceive the Mahdi's lookouts by stretching canvas between the watchtowers until he could complete the real earthworks; he had women and old men paint the canvas to make it look like stone. There was not much barbed wire, but he rolled out what he had at the foot of the walls. Gordon himself was everywhere, bullying, cajoling, rewarding, punishing, and joking in French and bad Arabic. He struck medals of his own and held regular investitures. To avoid theft and desertion he printed his own money and declared all other currency invalid. Most of the time he was in good spirits, though occasionally he confided doubts to his diary: 'What holes do I not put myself into? And for what? So mixed are my ideas. I believe ambition put me here in this ruin. . . . However, if I am humbled, the better for me.'

The Mahdi did not know of these doubts, but heard of the high morale of the garrison (8,000 men and fifteen European officers), of the fact that even the Muslim clergy accepted advice on appropriate texts to use in their services, and that most of the traitors and spies had been identified and expelled from the city. He was full of admiration and sent emissaries to Gordon offering him the command of an army, a priesthood, anything. Gordon likened it to the temptation of Our Lord in the desert.

Back in Britain, the Press and public became aware that direct communication with Khartoum had ceased; there were stirring editorials in the newspapers and mass meetings were held in London on 5 and 9 May and in Manchester on 11 May. After the 9 May meeting in Hyde Park Gladstone, who unlike Disraeli had no taste for imperialist adventures, said in the House of Commons: 'There is no military or other danger now threatening Khartoum.' This was so obviously a lie that he was hissed and abused inside and outside the House. He was reminded that the Mahdi had already slaughtered Hicks and his 10,000 men, conquered most of the north and west Sudan and had about 50,000 well-armed men ready to invest Khartoum when he gave the word. The Royal Geographical

Society felt that something should be done, and suggested an expedition from the Congo, in conjunction with the Belgian King, the Queen's cousin and Gordon's erstwhile employer. The philanthropist Baroness Burdett-Coutts launched a general appeal for funds, and there was even a get-together by big game hunters who suggested the formation of a commando force mounted on camels and elephants. Prayers were offered up in the churches ('Is not this what the godly man, the true hero himself would wish to be done?'). Innumerable questions were asked in the House.

Gladstone was very angry. He did not like being called a traitor and a liar. His old friend Archbishop Manning had called him a traitor. The Tory Party, which had first given him a pocket borough, called him a traitor. Now vicars and colonels, Radicals and Imperialists were all accusing him of having betrayed Gordon's trust in him. This was an unjust accusation – Gordon never trusted politicians and had known from the start that Gladstone would never voluntarily lift a finger to help him. Gordon and his friends hoped that Khartoum could be saved in spite of Gladstone, that he would leave the campaign to the Foreign Secretary and the Minister for War, Lord Granville and Lord Hartington, though they had vague orders neither to shed blood nor to spend money.

Gladstone did not know what to do. He did not want the martyrdom of this mad soldier on his political conscience, but on the other hand he did not want him to return to England as a conquering hero, throwing in his lot with the Conservative Party which was pressing for a general election. Above all, as a man who prided himself on having God on his side, Gladstone was irritated by Gordon's religious pretensions. Why, the man had got the British government involved in some sort of bloody religious debate somewhere up the Nile. Gladstone decided to do nothing, ride out the storm and hope that both the Mahdi and Gordon, somehow, would go away.

Many European politicians, then as now, believe that if they can only hold out until the beginning of the school summer holidays no action on any front need be taken until September. But Gladstone had not reckoned with Lord Hartington's conscience. As Lytton Strachey wrote:

> It was not, like Mr Gladstone's, a salamander conscience – an intangible, dangerous creature, that loved to live in the fire; nor was it like Gordon's a restless conscience . . . it was a commonplace affair. Lord Hartington himself would have been disgusted by any mention of it. . . . And yet people seemed to have got it into their

heads that he had some kind of special faculty . . . that there was some peculiar value in his judgement on a question of right and wrong. In public affairs, no less than in private, Lord Hartington's decisions carried an extraordinary weight. The feeling of his idle friends in high society was shared by the great mass of the English people. . . . In Lord Hartington they saw, embodied and glorified, the very qualities which were nearest their hearts. . . . His fondness for field sports gave them a feeling of security; and certainly there could be no nonsense about a man who confessed to two ambitions – to become Prime Minister and win the Derby – and who put the second above the first. They loved him for his casualness – for refusing to make life a cut and dried business – for ramming an official despatch of high importance into his coat pocket, and finding it still there, unopened, at Newmarket several days later. They loved him for his hatred of fine sentiments; they were delighted when they heard that at some function, on a florid speaker's avowing that this was the proudest moment in his life, Lord Hartington had growled in an undertone that "the proudest moment of my life was when my pig won the prize at Skipton Fair". Above all they loved him for being dull.

Lord Hartington had started to become uneasy in mid-May, when the Cabinet seemed to be procrastinating over any plan for the relief of General Gordon. He wrote a letter to his Cabinet colleagues saying so. They ignored it. He approached Gladstone, who was evasive. Throughout June and July, The Derby, The Oaks, the cricket, he worried about the mind and intention of the government of which he formed part. On 31 July he decided that he would resign unless an expedition were organized for the rescue of Gordon in Khartoum.

Gladstone knew that he could ignore Lord Hartington's ruminations but not his resignation. The money for the expedition – £300,000 – which previously could not be found, was now found. Gordon's friend Wolseley was put in charge. Lord Hartington withdrew his resignation. Gladstone was relieved and everybody went on holiday.

Charles George Gordon knew nothing of all this. He did not know that he had been abandoned to his fate by Gladstone at the end of April, though he would not have been surprised. He would have been even less surprised had he known that he had been abandoned to his fate by Sir Evelyn Baring, who had left Cairo for Europe at the end of April to look after his banking interests. Nor did he know that, thanks to Lord Hartington, an attempt was being made to rescue him.

There was all sorts of drilling and training to get on with in Khartoum. This was now directed by Gordon's new right-hand man, Mohammed Ali – Colonel Stewart had been in a state of moral collapse since Gordon had shot the two Egyptian officers for cowardice. Several sorties were made against the Mahdi's troops, and a useful quantity of arms and ammunition was captured. A sort of floating fort was built where a spit of land projects between the Blue and White Niles at low water, the squiggle of sand which gives Khartoum its name, which means 'The Elephant's Trunk'. Camel trains were raided and their food commandeered. The little fleet of armoured launches and paddle steamers sallied forth to shell the enemy camps from time to time and caused havoc, as the slowly rising waters of the Nile forced the Mahdi's troops to move periodically to higher ground; these same rising waters also provided Gordon with a kind of moat which protected most of Khartoum's perimeter.

On the battle of wits and propaganda front things were also going well. The Mahdi, still hoping to win Gordon over, and reassured by the lack of activity in Cairo, had stayed away from what was not yet a siege – as Gordon wrote himself, commenting on the fact that he had been left an escape route, 'the square was always broken'. Gordon and the Mahdi waged a religious war during much of this time. The Governor-General could not print tracts in Arabic as easily as he could print money, but he held meetings with the Muslim religious leaders in the city and had them declare the Mahdi a false prophet. This false prophet infiltrated his own missionaries into Khartoum, and even sent Gordon an appeal to 'give up the world and its vanities, and look for the world to come, for everlasting happiness in Paradise. If you truly desire to come to God and seek to live a godly life . . . come out to accept your everlasting good fortune.' But Gordon was not tempted to put on the *jibbeh* with its patch of sin. He changed his own uniform daily, from Royal Engineers regimentals, to a Turkish field-marshal's full dress uniform, to his own version of the khaki cotton service dress which was to become universal in the British Army. Variously dressed, he harangued his subjects and made public appeals to the Mahdi to lay down his arms and join the Governor-General in prayer and a quest for spiritual satisfaction. It was an ecclesiastical stalemate of indefinite duration.

What brought the exchange of holy writ to an end was a rash excursion by Mohammed Ali. Perhaps over-excited by the confidence that this famous man had placed in him, forgetting what he had been taught about careful reconnaissance, he organized a sortie of his own against an enemy camp, and was ambushed and killed with a thousand men. This misfortune made Gordon realize that his situation was, from a military point of view, precarious. He could not be sure that the British government would try to save him. He knew that he was hopelessly outnumbered. He also knew that as soon as the waters of the Nile began to fall the exchange of religious exhortations would cease and he would be overwhelmed. He decided to evacuate the remaining European civilians. Some, such as the Greek doctor in charge of the hospital, refused to go, as did an Austrian priest. Eighteen Greeks and Italians agreed that there was no point in their staying. Power said he would go with them. Then, Gordon records:

> Herbin, the French Consul asked to be allowed to go. I jumped at his offer. Then Stewart said he would go if I would exonerate him from deserting me. I said you do not desert me. I cannot go, but if you go you do me a great service. I then wrote him an official [letter]. He wanted me to write him an order. I said, no, for though I fear not responsibility, I will not put you in any danger in which I am not myself. I wrote then a letter couched thus: '*Abbas* is going down. You say you are willing to go in her if I think you can do so with honour. You can go in honour, for you can do nothing here, and if you go you do me service in telegraphing my views.'

Late at night on 9 September *Abbas*, Gordon's best boat (it had little draught and was narrow-beamed, and the cataracts were covered with 30–40 feet of water), weighed anchor and slipped downstream. For a short distance it had an escort, to divert the sentries at the enemy camp on shore. There was a brief exchange of shots, then she was gone. Gordon had shaken hands with all on board and said he hoped to see them again in Cairo or Paradise. With the boat went his siege diary to date, and other papers addressed to the Chief of Staff, Sudan Expeditionary Force – though Gordon did not know if such a force existed. That same evening, Lord Wolseley, the Force's Commander-in-Chief, was sitting down to dinner in Cairo, having disembarked at Port Said that afternoon.

Historians have differed, as they have on so many aspects of Gordon's life, as to just why Gordon sent away, at a crucial stage in his joust with the Mahdi, all those on whom he might have been expected to rely. He had just lost the Egyptian who had taken Gessi's place in the command structure, though the assortment of

Nubian Sudanese and Egyptian troops was well disciplined, well trained and totally mesmerized by him. However for most people a little congenial company in the evenings would not have gone amiss – a fellow-national, a fellow-European. A normal man would have liked to have had somebody around, even just to criticize in his own language. The answer is that Gordon was not a normal man, then or ever. He had had his Palm Sunday. There was nothing left but the Crucifixion. As he wrote: 'May our Lord not visit us as a nation for our sins, but may His wrath fall on me, hid in Christ. This is my prayer, and may he spare these people, and bring them to peace.'

Whatever Gordon's motives may have been, and those of his former colleagues who left in the *Abbas*, they will never be known now. On its way through the wilderness of Monassir the boat struck a rock and was got ashore more by good luck than by skilful navigation. Scrambling on to dry land, Colonel Stewart saw some Arabs and naïvely assumed they were friendly. He explained who he was, and what his mission was. Within two hours the crew and passengers of the *Abbas* had been massacred (Egyptian sources claim that Stewart was not killed but only wounded, though he is said to have died in hospital at Gakdul in February 1885). The mass of papers, giving an accurate account of the state of the defences at Khartoum and Gordon's estimate of just how long they could hold out, were taken immediately to the Mahdi. He had the papers listed and a copy of the list sent to Gordon, with a courteous letter. The tone of the letter was that of one municipal librarian writing to another. So Gordon came to know that the boat had not reached Dongola, its destination, and the Mahdi that a relief expedition was being mounted.

When Gordon heard of the *Abbas* disaster, he wrote in his diary: 'If *Abbas* was captured by treachery, then I am not to blame. Neither am I to blame if she struck a rock, for she drew under two feet of water and fifty boats used to go down yearly to Cairo with high Nile; if they were attacked and overpowered, then I am to blame for I ought to have foreseen the chance and prevented their going.' He speculated on the likelihood of treachery by the Arab captain or *ries* (rais: chieftain). In the end, he assumed it was a judgement for his too hasty execution of the two officers whom he had shot for cowardice: 'I look on it as being a Nemesis on the death of the two Pachas.' He seems to have had some doubts at this time about the legitimacy of his position, and indeed of any 'relief expedition'. Nearly all the Sudanese sheiks had joined the Mahdi; Sheiks El-Obeid and Negumi, two of the most important, were now in command of the Mahdi's forces a few miles away from Khartoum. Whether they were right or wrong to do so was another matter, but he had been sent to Khartoum to evacuate British nationals and hand over the government to the local authorities, which meant those same sheiks. On 12 September he wrote: 'Note that I do not call our enemies "rebels" but Arabs, for it is a vexed question if we are not rebels since I hold the Firman restoring the Soudan to its chiefs.'

Legitimate or not, the relief expedition was on its way. The first battalion of infantry got to Dongola on 15 September and news of its rumoured arrival reached him, smuggled in by methods unknown, two days later. He was sceptical about the size and motivation of the force: 'I have the strongest suspicion that these tales of troops at Dongola and Meroe are all gasworks and that if you wanted to find Her Majesty's forces you would have to go to Shepeards Hotel in Cairo.' He was right to be sceptical, and the Mahdi was right not to be alarmed. The infantry battalion was immobile because the boats which were to move it up the Nile were just being offloaded at Alexandria, and the main body of troops had not yet left England. But he did not despair, though two-thirds of the population had fled and only half the rest was reliable. He wrote:

> During our blockade we have often discussed the question of being frightened, which in the world's view a man should never be. For my part I am always frightened and very much so. It is not the fear of death, that is past, thank God, but I fear defeat and its consequences. I do not believe a bit in the calm, unmoved man. I think it is only that he does not show it outwardly. Thence I conclude that no commander of forces ought to live closely in relation with his subordinates, who watch him like lynxes, for there is no contagion equal to that of fear. I have been rendered furious when from anxiety I could not eat, I would find those at the same table were in like manner affected.

But he knew that he had learnt to set a good example and kept his followers in stout heart: 'As for all that may be said as to why I did not escape with Stewart, it is simply because the people would not have been such fools as to let me go; so there is an end of these "greatcoats of self sacrifice" etc.'

Not all his journal was full of noble thoughts. There were very funny caricatures, too: Lord Granville, the Foreign Secretary, was shown reading *The Times* at his seat, Walmer Castle, startled to find that Khartoum had not yet fallen: 'Why HE [Gordon] said distinctly he could only hold out six months, and that was in March (counts the months). August! why he ought to have given in! What is to be done? They'll be howling for an expedition. . . . ' Sir Evelyn Baring was the hero of several comic strips, dribbling hypocrisy. Gladstone was there, too, chopping down trees at Hawarden Castle, pacifying Ireland, wearing his peculiar shirt collars and carrying his bulging bag. The journal also contains some snide swipes at the Woolwich curriculum: 'I think if instead of Minor Tactics or books on the art of war we were to make our young officers study Plutarch's *Lives* [he had had a copy given to him by Gessi] it would be better; there we see men (unsupported by any true belief – pure pagans) making as a matter of course their lives a sacrifice, but in our days it is our highest merit not to run away.'

By the end of September he had confirmation that something was happening at Dongola; he would have been upset, if not surprised, to read a letter home by an officer who noted: 'The expedition is planted and taking root here . . . there is nothing but confusion.' Gordon decided to send four of his armoured steamers still in commission downstream to El-Metemmah to meet the Expeditionary Force. With their experienced captains, they would advise the force's commander on how best to navigate the Nile and sidestep the Mahdi's hordes. He was reluctant to lose such a large part of his 'navy', valuing each boat at 2,000 soldiers in terms of firepower and nuisance, but he felt he had to make a gesture. Something had to be *done*. Messages a-plenty had been sent before the cable was cut, and he had continued to smuggle out carefully worded reports even after the wreck of the *Abbas*, but unlike Baring he was not 'preparing a great statistical work or using information for literary purposes'. Not knowing that Baring was absent from Egypt, he wondered what he was doing with all the facts and figures he had said should flow incessantly down the Nile: '[Baring] is like a man on the bank, having seen his friend in a river already bobbed down two or three times, who hails "I say, old fellow, let us know when to throw you the lifebuoy. I know you have bobbed down two or three times, but it is a pity to throw you the lifebuoy until you are in extremis, and I want to know exactly." '

The Mahdi was pleased to hear of the departure of the navy, and even more pleased when there was no sign of its return. On 21 October, the Muslim New Year (1302), he decided that the moment had come to take personal command of his forces in front of Khartoum. Gordon saw and heard him arrive. He heard the *onbeia* (elephant's tusk trumpet) and the *nahas* (war drums) and saw the red, black and green flags waving above the 40,000 or so troops pitching their tents just out of firing range. The Mahdi sent him a polite invitation to surrender. Gordon replied: 'Tell the Mahdi that it is all one to me whether he has captured 20,000 steamers like the *Abbas* or 20,000 officers like Stewart Pacha. I hope to see the newly arrived English, but if Mahomet Achmet says the English die it is all the same to me. I am here like iron.'

The Mahdi acknowledged the message calmly and settled down to wait for the waters of the Nile to fall. Had he known, he would have been relieved to learn that there was no feeling of urgency among the leaders of the relief force or its political masters in London and Cairo. There were even railway enthusiasts who thought there would be time to build a line between Suakim and Berber, and contracts were signed for the exploratory work. Royal Engineer officers were sent to Suakim to see if it were feasible to pump water from the coast 100 miles inland and 3,500 feet above sea level to the heights at Berber; they reported that it was possible, but that the cost was prohibitive and anyway the water boiled in the pipes after 4 miles. After this and sundry other futile experiments, Lord Wolseley decided to concentrate on a Nile expedition, and slowly the military machine began to rattle and move.

On 2 November Gordon made one of his regular surprise checks of arms, ammunition and supplies and discovered a hoard of grain put by against the event of a forced sale by one of his 'loyal citizens'. He had written on 24 October that 'if they do not come before 30th November, the game is up, and Rule Britannia'. Things now looked a bit better. He could hold out for another six weeks before 'the sponge must be thrown up'. On 3 November he had more good news. One of his steamers got through from Shendy with a letter from Lord Wolseley dated 14 October – Wolseley would set off from Dongola on 1 November. So he was on his way! There was also a note in cipher from Major (later Field-Marshal Lord) Kitchener, the Intelligence Officer, but the key had been lost with Stewart; Kitchener earned a caricature in the journal.

On 12 November the Mahdi ordered an attack on the two remaining steamers at Khartoum, the *Ismailia* and a Thames launch named the *Hussineyeh*. He had brought up some captured artillery and hired some gunners. On the morning of the thirteenth the *Hussineyeh* had been hit so hard that she had to be grounded to avoid sinking. Gordon watched the last moments:

I saw that poor little beast, the *Hussineyeh* fall back, stern foremost, under a terrific fire of breech loaders. I saw a shell strike the water at her bows; I saw her stop and puff off steam, and then I gave the

171

glass to my boy, sickened unto death. . . . My boy (he is thirty) said: *'Hussineyeh* is sick'. I knew it but said quietly, 'Go down and telegraph to Mogrim [the outpost at Omdurman], Is *Hussineyeh* sick?'

This disaster provoked a new wave of pessimism in the garrison, and Gordon noted: 'There is not one person on whom I can rely. . . . Nearly every order, except when it is for their interest, has to be repeated two, or even three times. I may truly say I am weary of my life; day and night, night and day, it is one continual worry.'

His morale was up again on the fourteenth, when he made some calculations and worked out that even shooting off 40,000 rounds a day – and he liked to make 'a noisy show' – he had shells and cartridges for another seven weeks. 'I feel quite indifferent for if not relieved within a month our food supply fails, and I like to go down with our colours flying.'

As the level of the Nile fell, the Mahdi moved in closer, ready to ford, cutting off communication by the temporary bridge with Omdurman and making it difficult for what was left of the 'navy', the *Ismailia*, to patrol the river forks. One of his last tricks in the game of psychological warfare he was waging with Gordon was to bring up European prisoners into the siege area, or try to make his rival believe they were there as hostages. One of the provincial governors, the Austrian Slatin, had been converted to Islam, probably to save his life, and wrote pathetic letters to Gordon begging for 'peace'. He was, of course, ignored. Gessi might have set aside his British nationality, but he had been punished for that materially. To give up the Lord for Satan was unforgivable. But was Hemmings (Emin Pasha) out there? And Lupton? It was impossible to be sure. What of the philosopher Ernest Renan, whom he had met at the Royal Geographical Society's rooms? He had said he was off to Africa, would never be seen in Europe again – 'If he comes to the lines and it is Renan, I shall go and see him, for whatever one may think of his unbelief in Our Lord, he certainly dared to say what he thought and he has not changed his creed to save his life.' And what about Oliver Pain? Rumour had it that he had been buried alive in the desert. Could that be true?

On 22 November he was still faintly optimistic, and thinking on paper about what he would do 'if the expedition comes here before the place falls (which is doubtful) and if the instructions are to evacuate the place at once and leave Massala and Sennaar etc., I will resign and have nothing more to do with the government of the place or of the Soudan, and this I have a perfect right to do, and no one, not even the Soudan troops or people, would say one word'. He would keep steam up in the *Ismailia* and withdraw upstream, ideally taking the southern provinces with him into the Congo. Three days later, he heard that the relief expedition was still at Ambukol, 200 miles away, and with the Bayuda scrub and desert to cross; however, he posted a proclamation to the effect that assistance was at hand and even struck a new medal for siege veterans.

By the beginning of December the bad news began to seem weightier than the good. There was still plenty of food (dull but adequate), arms and ammunition for the 14,000 people still in Khartoum. But the rate of desertion was increasing. He had only Sudanese Nubian troops left now, and they did not like the *dhurra* flour and biscuits; they were not as good shots, anyway, as the Arabs who had joined the Mahdi. To Augusta he wrote: 'This may be the last letter you will receive from me, for we are on our last legs, owing to the delay of the expedition. However, God rules us all, and, as He will rule to His glory and our welfare, His will be done. I fear, owing to circumstances, that my affairs are pecunarily not over bright.' He was, in fact, more worried about his finances and Augusta's future than about the likelihood of being killed. Since his days at Gravesend he had always given away most of his money. Sir William Butler records:

> When Gordon accepted the Soudan mission in January, 1884, he had no money. He had, in fact, to borrow a few pounds from the King of the Belgians in order to come to London after the receipt of Lord Wolseley's telegram. When Gordon came out from his interview with the Ministers, the fact of his poverty was discovered by Lord Wolseley putting the direct question to him, 'Have you any money?'. It was then after bank hours, and as Gordon was to leave for the Soudan at 8 p.m. there was not much time to procure a requisite sum. Borrowing ten or twenty pounds here and there, Lord Wolseley got together two hundred pounds in a bag, which he handed to Gordon as the train was about to start from Charing Cross. Eight days later Gordon met at Ismailia an old Soudan servant – one Mohamed Tuhami – who had formerly been his secretary at Khartoum but was now old, blind and in poverty. He gave this man one hundred pounds from the bag, and passed on to Cairo. Between that day and December 14th he increased this debt of two hundred pounds to eighteen hundred and thirty-six pounds, which he owed to the Foreign Office, and to a further sum of two thousand one hundred pounds due to Cairo.

Gordon also owed the King of the Belgians £570. He asked Lord

Wolseley to settle these debts and 'as it seems impossible we shall meet again in this world, I would ask you to see that my family do not lose by my death'.

On 14 December Gordon wrote the last page of his journal. Those in the city with whom he was on friendly terms were summoned to the palace and told they could send last messages out on the *Bordeen* (the Nile steamer which had rescued Gessi). The Mahdi had let it be known that he would let the *Bordeen* through, but that it would be the last. From this day on conditions rapidly deteriorated. With the taking of Omdurman, the square was now finally closed and the siege complete. All food was rationed and the rations got smaller every day. An account by one of the besieged reads: 'Soon actual starvation will begin; everything that can keep the light of life flickering a little longer in these wretched frames is tried – rats and mice, the leather of boots, the straps and plaited strips of native bedsteads, gum of mimosa, the inner fibre of the palm tree, have all been eagerly devoured.'

Gordon prepared for his last Christmas on earth by lighting huge candelabra in the palace windows in spite of the fusillades they attracted. He was heard singing Christmas carols in a cracked voice. He told Bordeini Bey, a half-Italian, half-Egyptian merchant whom he had known for years, and who was to survive the massacre: 'When God was portioning out fear to all the people in the world, at last it came to my turn, and there was no fear left to give me. Go tell all the people in Khartoum that Gordon fears nothing, for God has created him without fear.'

Nobody believed this, least of all Gordon, but such was his ascendancy that nearly 10,000 men kept him company during those last hopeless days. The Omdurman bridge was destroyed on 5 January 1885. There was now only one approach on foot.

A week later, the relief force had crossed the first part of the Bayuda and was halfway to El-Metemmah. Unfortunately, the desert march had been taken at such a pace that at Gakdul the camels were exhausted and had to be rested for sixty hours. On 14 January the column moved off again and fought the Mahdi's troops garrisoning Abu Klea, defeating them. Another defeat was inflicted on the nineteenth at Gobat near El-Metemmah and on the evening of the twentieth the whole force, victorious and in great spirits, was only 3 miles south of El-Metemmah. They could see Gordon's four armoured steamers, waiting patiently as they had been doing for 112 days.

Here another mystery, not yet solved, presents itself. Lord Wolseley had given orders that as soon as the troops in this first column, over a thousand in number, got to the Nile at El-Metemmah they were to sieze anything which was floating and get up the river from Gobat to Khartoum at full speed. A senior naval officer had been sent with the column, together with a cadre of sailors, in case any repairs or nautical manoeuvres had to be made. This naval officer found the four steamers in perfect condition, with trained crews anxious only to weigh anchor. Why did he wait for three days – three days which turned out to be fatal for Gordon and his garrison? Sir Herbert Stewart, who had started out in command of the force, had been killed on the nineteenth, but Sir Charles Wilson had been ready to take over. Could a simple change of command on the field have slowed down the embarkation? Were there quarrels about who should fly which flag on the leading steamer? Was there that curious mixture of ill-will and bungling at El-Metemmah as well as in London and Cairo? Did a boiler blow up – a *post facto* excuse? Nobody knows, for the *Daily Telegraph* and *Standard* correspondents, Herbert and Cameron, had both been killed at Gobat. All that is certain is that the expedition did not sail until late in the afternoon on 23 January. By that time the Mahdi had already seen that the Nile was shallow enough to cross, so that he could attack the city on all sides simultaneously. He gave orders to prepare for an assault before dawn on the twenty-sixth.

There was no way the assault could be resisted. The Nile had fallen far enough to expose even the lines of barbed wire at the Bourré and Messalamieh gates. The moat was dry. According to the few survivors, 'ten thousand howling dervishes', eager to take revenge for Abu Klea and El-Metemmah, poured through the gates and killed everyone in sight. There are several versions of Gordon's death. According to one he finished his last cigarette, then walked to the head of the main staircase in a freshly pressed white uniform and red fez. He had filled the cellars of the palace with explosive and was about to ignite it electrically when one of the Mahdi's generals transfixed him with a spear, then cut off his head. Another version has it that Gordon fought it out on the walls, with pistols and sword, killing a score of Arabs before he died.

The most likely version is that he had, indeed, mined the palace and set a slow fuse at dawn. Then he heard the yells of the Arabs as they swarmed over the ramparts, meeting only feeble resistance from the half-starved garrison. As the sun rose, the whole town was in their possession and the palace compound surrounded. According to one survivor, the Austrian priest, who told the story to Sir William Butler:

> Gordon left the palace and moved at the head of a small party of soldiers and servants, towards the Church of the Austrian Mission. . . . Walking a few yards in advance of his party, Gordon drew near the church. The short and mysterious dawn of the desert was passing into broader day – over the palm trees on the edge of the Blue Nile the eastern sky was flushed with the red of the coming sun. From the lost town, still lying in shadow to the right, the shouts of a victorious enemy and the cries of a perishing people rose in a deeper volume of sound. . . . Before the little band had crossed the open space between the palace and the church, a body of Arabs issued from a neighbouring street. For a moment the two parties stood almost face to face, then a volley of musketry flashed out at close range, in the yet uncertain light, and the bravest and noblest soldier of our time was no more.

Sir William adds: 'Thus fell in dark hour of defeat, a man as unselfish as Sidney, of courage dauntless as Wolfe, of honour stainless as Outram, of sympathy wide reaching as Drummond, of honesty straightforward as Napier, of faith steadfast as More.'

Gordon himself would have put it more simply. He had resolved not to be taken alive. He was not taken alive.

TEN

Too Late

Too late! Too late to save him.
In vain, in vain they tried.
His life was England's glory.
His death was England's pride.
  Popular song commemorating Gordon's death, 1885

At noon on 28 January 1885 Sir Charles Wilson's convoy came into sight of Khartoum, at the north end of the island of Tuti. The Blue and White Niles, as yet unjoined, flowed sluggishly downstream. A few corpses floated by. No flag was flying on the staff on the flat roof of the Governor-General's palace. Instead of a welcome from the beleaguered garrison, Sir Charles and his troops were fired on from all sides by the Mahdi's dervishes, waving their battle flags and screaming in triumph. The relief expedition was too late.

Too late! That was the burden of the popular songs, of the newspaper headlines, of the cartoon captions in *Punch*. The government tried to hold back information, but by the morning of Thursday 5 February the news of the fall of Khartoum had reached London: 'General Gordon's fate uncertain'. Next day the fate of the hero was certain. A government Blue Book was published 'proving' that nobody was to blame. A rival 'Egyptian Red Book' came out, proving the opposite. Gladstone was portrayed marching with his Cabinet, in the manner of the Salvation Army, playing various instruments and wearing buttonhole badges saying: 'Too late'.

The political consequences for Gladstone were disastrous. It is certain that Queen Victoria was genuinely distressed by Gordon's death – 'Would you express to your other sisters and elder Brother', she wrote to Augusta, 'my true sympathy, and what I do so keenly feel, the *stain* left upon England, for your dear Brother's cruel, though heroic fate.' It is equally certain, however, that she was glad to have an opportunity to attack her old enemy: in her diary she wrote that 'the Government alone is to blame', and this was what she said in an uncoded wire to her Prime Minister, hinting that he should resign. It was an unheard of and unconstitutional thing to do. Victoria even took the equally unconstitutional step of passing state papers secretly to Lord Salisbury and the Conservatives, thus hastening Gladstone's final fall from power. In fact, the Liberal government fell later that year in spite of his protests – 'The Prime Minister is not altogether able to follow the conclusion which Your Majesty has been pleased thus to announce' – and though re-elected in February 1886 he survived only until July. When he returned to power in 1892 he was so harassed that he retired from politics altogether the following year.

Other nations rejoiced at the tragedy. Russia immediately made threatening noises about the 'liberation' of Afghanistan, and war was only just avoided. The poet Rimbaud, on business at Harrar in present-day Ethiopia, summed up the French attitude: *'C'est justement les Anglais avec leur absurde politique qui minent désormais le commerce de toutes ces côtes. Ils ont voulu tout remanier et ils sont arrivés à faire pire que les Egyptiens et les Turcs, ruinés par eux. Leur Gordon est un idiot, leur Wolseley un âne, et toutes leurs entreprises une suite insensée d'absurdités et de déprédations.'* (It is in fact the English with their absurd policies who ruin all business around here. They wanted to put their hands on everything and have ended up worse than the Egyptians and Turks they ruined. Their Gordon is an idiot, their Wolseley an ass, and all their enterprises are a senseless sequence of foolishness and depradation.) The French government tried to take advantage of this supposed foolishness by occupying formally vast tracts of land in West, Central and North Africa, though this only provoked successive British governments into reluctantly colonizing the Gold Coast and Nigeria and reinforcing the trading stations in the Gambia and Sierra Leone. The Germans and the Belgians pushed ahead with their plans to colonize Central Africa, with some success, but again only provoked a British reinforcement of existing interests in East and South Africa. So Gladstone's reluctance to strike an imperialist pose only turned the middle classes, and the partly enfranchised working classes, into imperialists and jingoists ready to cheer the unfurling of the Union flag anywhere on the globe. The Russians, after being discouraged in Afghanistan, turned their attention to the Far East.

King Leopold II of the Belgians was probably just as upset as Queen Victoria at the death of a man who was not only formally on leave from his service, but also one for whom Leopold had an immense regard. The King of the Belgians was a much caricatured man, accused of having helped himself to the fortunes of his sister and his daughters; he always said he merely managed their affairs and made them richer, but he certainly did not allow them to live in royal style. It was said that he was a petty dictator, but when some papers blew off his desk one day and a minister sprang to pick them up, he pointed to his heir, Albert, made him collect the papers and commented: 'A constitutional monarch must learn to stoop.' Had Gordon not been killed, Leopold might well have carried through his plan, with Stanley, to develop the Congo and 'get all nations to join in a philanthropic organisation under his own presidency dedicated to freeing the Congolese from slavers'. But he needed Gordon's prestige and ability. When he lost them, he created the Congo Free State, a sort of private protectorate, out of which he made another fortune and later earned the opprobrium of the world for what, with or without his knowledge, went on up the Congo.

Gordon would not have been surprised by the Casement Report in 1901, which described Leopold's savage exploitation of the natives in the Congo and resulted in Belgium taking over the Congo as a colony, nor by what happened there later in the twentieth century. He always believed that Great Britain had the only genuine civilizing mission. He would have been pleased to know that Queen Victoria received the Zulu chief Cetewayo after his submission and treated him kindly, as she did the Maori chiefs. The Colonial and Indian Exhibition of 1886, with its attendant natives, stirred public opinion and made it a little less racist. After his bitter experience in Basutoland, he would not have been surprised by the insensitivity and mismanagement which drove the Boers to rebellion at the turn of the century.

He would have been surprised by the rapidity of the decline and fall of the British Empire, with the possible exception of India; he had seen enough of senseless luxury in his very short time in Bombay to be able to reason that a people so oppressed and exploited would become ungovernable again. He never liked intellectuals, especially well-meaning ones, but he would have been startled by the ease with which the Empire was sabotaged from inside by Fabians and their friends who believed that Africans, Asians, even Solomon Islanders, really wanted independence and parliamentary democracy. He would not have been surprised when military dictatorships were established almost everywhere a few years after the Union flag was taken down. Nobody took any notice of Gordon's wise advice that natives had to be either sincerely befriended or 'smashed', but if governed justly would prefer foreigners in their palaces to corrupt and inefficient fellow-countrymen. So an Empire acquired almost by accident and certainly without much enthusiasm, though at the cost of many lives, was handed back to the fanatics, the bigots, the slave traders, in some cases the cannibals.

China, which Gordon liked more than any other country in which he served, came off rather better than most. The Empire fell in 1912 and an ideologically new sort of Heavenly Kingdom took its place, a kingdom which became a politically wise and industrious new China. Two other generals, Marshall and MacArthur, advised the United States government of the day that Mao Tse-Tung, the new Heavenly King, would defeat Chiang Kai-Shek, but their advice was ignored, too. Gordon would have admired the razor's-edge diplomacy which re-established friendly relations between the United States and China, and which has kept the People's Republic out of a war with Russia, a war which he advised would inevitably be disastrous. He never knew anything of Japan, hardly awake in his day. He would not have been surprised to find Russia transformed from being the mainspring of a Tsarist Empire to become the mainspring of a Soviet Empire; further territorial aggrandizement had been predicted to him by Colonel Khleb in the 1850s.

And what of the Middle East, where he spent most of his active life? The shadows of coming events which fell on Gordon proved to have substance. The Turkish Empire did disintegrate, though Gordon, who had a low opinion of all Turks, did not foresee a Kemal Ataturk, a national renaissance, albeit short-lived. Egypt went on being a British protectorate even if nominally independent from 1922, and even if the Khedive changed his title to King. The fall of the monarchy after the withdrawal of British troops in 1952 would not have come as a surprise, though the nationalization of the Suez Canal would have pleased the old Governor-General, as 'the bankers and merchants were swept away'. He would have been ironical about the failed British, French and Israeli invasion – too late! He would have disapproved of the Balkanization of Syria–Lebanon–Palestine, even after French and British tutelage. He would have opposed the establishment of the State of Israel, not because he was vaguely anti-semitic but because he would have seen that to add yet another militant creed to the pot would make it boil over.

180

It was the Arabs (not including Egyptians, whom many people do not think of as 'proper Arabs') whom he always felt were on the brink of a great religious revival, though he knew all about the tensions between Shiite and Suny Muslims, and that a theocracy in power in Iran made war with Iraq and civil war in the Lebanon inevitable, as inevitable as the 300-year-old civil war in Ireland. He knew, in 1885, that disenchantment with Christian capitalist values was complete, and he would have been mildly amused when the oil sheiks held the industrial world to ransom. Oil-derived wealth will not abolish repression and aggression as poverty is being abolished. The reverse is true. Islam will become more fundamentalist, as Gordon believed Christianity was destined to become again – Early Church fundamentalism rather than Puritan fundamentalism. He would have approved of Pope John Paul II, the prophet of ecclesiastical co-existence within a strong Christian union. Maybe even his tracts would have had a wider circulation at the end of the twentieth century, though they were unread in his day. Major-General Emma Davies of the Salvation Army once commented that Gordon had always been an inspirational figure for General Booth and his successors, an inspiration in thought and good works.

As for the Sudan, where Africa meets the Arab world, he would have been sorry to learn that the Mahdi survived him by only six months, without having been 'given his chance'. He would have said it was a Nemesis, because the Mahdi had spiked his head on a tree and used it for target practice – not a gentlemanly way to treat an enemy or even part of an enemy. He knew the Mahdi's successor, the Caliph Abdullah, and did not like him, so he would not have been surprised to learn that the Sudan returned to slave trading. In 1897 Kitchener, the Intelligence major in Cairo in Gordon's last days, mowed down Abdullah and his troops with the new machine guns; Lytton Strachey comments: 'At any rate, it had all ended very happily – in a glorious slaughter of 20,000 Arabs, a vast addition to the British Empire and a step in the Peerage for Sir Evelyn Baring.' But the so-called Anglo-Egyptian Condominium of the Sudan was never quiet. In neighbouring Libya, Italian after 1912, a new Prophet, Omar-el-Muktar, became head of a religious community at El-Gsur and disturbed the peace from 1880 to 1931, when he was hanged by Marshal Graziani on Mussolini's behalf. Soon after independence in 1955, the Sudan again began to murmur with religious discontent, which was later fermented by the rise of Ghaddafi in Libya and Khomeini in Iran. Gordon, who had much in common with Rodolfo Graziani and was much admired by him, would have advised the 'smashing' of them all if they would not unite and channel their fervour into peace and prayer instead of holy war. The Sudan in the 1980s is fundamentalist again.

Had he lived, would Gordon have been consulted about Middle Eastern policy? Would he have become a peer, perhaps have been charged with Army reform and so saved millions of British lives?

It is pointless to speculate further – more fruitful, perhaps, to ask whether or not Gordon really wanted to be rescued. Is it not possible that he wanted to die as he did, in a sort of holy war?

There is no doubt at all that he could have escaped until almost the last moment. The Mahdi did not want to kill him. As Slatin Pasha wrote afterwards, hope was never lost that the Governor-General would be converted, like Slatin himself, and together Gordon and the Mahdi would conquer and rule all Central Africa in the name of Allah. This was never possible, but then hope and possibility are always strangers to each other. Though the exact place and manner of his death are unclear, most accounts have it that Gordon made no attempt to defend himself and virtually walked on to a dervish's spear. What did go through his mind during that last month in Khartoum, surely the only month of his life not chronicled by him in detail? Some authors have hinted that he went mad, and point to signs of megalomania during the latter part of the siege – striking medals of his own, printing money with his own signature on the notes, dressing up in different uniforms, singing hymns on the battlements. Perhaps he was setting the scene for his death, a heroic death to make up for the wretched slide of his grandfather, William Augustus, from hero of the Heights of Abraham to rejected Barrack Master at Exeter.

Whether he was mad or not, he was certainly a frustrated and disappointed man. In *Gordon: Martyr and Misfit* Anthony Nutting, a former Foreign Office Minister, contended that 'his whole life was one continuous conflict between an innate idealism and an iron discipline'. He was certainly not an 'oily diplomat' and would not have got through the selection procedures for the Foreign Office. But then these procedures have come into disrepute lately, as a number of 'oily diplomats' have turned out to be sexual deviants or traitors or both. Again, he was an expert and the Foreign Office does not like experts; it is still standard procedure to move diplomats around so that they never gain deep, expert knowledge of any one country and so do not embarrass their unashamedly ignorant colleagues. If Gordon felt he was a misfit, and this is doubtful, it was because successive Foreign Secretaries made him feel that he did not belong in the councils of state. There was certainly no conflict between 'innate idealism and an iron discipline'; an iron discipline was one of his ideals.

The Army had treated him very badly, the Royal Engineers even worse, and he certainly resented it. In Gordon's day there was a distinction between army and regimental ranks. The Army was more or less compelled to promote him rapidly, if only because he was a high-ranking officer in other armies, though he never reached his father's rank and was taken off the Active List at the age of forty-nine. A more active man in that limbo would have been hard to find. The Royal Engineers had other ways of showing their disapproval, envy and hatred. They slowed down his promotion until it looked absurd. He was promoted to army major on 30 December 1862, but he remained a captain of Engineers until 5 July 1872, and he was never promoted beyond lieutenant-colonel (1 October 1877) RE. This was a subtle way of making him difficult to place, at home or abroad, and virtually ensured that he would become a soldier of fortune. The very phrase 'soldier of fortune' had been anathema to his father.

At the end Gordon had been made to feel old and unwanted. True, he had a job, as whatever he liked to call himself in the Congo, but that would be working for a foreigner, too. He did not share the general opinion of Leopold, which thought him only greedy and ambitious, and had been the recipient of many kindnesses from him. The King flattered him, gave him money, and kept his doors always open to a man whom he wanted in his service more than any other.

And, undoubtedly, he missed Romolo Gessi. For over a quarter of a century this shrewd, brave extrovert had been coming in and out of Gordon's life, cheering him up, shocking him sometimes, occasionally out-soldiering him. There could have been no greater contrast than that of Gessi with Gordon's first great friend, Drew of the 11th, nor between the Gordon household and that of the Gessis in Bucharest. In so far as Gordon was able to relax, it was because he had been taught by Gessi to do so. And, of course, he owed his reputation as the pacifier of the Sudan in part to this former Garibaldino.

Maybe he felt he had just lived too long and ought to be forgotten. He would have been astonished to learn that after his death, suicide or martyrdom, he became a cult figure, the pure and perfect hero, *chevalier sans peur et sans reproche*. Books were written about him, odes were dedicated to him, statues put up, stained glass windows subscribed for. Boys' homes were set up and named after him and a new generation of 'Wangs' was trained in piety and put into useful jobs. He was an example to all, and after Kitchener's victory at Omdurman in 1898 a memorial service was held even in Khartoum, at which a band of Sudanese buglers blew 'Abide with Me'. A Gordon College was set up in the Sudanese capital. £20,000 was settled on his family, on Augusta and her surviving elder brother and three sisters.

But time passes, and officialdom has always wanted to forget Charles George Gordon. In Southampton, the family home for so many years, there are roads named after Omdurman and Khartoum, but the only Gordon Avenue bears the name of a speculative builder who was no relative. A memorial (by two well-known local gravestone carvers, Garret and Haysom) stands in Queens Park, facing the entrances to the Eastern Docks; it is undistinguished, to say the least, consisting of a mound surmounted by four columns of Aberdeen granite on a marble base, a floriated capital and cross. There is a plaque on the front of 5 Rockstone Place which reads: 'In this house lived the hero of Khartoum. General Charles George Gordon. Chinese Gordon. B.1833. D.1885.' The last member of the family to live there, a niece, Mrs Moffitt, died there in 1919, and 'the Remaining Capital Old Fashioned Furniture, Books, Indian and Chinese ornaments' were sold off by public auction. From 1888 to 1938 there was a Southampton Gordon Boys' Brigade, but only the foundation stone survives at 6 Ogle Road, with the motto *Semper Fidelis*. There is nothing more to remind visitors that for thirty years on and off this 'soldier, administrator, philanthropist' lived in the city.

Gravesend retains a few official traces still. There is a statue in Fort Gardens, a Gordon Promenade, a Gordon School and a Gordon Mission Church. There are some publications in the libraries, especially in the Gravesham Local Collection, and there is a three-page local history pamphlet about him, published in May 1983, in addition to a mention in *The Gravesend Forts* of November 1982. The people of Gravesend seem to have been affected *en masse* by his death. Augusta wrote a Preface to a little anthology of poignant memories compiled by an RE clerk there. A lady of fashion recalls that, for an attack of *ennui*, Gordon prescribed a 'good long day's washing'. An RE chaplain names Gordon's two most prized books after the Bible: Hall's *Christ Mystical* ('Read prayerfully') and Hill's *Deep Things of God*. Men and women from Peppercroft Street and the slums of Passenger Court and Pump Alley, distinguished citizens and occupants of the workhouse infirmary, all recalled 'his sense of humour, hatred of deceit, deep humility, love of humanity and hatred of Pharisaism'. One of his lads reminded readers of the slogan 'God bless the Kernel' once whitewashed on the walls of the Fort.

The Foreign Office and the Ministry of Defence (War Office) do not welcome inquiries about this awkward hero, though the Royal Military Academy Sandhurst has the Registers and Muster Rolls on which the family appears, and the Royal Engineers at Chatham are helpful to those who are interested. There is one remaining Gordon Boys' School, at Woking, and it has a good museum. Romolo Gessi does not figure in any UK collection, though the Biblioteca Classense in Ravenna has its Gordon niche. The Royal Geographical Society remembers its former Fellow with affection and keeps his letters, to Sir Samuel Baker and others, and some beautifully drawn maps. The Public Record Office at Kew has the rest of the maps.

All that is left of the corporeal man is somewhere in the desert of the Sudan – in two places in fact. The last attempt to find his remains was made in 1909 when officers of the Camel Corps proposed a Nile Expedition to locate them and bring them home.

The official oblivion to which he has been confined would not have surprised or displeased this admirable man. His soul is no doubt content to know that his body is part of the sands of the Nile. Had it been found soon after his death he would have had, by royal command, a state funeral to rival that of Sir Winston Churchill many years later. That would really have upset him.

Select Bibliography

Allen, Bernard M., *Gordon and the Sudan* (Macmillan, 1931).

Allen, C. H., *The Life of Chinese Gordon* (Kingdon, 1884).

Arfelli, Felice, *Romolo Gessi alla Navigazione del Lago Alberto* (L'Oltremare, 1933).

Avelardi, Arture, *Romolo Gessi Pascia nel Sudan Niliaco* (Paravia, 1932).

Barnes, Rev. R. H., *Charles Gordon: A Sketch* (Macmillan, 1885).

Bennett, D. A., *A Handbook of Kent's Defences* (KDRC, 1972).

Blunt, W. S., *Gordon at Khartoum* (London, 1886).

Boulger, D. C., *The Life of General Gordon* (Unwin, 1897).
General Gordon's Letters from the Crimea, the Danube and Armenia 1854–1858 (Chapman and Hall, 1884).

Bourdman E. P., *Christian Influence upon the Ideology of the Taiping Rebellion* (University of Wisconsin, 1952).

Buchan, John, *Gordon at Khartoum* (Peter Davies, 1934).

Butler, Col. Sir William, *Charles George Gordon* (Macmillan, 1892).

Carrick, C., *Serious Reflections on the Death of General Gordon* (Canterbury, 1888).

Cesari, Cesare, *Orme d'Italia in Africa* (UEI, 1937).

Churchill, Major S., *General Gordon, a Christian Hero* (Nisbet, 1890).

Churchill, W. S., *The River War* (Longmans, 1899).

Colquhoun, Major, *C. Gordon* (London, 1885).

Compton, P., *The Last Days of General Gordon* (Hale, 1974).

Cromer, Lord, *Modern Egypt* (London, 1904).

Dainelli, Giotto, *Gli Esploratori Italiani in Africa*, Vol. 2 (UTET, 1960).

Delebecque, Jacques, *Gordon et le Drame de Khartoum* (Hachette, 1935).

Elton, Lord, *General Gordon* (Collins, 1954).

Foreign Office Papers (Public Record Office, Kew) FO 78/1406 (service in Turkey), FO 78: 3227–3230 (Danube Commission) and FO 195/979 (British Embassy in Constantinople).

Garrett, R., *General Gordon* (Barker, 1974).

Gessi, Romolo, *Sette Anni nel Sudan Egiziano* (Alpes, Milan, 1930).

Giulietti, G., *Memorie su Romolo Gessi* (Soc. Geog. Ital., 1881).

Gordon, Sir H. W., *Events in the Life of Charles George Gordon* (Kegan Paul, 1885).

Graham, Sir Gerald, *Last Words with Gordon* (London, 1887).

Gravesend Reporter, The, 1865–71.

Hake, A. Egmont, *Journals of Maj-Gen. C. G. Gordon at Khartoum* (Kegan Paul, 1885).

History of Chinese Gordon (Kegan Paul, 1885).

Private Diary of the Taiping Rebellion of C.G. Gordon (Kegan Paul, 1890).

Hope, Eva, *General Gordon the Christian Hero* (Walter Scott Publishing, 1885).

Kelen, B., *The Mistresses*.

Lilley, W. E., *The Life and Work of General Gordon at Gravesend* (Kingdon, 1885).

Marchini, Marco, *La Storia Meravigliosa di Gessi Pascia* (Bemporad, 1928).

Milani, Mino, *Nel Inferno del Sudan* (Mursia, Milan, 1968).

Mossman, S., *Private Diary of His Exploits in China* (1885).

Nutting, A., *Gordon: Martyr and Misfit* (Constable, 1966).

Ohrwalder, J., *Ten Years of Captivity in the Mahdi's Camp* (Bibliothek Vertwoller Memoiren, 1908).

Petermans Geographische Mitteilung (July 1878).

Rosenbaum, R. A., *Earnest Victorians* (Heinemann, 1961).

Shukry, M.F., *Equatoria under Egyptian Rule* (Cairo University Press, 1953).

Swaine, Rev. S. A., *General Gordon* (Cassell, 1885).

Stocchetti, Francesco, *Romolo Gessi* (Vallardi, 1956).

Strachey, Giles Lytton, *Eminent Victorians* (G.P. Putnam's Sons, 1920).

Symons, J., *England's Pride* (Hamish Hamilton, 1965).

Tames, Richard, *General Gordon* (Shire, 1972).

Trench, A. C., *Charley Gordon* (Allen Lane, 1978).

Turnbull, P., *Gordon of Khartoum* (Bailey Bros and Swinfen, 1975).

War Office Papers (Public Record Office, Kew) WO/32 Codes O(AJ), O(S), 46(A) and 53(C).

Zavatti, Silvio and Carlo, *Gordon, Gessi e la Riconquista del Sudan* (University of Florence, 1947).

There are innumerable articles about Charles George Gordon in historical and other journals; an intriguing recent analysis of one of his interests is F. Plaut's 'General Gordon's Map of Paradise', in *Encounter* (June–July 1982). The Royal Geographical Society in London has the best collection of correspondence; the Gordon Boys' School, Woking, and the RE Museum, Chatham, the largest collection of memorabilia.

Index